LIEUTENANT GENERAL
EDWARD A. CRAIG

LIEUTENANT GENERAL EDWARD A. CRAIG

Warrior Six: Combat Leader in World War II and Korea

COLONEL RICHARD D. CAMP USMC (Ret.)

CASEMATE

Philadelphia & Oxford

Published in the United States of America and Great Britain in 2023 by
CASEMATE PUBLISHERS
1950 Lawrence Road, Havertown, PA 19083, USA
and
The Old Music Hall, 106–108 Cowley Road, Oxford OX4 1JE, UK

Hardcover Edition: ISBN 978-1-63624-236-1
Digital Edition: ISBN 978-1-63624-237-8

A CIP record for this book is available from the British Library

Printed and bound in the United Kingdom by CPI Group (UK) Ltd, Croydon, CR0 4YY.
Typeset by DiTech Publishing Services.

For a complete list of Casemate titles, please contact:

CASEMATE PUBLISHERS (US)
Telephone (610) 853-9131
Fax (610) 853-9146
Email: casemate@casematepublishers.com
www.casematepublishers.com

CASEMATE PUBLISHERS (UK)
Telephone (0)1226 734350
Email: casemate-uk@casematepublishers.co.uk
www.casematepublishers.co.uk

Cover image: Lieutenant General Edward Craig. (USMC)

Dedication:

Suzanne Mary Pool-Camp
Extraordinary woman

In the subtitle, "Warrior Six" refers to General Craig's radio call sign in Korea. The term "Six" is the military abbreviation for commander, i.e. A subordinate asking to talk with the "six" (commander).

Contents

Part IV Korea

Preface

I first met General Craig when I came back from a morning run at the Marine Corps Recruit Depot where I was stationed. As I walked back to my office, a tall, slender, white-haired gentleman met me in the passageway. I asked if I could help him. He introduced himself as "Ed Craig" and mentioned that he came to see me because of an article in the base newspaper about my interest in resurrecting the small base museum. We chatted for a brief time (I was dripping wet with sweat) and then he departed, but not before handing me his card and inviting me to his home. As he went through the hatch, I took a good look at the card and noted his name wasn't just "Ed Craig," it was Lieutenant General Edward A. Craig USMC (Ret). That chance meeting began a friendship that lasted almost two decades.

I often visited General Craig at his home whenever I happened to pass through San Diego. Not only did he and his wife welcome me with stories of his 34 years of service, but he also gave me military relics from his days in the Corps, including a Japanese samurai sword that he "picked up" on Guam during the invasion of the island during World War II. He handed me the sword just as I was leaving for a flight back to San Francisco, where I was stationed at the time. I thanked him profusely, but all I could think about was, "How the hell am I going to get the sword through the airport and onto the plane without getting shot!"

After a harrowing walk through the airport (before TSA) I stepped up to the ticket counter. The agent took one look at the sword in my hand, shook his head, and said, "You've got to be kidding." He finally took the sword and through some machinations, was able to get it to the plane's flight deck crew, who secured it. I was handed the sword upon arrival in San Francisco. Thank you, General Craig.

During one of my visits, General Craig gave me his typewritten Incidents of Service 1917–51, a 200-page manuscript detailing his service in the Marine Corps. At the time, I was fully involved in continuing my own career in the Corps and did not have time to do anything with his manuscript.

Upon retirement, I started a second career—mainly as a hobby to keep me off the streets—as an author of magazine articles and non-fiction books, including a biography of General Raymond G. Davis entitled *Three War Marine Hero*, published by Casemate in 2020. Its publication "fired me up" enough to haul the Craig manuscript out of my footlocker, dust it off, and start researching Craig's background to augment his Incidents of Service.

I started by visiting the Marine Corps History Division archives to review their wonderful files (I knew what they had, having been the Acting Director), including Craig's oral history. Next, I "hauled out" my personal copies of the official histories of the U.S. Marine Corps, namely U.S. Marine Corps Operations in World War II, Central Pacific Drive and Isolation of Rabaul and U.S. Marine Corps Operations in Korea, Volumes 1 and 2. I also used the excellent Marine Corps Monographs, Bougainville and the Northern Solomons and The Recapture of Guam, and the many excellent histories of World War II that are noted in the bibliography. Finally, I would be remiss if I didn't mention the veterans that I interviewed over the years; General Raymond G. Davis, General Lemuel C. Shepherd, and, of course, Lieutenant General Edward A. Craig.

Finally, I put pen to paper and a year later produced a manuscript for submission to Casemate's Publisher, Ruth Sheppard.

PART I

Formative Years 1917–21

CHAPTER I

Commissioning: "A day late and a dollar short"

Edward A. "Eddy" Craig was born on November 22, 1896, in Danbury, Connecticut. A service junior, he spent much of his childhood moving around the country from Army post to Army post. His father, Colonel Charles Franklin Craig, was a career officer in the U.S. Army Medical Corps, and an international authority in the fields of bacteriology and preventive medicine. He was very close to his parents and attempted to write to them every Sunday, if only a few words, regardless of where he was located. His letters were upbeat and showed concern for their health. He always ended his letters by telling them not to worry about his safety.

Craig had little knowledge of Marines. "My first experience with the Marine Corps was when I was a boy about 10 years old. I was living in Washington and went down to the Washington Naval Yard to sight see and took my camera along. I was taking a picture of one of the naval guns that was sitting out in the park, when a Marine sergeant came up and arrested me and took me to the officer of the day. He informed me that I could not take pictures in the Navy Yard and took the film out of my camera. He let me go, but that was my first experience with the Marine Corps and even then, I did not know what Marines were."[1]

War

A somber Woodrow Wilson slipped into a side room off the main lobby of the White House, took pen in hand, and scribbled his signature on the document that lay before him on the highly polished walnut table.

A buzzer sounded in the executive office and a Navy aide, Lieutenant Byron McCandless, ran out onto the White House lawn and semaphored to a fellow officer peering out a window of the Navy Department office across the street. The signal immediately flashed to every ship and shore installation: "WAR."

The April 6, 1917, newspaper editions proclaimed President Wilson's call to arms— "Make the World Safe for Democracy," sending the nation's collective blood pumping. Thousands of young men streamed to the colors. Among them was 20-year-old Edward A. Craig, a student of St. John's Military Academy, Delafield, Wisconsin. He recounted, "I was in school at the time, and on my own. When World War I broke out I immediately set out to get in the service. I couldn't get in the Army until I was twenty-one with a commission ... and twenty in the Marine Corps based on having completed four years of Reserve Officers Training Corps (ROTC) at St. John's."[2]

Craig was attracted by the Corps' slogan, "First to Fight." "I'd seen the posters all over, and I wanted to get to Europe with the Marines and see what was going on and help out over there." Craig sent a telegram to his Army doctor father: "I'm entering the U.S. Marine Corps. I have a chance for a commission." He received the following reply from his father: "Do not join the U.S. Marines under any circumstances. A terrible bunch of drunks and bums, Signed, Father." His father had gained a dislike of Marines while stationed at Fort Leavenworth. There were several Marines attending school who were heavy drinkers. He changed his mind after World War I and became very pro-Marine.[3]

Despite the admonition, Craig was determined to join the Marines and reported to the Marine Corps Recruiting Station on the tenth floor of a ratty looking building in Chicago, where he joined other volunteers for the pre-commissioning physical examination. Everything went well until the eye test. "I could not read the chart they had in a rather dark office," and he was disqualified. "I was of course broken hearted, and after some letters written by my father, and telegrams to Headquarters Marine Corps by myself, I was granted a reexamination. The same light conditions in the same examining room threw me out again."[4]

He returned home, resigned to the fact that he could not go to war. "Life to me about that time was pretty black, and my father sensing my disappointment wrote a personal letter to the Commandant asking if I could have another examination." The Assistant Commandant, Major General John A. Lejeune, whom I later served as his aide, responded and authorized one more examination. Craig hopped a train to Washington and was given an appointment with the Corps' leader. "The Commandant, Major General George Barnett, talked to me personally, ending with the statement that if I did not pass the exam this time, there would not be another chance. I appeared before a board on which Colonel Ben Fuller, a future Commandant of the Marine Corps, was president." Craig was vindicated. "I took the exam that same day and passed without any difficulty and was given a commission a week later as a second lieutenant in the Marine Corps Reserve, with a date of rank of August 27, 1917."[5]

Unfortunately, the five-month delay in receiving a commission was costly. "I found that my failure in passing the physical examination had a great effect on my future in the Marine Corps. Hundreds of officers had come into the Corps since I originally tried to enter, and of course that had a great effect on my position on the lineal list." At the start of the war there were 511 officers and 13,240 enlisted men. A year later there were 2,400 officers and 70,000 enlisted men. The Corps' rapid expansion brought quick promotion. "Those that took the exam with me the first time were now captains," Craig stated, "while I was just a second lieutenant." In Marine parlance, Craig was a "day late and a dollar short." The selection law which came in many years later eased the situation for Craig considerably however, and he finally emerged about on par with my contemporaries.[6]

The selection law that Craig mentioned was introduced by Texas Representative Clark W. Thompson, a World War I Marine veteran, to regulate the distribution, promotion, retirement, and discharge of commissioned officers in the Marine Corps. The Act of May 29, 1934 introduced a system of promotion by selection and eliminated promotion based solely on time in grade. Thompson discovered that under the promotion system then in place, the average rate of promotion was so slow that a junior officer had to spend most of his service in the lower grades and could reach the higher grades only a short time before retirement at the age of seventy. Because of the stagnation and lack of promotion in the Marine Corps, 29 percent of the colonels, 98 percent of the lieutenant colonels, 72 percent of the majors, and practically 100 percent of the captains and first lieutenants were then over-age for their respective grades. In ten years without relief, 88 percent of the colonels and 100 percent of all other junior officers then in the Corps would be over-age in grade. The year prior, there were so few promotions that, in future years at the same rate, it would require fifty-five years to pass through the grade of captain, and twenty-five years to pass through the grade of major.[7]

CHAPTER 2

A Bit of Flanders in Virginia

Upon reporting to Quantico, Virginia on August 23, 1917, Craig was assigned to the First Officer's Training Camp at Quantico for the three-month course. Quantico was nothing more than a whistle stop on the railroad trunk line 34 miles south of Washington and 80 miles north of Richmond, in the semi-wilderness part of Virginia.[1] The reservation had only been in existence for four months when the Marine Corps "leased 5,300 acres of land, enough room to accommodate 7,000 men with maneuver areas and space for infantry and artillery target ranges."[2] Quantico's main purpose was to train Marines for combat duty in the American Expeditionary Force (AEF) in France. However, "The 5th and 6th Marine Regiments had already been formed and officered and that threw me out of chance to go to France."[3]

When Craig arrived, "the base at the time was a big mudhole. It was a mass of tree stumps, mud, and half-finished wooden barracks." Marine engineers struggled to clear the heavily forested land. "I remember the day I reported," Craig recalled, "there were trucks stuck all along Barnett Avenue [main road], and the stumps sticking out all over had not been taken out." Barracks consisted of rough-hewn board shacks that barely kept out the weather. "The rooms had open cracks that did not have any batting over them, which allowed the wind and rain to come through. When winter came, it was pretty cold ... unless you sat by the stove in the center of the room." Craig was assigned to one of the poorly build barracks, which housed 75 to 100 men. "Companies had their own mess halls, kitchens, and showering and toilet facilities."[4]

Officer Trainee James M. Sellers wrote: "There are rows and rows of unpainted wooden shacks ... the small streets between are all cut up with rain wash, and we stumble over what is left of a former small forest, roots and stumps, and sewer excavations."[5]

The first issue of the base newspaper noted, "Quantico in the Indian tongue means 'slippery mud.'" Captain John Craige noted, tongue-in-cheek, "Rumor had it, that after a hard rain the hay wagons would frequently sink into holes in the street until only the horns of the oxen and the heads of the drivers were visible."[6] "I found myself in Company D," Craig noted, "which was already one month through the course but my ROTC training stood me in good stead, and by the second month I found myself in charge of a platoon of officer trainees."[7]

"The training was rugged," Craig remembered. Reveille was at 0545, physical drill 0600, breakfast 0630, drill 1300–1430, 1500–1600, supper 1800, study 1900–2100, taps at 2200.[8]

"Each morning before daylight, we were out setting up exercises, then rifle calisthenics, and this was followed by a half-mile run in company formation under arms through the streets of Quantico to the old railroad station and back. I found that by breakfast time I was so tired that I could not eat very much. Then by nine or ten in the morning I would be ravenous."[9]

The training was realistic and often taught by French and British veterans. Bayonet training included boxing. Craig remembered "a British officer instructor that taught this phase. He was tough, a huge man, who had been through the fighting in France. He meant to make everyone learn the art of killing or get killed themselves. I was once one of those he picked out to box with him. He would take us on with boxing gloves, one at a time. He almost knocked me silly. I was glad when I saw the last of him!"[10]

"Most of our training at Quantico at that time consisted of trench warfare. We constructed a complete trench system as learned from the war in Europe." Craig's training company dug miles of revetted trenches, bombproofs, and posts of command (CPs). A miniature battlefield was created, "a bit of Flanders in Virginia." They "practiced" war games, one side defending and the other attacking under simulated combat conditions.

Unfortunately, Craig recounted that he "never did have occasion in my career ... to put any trench warfare training into practice. However, the pick and shovel work tended to get us into shape physically."[11]

Craig found himself in big trouble one night when he was assigned as "Charge of Quarters." Time for study rolled around 1900 and he was responsible for ensuring everyone was quiet and studying. "However, a group of officers put on an impromptu play, and everyone was having a good time watching the performance and I lost track of the time," he remembered. "Suddenly, the Officer of the Day appeared and wanted to know who was in charge." Craig admitted his culpability and was told to report to the commanding officer next morning. "I stood quaking in my boots, standing at attention before the major. He proceeded to really read me off and ended by saying he was going to give me a general court-martial! After I digested this, he then said that because of my age and inexperience, he would hold it in obeyance. I left his office with pretty shaky knees, but the incident taught me a good lesson, 'do your duty,' which I always remembered."[12]

CHAPTER 3

Expeditionary Duty: 8th Marines

Shortly before graduation, Craig received orders to report to the 8th Marine Regiment's 1st Battalion, which was forming up as part of the Advanced Base Force, a brigade-sized unit designed to protect U.S. interests in the Caribbean against the possibility of German attack. "The regiment left Quantico with only what we carried on our backs, with orders to go to Philadelphia and board the USS *Hancock* with our destination unknown."[1]

Craig was assigned as adjutant and signal officer. "I reported to 37-year-old Major Ellis B. Miller, a real martinet and stickler for detail, as well as a strict disciplinarian, who never hesitated to speak his mind on the quality of my work. In those days the adjutant also carried out the duties of executive officer, training officer, and intelligence officer, so I found myself up to my neck in work." The assignment was a rough row to hoe for a young second lieutenant.[2]

Craig related that "not knowing anything about Marine Corps paperwork or administration, I was often called in before the battalion commander on something I had messed up. Fortunately, we had an acting sergeant major by the name of Wisner and I had enough sense to go to him and ask questions and get help when I found myself in difficulties. Old Sergeant Wisner would invariably be in the office and speak up to give a plausible explanation of the incident which would leave Major Miller satisfied."[3]

The two became fast friends, despite the difference in rank. Craig related an amusing incident the first time he conducted an inspection for the battalion commander. "I had just entered a mess hall when Sergeant Wisner, who was behind me, yelled 'attention' at the top of his voice. I snapped quickly to attention and stood there frozen in my tracks until I heard a whisper from behind me—'Lieutenant, you are the inspecting officer.' It was then that I finally realized the situation."[4]

Wisner was one of the old Corps Marines who had been broken in rank several times because of his love for "demon rum." Despite being an alcoholic, "he was a very fine man and a very efficient sergeant major when he was sober." His overindulgence eventually caught up with him. "Later in Santo Domingo I attended Wisner's funeral and saw his body placed aboard a transport for the States," Craig recounted. "The tropics and rum had been too much for him."[5]

> I learned through Wisner to rely on my noncommissioned officers, which I did from then on, and they never let me down. The same thing applied to my staff. When I became a commander of a unit and had staff officers, I gave them full rein and trusted them; and they too, never fell down on me. I believe that what success I have had in the Marine Corps was the result of the work of these officers and men.[6]

Despite the battalion commander's demands, Craig thought Miller was the best commander in the regiment ... "and I always appreciated the chance to serve under him." The 2nd Battalion Commander was different. "He was quite old for his grade and when he went in the field to check on his battalion, he was not always too sure which officers and which companies were his ... and often gave orders that he had no authority to give," Craig related. "We grew used to this in time and nothing was said or done, and this lessened the confusion which existed at first."[7]

CHAPTER 4

Disappointment: No "Over There"

Shortly after his assignment to the 1st Battalion, secret orders arrived directing the entire regiment to leave for an unknown destination within twenty-four hours. Rumors were rife—"France, here we come"—and the men entrained in high spirits. A few hours later, the train stopped for water and the regimental commander, executive officer and adjutant got off to stretch their legs. While they were at the far end of the platform, the train started up and rapidly gained momentum, leaving the three officers running to catch up. "I was in the rear car and I will always remember the look on their faces as the train pulled rapidly away and they finally faded from sight."[1]

The regiment arrived in Philadelphia and immediately boarded the USS *Hancock* (AP-3). By late afternoon, the ship was loaded and had "singled up all lines," preparing to shove off. The hawsers were hauled in and the transport started to swing away from the pier. The deck was lined with officers and men, including Craig. "It was at that moment the Colonel and his staff appeared, pounding down the dock at full speed. Jacob's ladders were lowered over the side, and, amidst a chorus of cheers and catcalls, they climbed aboard, never to live the incident down."[2]

Hancock sailed into the Atlantic, her destination still secret. Craig was bitterly disappointed when "we got clear of the land and headed south [and were told that we] were not on our way to France. The 5th and 6th Marine Regiments had already been formed and officered, and that threw me out of a chance to go to France." After a week at sea, the ship docked at Galveston, Texas. "We had been sent south due to trouble in the oil fields at Tampico, Mexico. German agents had fomented trouble there, which was a danger to the oil supply for our fleet."[3]

"The situation was further exasperated when the German Foreign Secretary Arthur Zimmermann sent his infamous telegram* to the Mexican government in January 1917, encouraging the Mexican government to invade the United States and reclaim Texas, New Mexico, and Arizona."[4] The Mexican government was unstable and disjointed after years of revolution. "The allies at that time were depending largely upon the Mexican oil fields for fuel. It was feared that the Germans would take advantage of the generally chaotic condition in Mexico and interrupt oil production ... in the Tampico fields."[5]

"The townspeople turned out to watch the strange-looking 'soldiers' as they hiked through the city to the Army post at Fort Crockett. They had never seen Marines in green uniforms before and thought they were Canadians, much to the chagrin of the proud Leathernecks."[6] Private Raymond H. Stenback, a member of the 112th Company wrote home, "We arrived here at Galveston, Texas, yesterday evening and have been busy unloading our necessary equipment for a short stay."[7]

In the confusion of unloading the equipment by hand, much of it disappeared—cases of revolvers and field glasses—as each unit took what it needed regardless of ownership. Craig helped himself to a set of wheels. "I secured a nice new Indian motorcycle and sidecar and was driving that around for over 10 days until the Quartermaster, Captain

---

* "We intend to begin on the first of February unrestricted submarine warfare. We shall endeavor in spite of this to keep the United States of America neutral. In the event of this not succeeding, we make Mexico a proposal or alliance on the following basis: make war together, make peace together, generous financial support and an understanding on our part that Mexico is to reconquer the lost territory in Texas, New Mexico, and Arizona. The settlement in detail is left to you. You will inform the President of the above most secretly as soon as the outbreak of war with the United States of America is certain and add the suggestion that he should, on his own initiative, invite Japan to immediate adherence and at the same time mediate between Japan and ourselves. Please call the President's attention to the fact that the ruthless employment of our submarines now offers the prospect of compelling England in a few months to make peace." Signed, ZIMMERMANN.

Baugh, saw me hung up on a railroad track ... he came over, and after a severe dressing down told me to turn it in. It was many months until poor Captain Baugh got most of his property back and then only after a complete shakedown of all the company storerooms in the regiment." A board of investigation finally cleared Baugh because he did not know what he had aboard the ship. It had been loaded before he even saw it.[8]

> We had been at Fort Crockett just a short time when a storm called a 'Norther' hit. Cold rain and sleet were falling. Our regimental camp was pitched in sandy soil and the tents held down with regulation tent pegs. Every tent in camp went flat and we spent a sleepless night searching for our gear, which had been blown all over the place. Many would appear at formation covered with mud.[9]

After some months on the staff, Craig requested duty with a line company. It was granted and he was transferred to the 105th Company as a platoon commander under Captain Galen Sturgis. Right after joining the company, Craig was severely injured when a motorcycle hit him. "I was walking behind the last squad down a main highway past a line of trucks. Suddenly a motorcycle and sidecar hit me and knocked the rear squad down. I only remember a terrific jolt in the back and then flying through the air over the handlebars and landed on my head. I woke up the next day in the field hospital with a terrific headache and bad cuts and bruises on my head and body. I had a bad concussion and two days after my release from the hospital I was found wandering around camp not knowing where I was. I went back to the hospital for a week's treatment and rest before being released again."[10]

Fully recovered, Craig soon found himself back in the trenches, "a bit of Flanders in Texas." A large, entrenched area was made to resemble a typical French battlefield, with revetted trenches, bombproofs, and sophisticated defensive wire barriers. Sometimes, however, the training was too realistic. Craig related how the "boys" got a little carried away on simulated raids. "Raids were conducted by Marines armed with wooden rifles, tennis balls over the bayonets to prevent injury, to capture prisoners from the defenders." Marine being Marines, exuberance was the order of the day, and "many times the tennis balls would be accidentally removed. Prisoners were often removed in a limp condition."[11]

The "Texas" Marines didn't just sit on their hands. Their daily routine was taken up with qualifying with individual and crew served weapons, physical training, close order drill, and tactical exercises.

Craig was not immune to a little youthful indiscretion. "I had been assigned to take a patrol and reconnoiter through and behind our regimental lines. My patrol was acting as the enemy for the exercise. We crossed a small stream and successfully penetrated the defensive line. I ran into the commander's CP. Sneaking silently towards it, we cut all the telephone lines and rushed in to find everyone asleep. When I pulled open a door, Major Miller came out like a tiger, cursing me for taking them prisoner. He raised even more hell when he found out we had cut the wires. Being just a low-ranking lieutenant without much experience I apologized, and after some more pointed instructions, I returned muddy and wet to my company. Fortunately, the incident was soon forgotten when the 9th Marines arrived in August."[12]

The 8th and 9th Marines formed the 3rd Brigade of the Advanced Base Force and embarked aboard the Hancock for Guantanamo Bay, Cuba. Craig observed an incident involving Colonel George Reid, commanding officer, 9th Marines. "He had been ashore and was returning to the ship aboard a motor sailor. The colonel had a big package under his arm, and one of the gunnery sergeants, who was quite a bit under the weather at the time, insisted that he help the colonel with his package. The colonel however, would not give it up. All the way back to the ship, the gunnery sergeant would say, 'Colonel, I've got to carry your package for you. You shouldn't carry a package.' Just as we reached the ship, the colonel started to get out and was just stepping onto the gangway when the gunny grabbed the package and promptly fell overboard. The colonel was madder than a wet hen. The package contained two gallons of rum, which was not recovered."[13]

A few days later the Henderson docked at Port-au-Prince, Haiti, where Craig joined the 1st Provisional Marine Brigade, which was occupying the country. "I stayed for a short while until I was transferred to Santo Domingo. I was very happy when the orders came." Craig found himself reassigned to the Marine Brigade, in the Dominican Republic.[14]

PART II

Banana Wars 1919–31

Dominican Republic 1919–21

America's victory in the Spanish-American War of 1898 began a period of overseas expansion, invigorating a heretofore moribund Navy and gaining the U.S. Marine Corps a hard-earned reputation as an expeditionary corps par excellence. Safeguarding these newfound possessions, particularly in the Caribbean where internal strife and revolution was almost a way of life, required a highly mobile, rapid-reaction force, just the forte of the Corps. In the first three decades of the 20th century, Marines became the intervention force of choice, protecting American interests and promoting economic, political and social stability in the Caribbean. An entire generation of Marine leaders—officers and noncommissioned officers—earned their spurs in the jungles of Nicaragua, Haiti and the Dominican Republic.

CHAPTER 5

A Parrot, Fowl Weather, and Field Duty

In 1916, Marines landed in the Dominican Republic to protect the indigenous population of the country and American economic interests. The Marines provided the backbone for a United States military government which was trying to bring stability to the troubled island republic. While there, Marines performed a variety of functions not normally assigned to an occupying military force, and they gained experience which helped to provide a pool of combat-trained leaders for future conflicts. In addition, several themes emerge. The first of these is the vital role played by the Marine Corps in establishing and training a local constabulary capable of maintaining order after the Marines withdrew. Secondly, effective tactics for the conduct of counterinsurgency operations emerged from these interventions: for example, the coordinated use of air and ground forces began during these campaigns. The third important theme was the gradual development among Marines stationed in these Latin republics of the concept of what would be called in Vietnam "civic action" efforts by the occupying troops to "win the hearts and minds" of a suspicious and wary indigenous population.

Craig and six other officers were given passage aboard the USS *Kwasind* (SP-1233), a converted steam yacht manned by reserve naval officers and commanded by Lieutenant Commander William W. Ramsay. Space was at a premium, and they had to bed down on the deck in the wardroom. The captain's beloved parrot perched above, occasionally showering them with bird droppings to their great annoyance. The parrot's noxious muck and a West Indian hurricane, with its high winds and towering waves, made it the voyage from hell. To top it off, their field lockers containing their uniforms were lashed down on the stern, close to the water, and as the heavy seas constantly flooded it, everything they had in them was ruined.

"Early the next morning, after a most uncomfortable and rough night we looked out the portholes and found we were out of sight of land," Craig bemoaned. "The captain got lost. He could not find the entrance to the harbor and we wandered around for two or three days until we got our bearings and finally arrived in Santo Domingo City. We looked down our noses when the captain came into the wardroom and gave us a dressing down for throwing cigarette butts on the deck." One of the exasperated lieutenants remarked in a stage whisper, "How about that damn parrot crapping all over the deck!"[1]

The 2nd Marine Brigade headquarters was located in Santo Domingo City. It was deployed as an Army of occupation to enforce the decrees of the military government and maintain public order. Initially the country was divided into two military districts: the Northern District, with headquarters at Santiago, was garrisoned by the 4th Regiment while the Southern District had its headquarters at Santo Domingo City and was the responsibility of the 3rd Regiment. In 1919, the military government created an Eastern District composed of the provinces of El Seibo and Macoris, the centers of banditry and political unrest, garrisoned by the 15th Regiment.[2]

"Upon reporting to the 2nd Marine Brigade Headquarters, Colonel Rufus Lane, the Chief of Staff, informed me that I would leave the next morning for La Romana in the Eastern District and take command of the 70th Company, 3rd Regiment." The 70th Company was composed entirely of old timers, pre-war Marines, who had been with it since 1917. The previous company commander, Captain Charles F. Merkle, was a German-born "Prussian" type officer, who had dealt harshly with the local Dominicans and his men had followed his lead. To the people of the province, he was known as the "Tiger of Seibo" because of his notorious brutality. He deprived suspected bandits of water for days, opened the wounds of detainees with sticks to pour salt in them, and cut off their ears. An investigation found Merkle guilty of severely beating and disfiguring a local prisoner and for ordering four other Dominicans shot near *Hato Mayor* in the Eastern district. In one documented statement against Merkel, Gunner David H. Johns claimed that the captain cut down four prisoners with machine gun fire and "unjustifiably [b]urned down or caused to be burned down many houses in Seibo Province ... in direct disobedience of ... orders received from his commanding officer." On September 30, 1918, Merkel's commanding officer placed him under arrest and sent him to solitary confinement to await a general court martial. Before his court martial, however, on October 3 Merkel committed suicide in his cell with a .38 revolver.[3]

"On my first inspection of the company I found that without exception, each man had dumdum bullets (the tips had been cut off) in the pockets of their cartridge belts." The bullets were designed to expand and cause larger wounds but were prohibited by the Hague Convention of 1899. "The men were pretty 'hard boiled' in their dealings with the locals, but they were a well-disciplined and trained outfit ... and it was a pleasure to serve with them."[4]

Before taking command of the company however, Craig, now a temporary captain, was directed to report to the 1st Air Squadron. "I was to spend a week and make daily flights over the eastern district in order to orient myself and learn the principal trails, rivers, and mountain ranges. This was a most valuable experience and stood me in good stead when I headed combat patrols later." The exhilaration of flight in the backseat of a Curtiss Jenny never left him. He developed a keen appreciation for the potential of aviation. "I became air minded. My interest in Marine aviation and its capabilities never left me from then on."[5]

The 1st Air Squadron, composed of nine officers and 131 enlisted men, was commanded by Captain Walter E. McCaughtry, a former warrant officer who rose through the ranks. Equipped with six JN-6 (Jenny) biplanes, the squadron began operating from an airstrip hacked out of the jungle near San Pedro de Macoris in February 1919. It later moved to an airstrip near San Isidro, close to Santo Domingo City. The squadron adopted the ace of spades as its insignia. The squadron's insignia was designed by then Second Lieutenant Hayne D. "Cuckoo" Boyden, a member of the squadron. The distinctive emblem bore the letters "A" and "S." As conceived by Boyden, the ace being the first card in a suit stood for "First" while "A" and "S" represented the words "Air" and "Squadron." This design is the first official unit insignia to appear in Marine Corps aviation. The squadron engaged in some direct combat with the bandits, but its greatest benefit was supporting the brigade in the field by delivering supplies, mail, and personnel to the far-flung outposts.

An article in *Time*, noted that in Craig's youth, "he was something of a gay blade. On weekends he used to ride at breakneck speed into the town of Pedro de Macoris on a noisy, dust-spurting motorcycle, seriously disturbing a Marine captain attached to Santo Domingo's Guardia Nacional, who rode into town at the same time on a mule named Josephine."[6]

Craig's company was located in a remote area of the country. He set out to join his new command aboard the only transportation available, a small local boat, known as a "gasolina." "I was the only American on the trip, and practically every available space was occupied by locals. My accommodation consisted of a small space on the forward deck where I was surrounded by a local family complete with chickens." The locals were friendly, even sharing their meager food with him. "Being a small craft and with the fumes of gasoline permeating it, seasickness was prevalent as soon as we left the harbor and encountered the heavy seas which prevail along the coast of the island. After having motor trouble and drifting perilously close to the jagged rocks lining the shore, we finally arrived at La Romana, a large sugar estate, which became my home base of operations for the next eight months."[7]

The camp was located between the town and the sugar estate. Housing consisted of nine-feet-square wall tents for the men, while Craig and his assistant bedded down in a wooden building, which also housed their office, storeroom, and sickbay. A small company store stocked a few treats. Craig recalled, however, "We had little time to enjoy the luxuries because the bandit situation was critical. Several large groups were operating in this section of the republic. I found myself in the field inspecting outposts or leading patrols searching for bandits most of the time."[8]

Craig's first 10 days were spent inspecting his outlying outposts: Gato 10 miles, Yuma 42 miles, and Higuey 35 miles. The prevalence of banditry and the extent of country to be covered required wide dispersal of the Marines. "Travel was by horse and mule, or by foot with a patrol of six to eight Marines. Each month I made a trip to each outpost to inspect and to pay the men. It would mean about an 80-mile hike or ride round trip."[9]

Each outpost was manned by a platoon; around two dozen men, with a noncommissioned officer or sometimes a lieutenant in charge. They were supplied by pack train and sometimes the inventory of food was low. "In one outpost that I served in, Vinentillo, which was one of the furthest out, my entire commissary store consisted of bacon, flour, canned corn, and canned jam. Fresh meat we obtained locally. We got a certain amount of fresh vegetables by bartering with the locals. We usually had many cases of canned sardines, which I think sold for five cents a can. We bartered them to the locals for eggs, chickens or whatever we could scrounge. I also found the men were bartering the sardines with the local women for other favors."[10]

The locals were sometimes friendly and sometimes not. Craig found that "We would find some that in order to obtain favors would be friendly, or if they were employed by the Marines—it meant jobs. Others, of course, were between the Devil and the deep sea. It they gave information to the Marines, the bandits would kill them; and if they didn't give information, the Marines would sometimes be hard on them." Craig developed a relationship with a local local guide by the name of Ramon. According to Craig, Ramon was "about 35, wiry, with a drooping moustache and missing his left arm. He always carried a .44-caliber revolver, and with his slouch hat, homemade shirt and blue denim trousers, and leather thong sandals, would have passed for a bandit anywhere."[11]

Ramon accompanied Craig on every patrol and proved to be a loyal and competent guide. "He also brought us many hot tips on the bandits who infested the area." At times, he left camp to visit his wife, who lived several miles away in another village. Craig worried: "I always hesitated in granting his request for I knew the danger he faced on the 15-mile ride down the mountain trails. He had made many enemies as [a] result of acting as a guide for the Marines. The average Dominican was quick to take revenge if the opportunity presented itself." One weekend he requested leave, which Craig granted. "I watched as he mounted his horse and, with his one arm flapping, trotted down the trail." A few hours later, Craig learned that "Ramon had been waylaid and killed. His head was found impaled on a fence post and his body horribly mutilated by machetes."[12]

Then, as now, it was difficult to tell innocent civilians from bandits. At one time Craig received orders that his men were not to fire on any armed man unless that man fired first! Craig found it a senseless order. "These were the most stringent orders I ever received. And, of course, they were very hard to carry out, because if you saw a local with a rifle pointed at you, you had a tendency to shoot first if you possibly could. And I think this is what happened on many occasions." He blamed the orders on the military government, which was out of touch with the situation faced by Marine commanders in the field. "We had a military government at that time, and the military governor was an admiral with a staff up in Santo Domingo City. During my time ... I never saw the military governor or his staff on any inspections."[13]

CHAPTER 6

Hunting Bandits

"My mission was to 'cover' the eastern district, which permitted me maximum flexibility, and as a company commander, I was allowed a great amount of latitude in my decisions. I could find nothing in the orders or files of the company that defined the area I was supposed to patrol. Consequently, I assumed that I could go anywhere in the eastern district that I desired."[1] However, Craig had to exercise extreme caution because patrols from other units were not coordinated. "One time, we had just entered a house when a bandit fled out the back door. I had a sergeant with me armed with a BAR (Browning Automatic Rifle). I said, 'open up on him.' Fortunately, the weapon jammed as the man ran down the hill toward a clump of bushes. Just as he disappeared into the bushes, I heard a fusillade of shots." The bandit had run into another Marine patrol that Craig did not know about. If the BAR had not jammed, the other patrol may have suffered casualties.[2]

Ramon Natera, known as "General Ramon Natera," headed the largest bandit (gavilleros) group in Craig's area. He also went by the title "El General," and was an important leader of the guerrilla resistance from 1918 to 1922. An ardent nationalist, he was considered one of the most important guerrilla fighters in the eastern provinces. He "assembled the largest force and used the most sophisticated political tactics," which by 1920 had caused the deployment of 2,500 Marines.[3] Natera would finally surrender to the Marines on May 5, 1922. Natera's band numbered 75–100 men, but it was extremely rare for the Marines to run into more than a few. "We hit small groups, six or eight at a time; and that was all.

These big groups would operate only on rare occasions; the rest of the time they were split up and operated against various villages and locals and would rob and burn and what not, as small groups."[4]

"I remember one patrol which I took out which lasted for 10 days." Shortly after taking to the field with 20 men, including one volunteer from the 15th Regiment. "For days we followed a hot trail never being able to contact the bandits but knowing that they were always just ahead of us. At times we would lose them and then after a day or so pick up the trail again. On the 7th day, we reached a high mountain ridge just as dark was setting in. We were exhausted and intended to make camp but looking across a wide valley we spotted many campfires burning on a small flat hill. We thought it was probably Natera's men and, from the number of fires, we estimated that most of his group was with him. I figured that it would take us about three hours to move down the mountain and across the valley and be in position to attack the camp just before daylight. Shortly after 1am we moved out. We left all unnecessary equipment behind and moved slowly and carefully to prevent any noise."[5]

"Just before daylight we were in position for the attack. Tensions were high and as we advanced toward the camp in a skirmish line, we were sure of a big killing. After days of hiking and living on the ground we had at last caught up with our quarry. I was to fire the first shot which would be the signal to open fire. We had almost reached the top of the small hill where we would be out of defilade and able to see the bandit camp when the volunteer fired his rifle prematurely. That did it!"[6] After firing a few scattered shots, the entire bandit group fled down the other side of the hill and although we captured a large quantity of supplies and a few firearms and ammunition, we did not get one single bandit. I had a hard time restraining my men from beating the volunteer to a pulp for giving the attack away. The man claimed that he was not familiar with the safety on the rifle he was carrying. My men believed he deliberately fired so that he would not have to engage in a closeup firefight."[7]

Natera normally employed elaborate measures to prevent surprise. "On this occasion they were apparently under the impression that we were on the other side of the mountain and had relaxed their guard. This patrol was just typical of the many, many patrols which we conducted in Santo Domingo with no results, and it was a most frustrating experience of my early career to hike many days, on poor or no rations, and my men suffering all the hardships of life in the field for days at a time and coming back with absolutely nothing to report."[8]

Craig received information from a reliable local contact that Natera had established a permanent base camp in his patrol area, and that he intended to lay low there for a while and reconstitute his force. "I took 20 of my men and established a base camp in the small hamlet and began operating from there." He used three undercover Dominicans to locate Natera's camp. "I followed a roundabout way and hit the trail leading to the reported site. The area was densely wooded but the trail was well worn by men and horses. As we proceeded further into the jungle, it branched out in many directions and became harder to follow." The patrol came across woodchoppers, older men, who had erected a small lean to against the rain. They seemed to be working industriously on large mahogany logs. The chopping could be heard loud and clear through the jungle. Shortly after, the patrol found a barrier of felled trees that extended into the jungle in both directions. "The trees had been felled toward our line of march and the branches sharpened, presenting a formidable barrier. After working our way through it, we suddenly came into a cleared area containing 10 or 12 long shacks and many lean-tos. It was Natera's camp, but he and his group had fled without firing a shot. They left behind three badly wounded men and a large quantity of supplies. We burned the camp and interrogated the prisoners but got little information from them."[9]

"We determined that Natera had ringed his camp with woodcutters who gave him a warning of our approach. It was a clever alarm system and it worked. Needless to say, when we retraced our way back over the trail, the woodchoppers were all gone. Piles of chewed sugar cane testified that they had been there for some time. This was the only permanent camp I knew of that Natera occupied as he was usually on the move."[10]

"On my return from the patrol, I found an order from the regimental commander directing me to return to La Romana immediately, as he considered that I had been too far from my regular patrol area because he had information that indicated that there were no bandits in the Jagual area. I took great pleasure in including in my patrol report to him that we had destroyed Natera's permanent camp."[11]

Craig spoke of the difficulties in fighting a guerrilla war. "Many patrols were fruitless after much hardship, and it was so difficult to come into contact with the bandits ... this type of duty was most discouraging. Occasionally our patrols would hit small groups and kill one or two, and on a number of occasions we were ambushed by bandits."[12]

CHAPTER 7

Humping the Hills

"Life on patrol was rugged," Craig declared. "We usually traveled by foot carrying the minimum of gear and a couple days rations on our backs. If we were going to stay out longer, we would sometimes take a pack mule to carry the Lewis machine gun and ammunition together with the rations. And if the food ran out, we would forage through the country, obtaining what we could from the local people. Food was prepared over open fires in canteen cups, mess pans, or such cans or pots as we could borrow.[1]

Craig's patrol area was lush jungle-covered terrain, crisscrossed by numerous rivers and streams. Dense undergrowth forced his patrols to use the trail network, making them vulnerable to ambush. Casualties were a tremendous burden. Craig did not have enough doctors or corpsmen to accompany every patrol. "We had to use make-shift litters with carrying parties of local men who were impressed for the job."[2]

On a patrol, one of Craig's men was shot through the groin, which left a gaping wound in his buttocks. A Navy doctor hiked in and started treatment. Sadly, though, gangrene set in. The wounded man was in terrible pain and "I suggested that we take him to the regimental hospital, but the doctor objected and would not permit his evacuation. Craig agonized over the decision. "From the odor and the condition of the man I knew he would die if we didn't evacuate him, so I overrode the doctor." The dying man was carried on a makeshift stretcher several miles over narrow mountain trails. "Halfway down, I almost lost my nerve and thought of turning back, but I decided it was the right thing to do.

He would die anyway if I didn't make the effort." Local carrying parties replaced each other every few miles to keep up the pace. They finally reached a road where an ambulance picked him up and transported him to the regimental hospital. The doctors performed emergency surgery and managed to save the Marine's life. "The doctor told me that if I had not brought him in, he would have been a goner." The man fully recovered and later returned to duty. "This was a terrible chance I took at the time, but I was never so happy over a decision in my life."[3]

Shortly after returning from a mounted patrol to La Romana from Higuey, "I was just getting cleaned up when a local runner brought the news that a large group of bandits had captured a local German storekeeper and his wife only six miles away. "We quickly formed a 12-man mounted patrol, including myself and Lieutenant Shields, and after a fast ride we came upon two armed local men, who jumped up and fired at the lieutenant before running into the brush. Shields had his pistol in hand and attempted to fire back, but it jammed and, in frustration, he threw it at the bandits. His frightened horse took off at a gallop." The rest of the patrol thundered along behind. Within a couple of minutes, they ran headlong into the bandits, who scattered in panic. "Hell of a thing," Craig remembered. "We came thundering right into the middle of them, yelling and shooting. We picked off four of them before they could get into the jungle." The Germans were released unharmed, however "mad-man Shields took quite a bit of good-natured ribbing. The troops teased him unmercifully for leading a charge, unarmed."[4]

Craig had to exercise extreme caution because the patrols were not coordinated. "One time, we had just entered a house when a bandit fled out the back door. I had a sergeant with me armed with a BAR. I said, 'open up on him.' Fortunately, the weapon jammed just as the man ran down the hill toward a clump of bushes. Just as he disappeared into the bushes, I heard a fusillade of shots." The bandit had run into another Marine patrol that Craig did not know about. If the BAR had not jammed, the other patrol may have suffered casualties.[5]

Colonel William C. Harllee assumed command of the 15th Regiment and launched a systematic drive to finish off the bandits operating in the Eastern District. "He arrived at a time when bandit activity seemed to be getting worse," Craig reported. He put out operation orders which provided for certain patrols and certain companies to arrive in certain areas at specified times. These patrols had orders to shoot any bandits seen and to bring in any prisoners that surrendered, and to gather in everybody between the ages of 10 and 70 years of age for interrogation and checking by a team of locals who had consented to identify bandits they knew.[6]

An interrogation center was set up under Captain Louis Cukela. "He was quite a character in the Marine Corps," Craig said. "He was a Medal of Honor man and had quite a number of other high decorations which he obtained in France. Cukela spoke Spanish fluently ... [and] his patrol, which had been operating secretly—consisting mostly of Mexican and Puerto Rican nationals who had joined the Marine Corps—had been disguised as locals. They were thoroughly familiar with the territory and with the people." Anyone the patrols captured were sent back to the interrogation center and brought before the informers who were behind a canvas screen. "Whether these informers always correctly identified bandits or their own enemies, I never found out. We did gather quite a bit of information and quite a number of bandits were identified."[7]

Cukela was later brought before a U.S. Senate committee and questioned about atrocities he committed in Haiti.

CHAPTER 8

A Hazardous Profession

After seven months, Craig was transferred to a mounted detachment, the 33rd and 44th Companies, stationed at a place called Chicharones, a railhead at the end of a macadam road that led to regimental headquarters. My main mission was to patrol the area and to run bull carts to the various companies and battalions in the regiment. I had some 20 bull carts, and each cart had six bulls. They were handled by local drivers, most of whom were Jamaican Negroes. Each bull cart train ordinarily consisted of some 15 to 20 carts and a guard of about 10 Marines. We would run them at night because the bulls couldn't stand the heat of the day. This was the only means of supply in the area. I think the bull cart train was one of the first such organization the Marine Corps ever used.[1]

The detachment sergeant, named Bill Hensley, was a former cowhand on the western ranches. Later he served in the Canadian Army in World War II. He was a wizard with horses. The mounts were Puerto Rican, much larger than the local mounts. They were fed on oats and hay and were well cared for, or "Sergeant Hensley would know the reason why." Craig described Hensley as "a typical Marine of the old Corps, every inch a soldier. He was well over six feet in height, powerfully built, straight as a ramrod, and always wore a mustache. He was one of the finest Marines that I have ever served with." Like all good sergeants, Hensley took care of his officer, even saving Craig's life on several occasions.[2]

Craig recalled one such occasion:

> We were headed toward our base camp when we hit a main bull cart trail. Heavy rains had made the trail deep in mud and almost impassable in places. Water

had collected and stood in pools and was such that horses could get mired. I was riding my favorite horse "Sublime," a big stallion and full of life. Even after four days of patrol carrying a load of heavy equipment and myself he was still spirited and nervous. As I was leading the patrol through an especially bad piece of ground, my horse bogged down up to his belly and began to plunge and rear, finally falling on his side and pinning my right leg under him. His subsequent movements tended to push my shoulders into the mud and part of my head was already going slowly under. I was having some bad moments when I felt a strong pull on my pistol belt suspenders and I found myself being dragged through the mud. Hensley, who had been directly behind me had spurred his horse forward and as he came opposite me, had reached down, grabbed me by my field equipment. He saved me from possible death.[3]

Later we secured a team of bulls from a nearby estate and dragged poor Sublime out of the bog, none the worse for wear, but thoroughly frightened, as the treacherous mud had almost closed over his head as he lay on his side struggling. Local coffee never tasted so good as that served to us by the friendly locals at the estate where we went to clean up.[4]

On another occasion, Craig's patrol had surrounded a cluster of local shacks after receiving a report that bandits were living there. "It was a bright moonlight night and I had just stopped a local who had come from one of the houses and was heading for the jungle. As I questioned him, he appeared surly and edged toward me. Just then Hensley came around the other side of the shack and, without even a 'by your leave,' he clubbed the local over the head with his rifle. As the local dropped, Hensley reached down and grabbed a razor-sharp knife from his hand. He had seen the flash of the knife in the moonlight and instinctively reacted. Bill Hensley and the moon shining on the knife gave me the break I needed."[5]

On one of the few occasions Craig was in camp, his "boy," a hired man who did housekeeping chores, dashed up screaming hysterically. Blood streamed down his face from a ghastly wound on the side of his head. A piece of mutilated flesh was all that was left of his ear. "My God man, what happened?" Craig exclaimed. The terrified man pointed to a tough-looking local across the street and, in halting English, explained that the man had cut his ear off because he worked for the Marines. Craig recalled, I "picked up my automatic pistol, which was lying unholstered on the table, and slipped the lanyard over my shoulder." As he strode across the street, he yelled "for Sergeant Hensley to get his gun and follow me. My intention was to apprehend and arrest the local before he could escape." Craig approached the desperado and started to question him. "He suddenly reached forward and grabbed my pistol, which I was holding cocked in my right hand, pointing at the ground." The two struggled, but the bandit was too strong and succeeded in turning the pistol toward Craig. At that moment, Hensley ran up, grabbed the goon in a headlock, forced his own pistol into the miscreant's face, and pulled the trigger. "As the man fell dead, he pulled me over with him," Craig related, "covering me with blood and brain matter. Hensley's quick reaction saved me from being shot with my own gun… I reported the incident to my regimental commander who convened a board of investigation. The matter was finally cleared up when the board found that both Hensley and myself had acted in the line of duty."[6]

"I will always remember an incident during a patrol against the bandits. We traced a group of them to an area dotted with coral caves. The opening to one was just a round hole in the ground. There was a seven-foot drop to the floor. A passageway led into another cave holding bandit supplies. I hesitated to drop down, not knowing what I would be facing. Sergeant Hensley sensing my hesitation, jumped down ahead of me with his pistol drawn, ready to shoot. Unfortunately, the bandits escaped through another entrance, and we had to be content with capturing their supplies."[7]

One of the more macabre missions Craig ever had to perform was to take the body of a dead Marine back to the regimental field hospital. "The rainy season was in full swing and trails were slippery and deep in mud as I started with my patrol down the mountainside. Locals [who] we had commandeered were carrying the body on an improvised stretcher." Craig reached a road, where the body was placed in a heavy wooden coffin and loaded on an old truck, which was the only vehicle available at the time. "About midnight, we reached a point about three-quarters of the way through thick mud in the pouring rain, when the truck stopped." They could not get it started; the battery was dead. "I decided the only thing to do was to break open the coffin and place the dead

Marine's body across a horse and continue on foot." He had orders to deliver the body by morning.[8]

The road ran through thick jungle, and the overhanging trees shut out any light and Craig did not have a flashlight. He had to work in the pitch dark. "I had only the driver and one other Marine with me. As we ripped off the lid of the coffin, a sickening odor hit us in the face. The tropics had begun to work on the corpse. The driver became sick, and it fell on the other Marine and me to lift the body out and secure it across the horse." Rigor mortis had set in, making it difficult to lash the body across the horse. "Every mile it seemed the gruesome load would shift, and we would have to tighten the lashings." They finally reached another road where they were relieved of their responsibilities.[9]

However, the successful delivery did not end the incident. About three weeks later, Craig received a letter from the regimental commander accusing him of losing the dead man's bayonet. "I often thought that if the regimental commander had been present when we arrived, completely covered with mud, hungry, tired, stinking, and carrying what we could salvage, he would have relented in his desire to make me account for the lost bayonet." Craig tried for three months to settle the issue, even offering to pay for it, before it was finally resolved. "The incident shows some of the small matters that were given great importance in those days," he remarked. "I remember there was a big surge to make people pay for everything ... and we went out of our minds collecting four cents apiece for missing tent pins! It was terrible."[10]

Craig was hardened, mentally and physically, by the constant patrolling and privation in the field. "Everything I owned, I carried on my back. My quarters were a 9 x 9 wall tent without a desk. I slept on a field cot ... with a small ration box as a table, the light of one oil lantern, when I had kerosene—a candle when I did not. I had no sheets or pillowcase and my pillow consisted of my musette bag filled with my extra underwear and socks. My blanket was the only covering, except for a poncho—and the nights were cold and damp in the mountains. If I wanted to bathe, I had to go some 100 yards into the jungle, where there was a cold stream running over rocks into a deep pool. The presence of bandit groups made it desirable to lay your pistol within easy reach. My eating utensils consisted of a GI spoon and knife, a mess tin, and [a] tin can to drink out from." Craig echoed an age-old lament of the field soldier: "It always seemed to me that the troops chasing the bandits and living in the far-flung outposts should have been the ones who received the best, but it was just the opposite. The ones in garrison were the ones where comfort was the rule."[11]

After two years of field duty, Craig received orders back to the United States. He looked back on those days with a sense of accomplishment. It was professionally rewarding, although "it was rugged duty, and the methods we used were not always those of the book. Most of the men had never been trained in jungle warfare, and it was necessary to train them on the march and bivouac." He was an experienced jungle warfare expert, joining a core of junior officers who would subsequently rise to command positions in World War II.[12]

Aide de Camp

"A few months after this I found myself on the USS *Henderson* bound through the Panama Canal to Norfolk, Virginia and the Marine Barracks, Washington, D.C., where I was assigned as Aide de Camp to Major General John A. Lejeune, the Commandant of the Marine Corps." In addition to his duties as an aide, Craig acted as a recorder to the examining board, in charge of the Navy building guard, and engagements for the Marine Corps band.[13]

"Each morning at seven o'clock I was required to be at the stables. General Lejeune would arrive promptly at seven and we would ride horseback for one hour, always at a trot." Lejeune used a McClellan saddle, "so he got well shaken up. One time his horse stopped suddenly, and he went over his head. I jumped off to help him, but he was on his feet and back on his horse before I could hardly get to him."[14]

"We would stay at headquarters from eight o'clock when we got back from the ride until six or seven at night. He would do much of his work after the main force went home, and the heads of departments at the time knew they might be called on any time. So, they generally stuck around until they knew the general's car had left. I had nothing to do during these periods, but I had to be there, so I was able to complete two correspondence courses—Company Officer's Course and the Advance Course—which I found helped me greatly later on when I attended the Marine Corps Schools at Quantico."[15]

"During the time I was with General Lejeune, we took many inspection trips. I'll always remember one trip in particular. We had been to Camp Perry at the national [shooting] matches and were on our way home by train. We had been sitting in the smoking car talking about 10 o'clock at night, when the general said, 'I think I'll go back and turn in. If you want to sit up here and read, go ahead.' So, I stayed in the car."[16]

"Just after the general started to the rear of the train, the train stopped; and I noticed they were switching cars. Shortly after, the train pulled out again; and I decided to go to bed. I got back to our Pullman car, and I saw the general sitting on the side of his bunk, looking very white faced and panting, as if he had run a long way. 'What happened, General?,' I asked."[17]

"He replied, 'I had the damnedest experience I ever had in my life. I was going back to the dining car when the train stopped. They closed both doors of the car, locking me inside, and the car was shunted off to the side. I tried to get out every way I could. I ran back and forth trying the doors and windows. I finally had to break a window and climbed out, just as the main train was pulling out. I ran and caught the last car.' I thought to myself, My God, suppose he hadn't gotten out of that car? I'd have arrived in Washington without the general. I never would have heard the end of that! I determined that I would stick pretty close to him after that."[18]

"The general was a man who thought very little of himself. As a consequence, he would appear many times out of uniform, his stewards having forgotten to put on certain ribbons or insignia. So consequently, I always carried a supply in my pocket or had them handy where I could check when he came in; and, if I saw one missing, I would simply pin it on him. On one trip to Camp Perry, I got up in the morning and the general called out, 'Do you have an extra scarf?' I did not have an extra one because I never thought he would be minus a scarf. But I called over and said, 'Yes, sir, I have one,' and I handed him mine. My only scarf then was my civilian tie, which was rather gaudy. I arrived in Camp Perry in uniform wearing a civilian tie; so, it didn't take me very long to get to the post exchange and buy one."[19]

Fraught with Danger: Duty with the Nicaraguan Guardia Nacional 1929–31

The political situation in Nicaragua had been growing worse and worse and there was pressure from Congress and the press to get the situation in hand. "General Lejeune decided to organize the 11th Marines and send them down to reinforce the Marines already there. The regiment left on two light cruisers from Parris Island. The general decided to go down with them and find out for himself what the situation was. I went along as his aide."[20]

"We were given quick passage through the Panama Canal and landed at Corinto, Nicaragua. On arrival, General Lejeune relieved the commanding officer of the 5th Marines, because the officer failed to carry out a plan to attack the bandit leader Sandino's stronghold, allowing him to escape."[21]

"As we traveled to all parts of the republic, I became interested in the Guardia Nacional de Nicaragua [Nicaraguan Army]. It had only been recently organized by the Marines, and all [of] its officers were detailed from the Marine Corps." The Guardia was organized in 1927 as a combination of a local police force and national Army, commanded by Marines but separate from the Marine brigade. Officers were "loaned" to the Guardia, advanced one grade, and paid a stipend, in addition to their regular military pay. Even with this incentive, there were not enough volunteers. Selected non-commissioned officers were breveted to lieutenant in order to make up the shortages.[22]

Craig liked what he saw. "Duty with the Guardia looked different from the regular Marine Corps, and I believed that I could be of some help, as volunteers for the outfit were not too plentiful." Shortly after returning to the States, General Lejeune retired. He gave Craig an opportunity to pick an assignment. "I asked him if I could be detailed to duty with the Guardia. He agreed and said [it] would give me good professional experience and training." In the months to come, Craig had cause to doubt Lejeune's prophesy. "I found life in the Guardia much different ... the good American food was gone, equipment was lacking, and the local troops were still not completely trained and in many cases were unreliable and dangerous." Craig found that, "In many instances the Guardias had mutinied and shot their officers, and desertions were frequent."[23]

"Being associated with a man like General Lejeune did much good for me and I have always felt that much of the success that I have had in the Corps was due to his good influence and some of the good traits that I might have absorbed from my association with him."[24]

CHAPTER 9

1st Mobile Battalion
Guardia Nacional

After General Lejeune's retirement, Craig found himself aboard the USS *Sirius* headed for Corinto, Nicaragua. "I reported to the Jefe Director of the Guardia, Brigadier General Douglas McDougal USMC, at his headquarters in Managua. His staff briefed me on the general situation, and I learned that the bandit situation was still acute and that Sandino, the principal bandit leader, was still at the head of a large force."[1]

> I was assigned duty with the 1st Mobile Battalion,* Guardia Nacional as battalion executive officer. My duties consisted of inspecting outposts, usually on horseback, sometimes on foot. I found the outposts seriously undermanned. Most of the outposts were manned by local soldiers who were not too well trained, as they had just been organized. But, they learned fast and made excellent soldiers. "If they liked you, they were very loyal, but if you crossed them or did not keep your word, they could be just the opposite. In some cases, they killed their Guardia officers and in other cases, they kidnapped them and joined the bandits.[2]

As the executive officer of the 1st Mobile Battalion, Guardia Nacional, Craig found the duty interesting, but he wanted something more exciting. He requested assignment to a newly formed company slated for duty in a remote part of the country. "My company was composed of drafts from the other companies of the battalion. On the morning of our departure, men released from the brig filled up the vacancies in the

---

* The mobile battalion was organized by an agreement between the U.S. State Department and the government of Nicaragua. It was to be manned by 200 to 250 volunteers and used in active operations against the bandits, under the command of a senior U.S. Marine officer. (Foreign Relations of the United States, 1929 Volume III)

company. It was a mongrel outfit." With some degree of trepidation, Craig and his second in command, Second Lieutenant Kurchov, Guardia Nacional (corporal, USMC), a good professional Marine of Russian ancestry, marched his "crack" troops into the jungle. Craig remarked rather dismissively that "Being the only Americans among these local troops, with only a poor command of the Spanish language, could be a nerve-wracking experience." He had every right to be concerned. Just a few hours after starting out, one of the wrongdoers tried to shoot Kurchov. Unfortunately, for the evil doer, the lieutenant *née* corporal wrestled the rifle away and brained the men with his own weapon. The bashing quickly ended the abortive mutiny.[3]

"I found that much of my time was necessarily spent in the field either on patrol or on patrol inspections of the many outposts." Craig admitted that patrolling with the Guardia was very different than with the Marines. The Guardia carried a Krag rifle, a few with Springfields, rifle grenade dischargers, two hand grenades per man, a web belt of ammunition, a canteen and first aid pack, plus either a blanket or poncho. "I found that blankets usually got soaked in the rainy season and were of little use and simply a burden to carry. Most of us just used ponchos to sleep under at night."[4]

"Rations were meager and ordinarily carried in a small canvas bag attached to the belt. Many times, food would run out. We would have to live off the land, buying from the locals—usually red beans, sometimes ears of corn and sometimes coffee, very seldom tortillas. The only time that we would find tortillas was when we came across someone with a large supply of beans, tortillas, and rice. These were usually being prepared for the bandits, so we usually helped ourselves."[5]

Craig remembered one patrol where they had been out a number of days without ordinary rations. The Guardia shot several monkeys and stewed them up that night for dinner. "I could not bring myself to eat monkey meat."[6]

The men wore campaign hats. Leggings were seldom worn. Marine issue boon dockers and high shoes with cobble nail were issued to the Guardia. "I found many times that on the march, especially in wet weather, they would take off their shoes and carry them over their shoulders; and if approaching a town, they would stop, put on their shoes, and march through, then take them off on the other side."[7]

Craig was totally surprised on one patrol that was transferring a detachment of Guardia to another station. "I left with them early that morning before daylight; and looking back when daylight came, I saw that two of the Guardia had women on the back of their horses! I soon found out this was SOP in the Guardia, to take your wife where you were stationed. They went right along with the patrols. The women were very handy at these small outposts for cooking and washing, so I never raised any objections to women being on this type of patrol."[8]

"The outposts were spread over a wide area which was mountainous and sparsely settled. Only narrow muddy trails connected the various small towns where the Guardias were stationed. Life on patrol was even tougher than I had found it in Santo Domingo. Distances were greater and commanding local troops was a constant strain. In some instances (as previously mentioned), the Guardias had mutinied and shot their officers and desertions had been frequent. Fortunately, I never had such troubles with my men except in one instance when five men deserted with their weapons and equipment. However, this was in connection with an order given by another officer."[9]

Soon after reaching the post, Craig received word that a Guardia detachment had mutinied and kidnapped their officers. It was expected that others might go over to the bandits. "At the time Kurchov was out on patrol, and not knowing my men too well, I was pretty nervous when I turned in that night." Craig slept with a BAR under his cot. The next day one of the sergeants asked if the detachment could serenade him after work. "It was not unusual to serenade people in Nicaragua, but I thought it strange under the circumstances. As darkness set in, I became more nervous when they did not appear. About eight o'clock there was a knock on my door, and when I opened it, every man who was not on duty was standing there." The men requested to come in. Craig really did not have a choice. "I thought to myself, well, this is it, they have me cold." Bandit groups were reported in the vicinity which did not help his peace of mind either.[10]

The men squeezed in and arranged themselves around the small room. A small kerosene lantern provided a weak light as the hard-looking group crowded around Craig. "To say I was afraid would be putting it mildly." Finally, a man started strumming his guitar—and the whole group broke into song. "The group loosened up when I passed out cigarettes and coffee. They cracked jokes and smiled. I finally understood, they were showing me their loyalty. I never had trouble with the men after that, and always felt secure when with them."[11]

Jinotega, A Depressing Place

Three days later I was on my way by plane to Jinotega, the capital of the department, located in north-central Nicaragua, under Major "Plug" Lowell. Jinotega was a depressing place. High in the mountains it was subject to frequent rains and clouds which hung low, usually causing a drizzle. The dirt streets were poorly drained and as a result were muddy or very dusty according to the season. The nights at times were really cold, and in the large local house where I lived with Major Lowell and other Guardia officers, we sometimes lit off a fire in the big fireplace during the evening. It was the custom in Nicaragua for women who had lost close relatives to wear black for many months. Due to the high death rate in the town, practically all the women wore black. This increased the feeling of depression and isolation. The locals were not friendly. Many of them had friends or relatives operating with Sandino's forces and resented the presence of the newly organized Guardia Nacional, and especially their white officers. In view of this our social life was rather restricted.[12]

Fourth of July was coming up and we decided to make our life with the locals a little more friendly by holding a fireworks display for the populace. A large supply of pyrotechnics of all kinds had been left in Jinotega by the Marines. On the night of the 4th, we hauled the fireworks to the middle of the plaza and dumped them in a pile. Hundreds of locals were invited, and they lined up on three sides of the plaza. The first rockets were set off and went up with a great whoosh, accompanied by the cheers of the locals. The second rocket was set off. It veered to one side and circled back into the plaza and landed directly on the large dump of pyrotechnics. Immediately all hell broke loose. Fireworks of all descriptions were shooting in every direction. I took cover behind a large tree and lay flat on the ground as rockets whizzed by. Everyone else was doing the same thing. The unscheduled display lasted for some time until finally the last pyrotechnic ignited and there was a momentary silence. Then, as everyone rose from the ground, the locals broke out into exited yells, as groups related their experiences. Fortunately, no one was seriously hurt, and the Americans' 4th of July celebration gave the populace much to talk and laugh about for many days afterwards. It did help to break the ice, and our relations with the locals were noticeably better afterwards.[13]

At this time the Guardia was in the process of taking over many of the outlying outposts which the Marines had previously manned. I found life in the Guardia much different from what I had been used to as a Marine. Some professional jealousy seemed to exist between the officers of the Marine Brigade and those detailed to the Guardia. A sad example of this came to my attention when a detachment of Guardia sent to relieve the Marines at San Rafael found that the Marine commander had deliberately destroyed much equipment which he could not take with him ... and could have been most useful to the Guardia. The past finally caught up with him when he was passed over for promotion.[14]

Yali, An Isolated Outpost

After a short time at Jinotega, Craig received orders to take command of his own company at Yali, a small, isolated town of approximately 250 individuals, situated in the high mountains about 30 miles from Jinotega. "We were the first Guardia to take over a town in this area and the people were afraid of the Nicaraguan troops and undoubtedly sided with the bandits in most cases. The townspeople were mostly hostile to the Guardia troops. The town was connected to several small adjoining hamlets by a narrow trail through rugged terrain—one high mountain after another with few trails and no roads—which made routine patrolling exhausting and frustrating. My junior officer was a corporal named Kurchov, who was serving as a second lieutenant in the Guardia. The first sergeant was named Navarrete, my most reliable Guardia. He was a higher-class Nicaraguan then the usual rank and file and was later commissioned in the Guardia."[15]

"The company had been formed in a hurry to take over the town from the Marines as they pulled out. It was composed of drafts from other companies of the battalion. Our mission was to suppress banditry, act as a police force, and build roads. On the morning of our departure from Jinotega, the vacancies in the company were filled by men released from the brig. At the time in question the Guardia detachment at Telepaneca which was located north of us had mutinied and kidnapped their two white officers. Sometimes, between my Guardia and the workers, I had a hard time deciding who to trust."[16]

The Guardias lived in a long low adobe building with a heavy adobe tiled roof that faced a plaza. "I had a small cubicle partitioned off with a frame covered with old ponchos in one corner of the main squad room. This frame was only about six feet high, so for all intents and purposes, I was practically in the same room with my troops." Craig and his lieutenant cooked their rations over a small outdoor fire. "Indigestion was often the result," he said. "I spent a week in the Brigade field hospital under treatment for a stomach ailment [probably an ulcer, which plagued him during the Iwo Jima operation in 1945]. I will never forget the morning I woke up in a clean bed and heard the band playing. I saw a battalion of Marines marching by with the National and 5th Marines colors. After months I had spent with the Guardias, who were usually comparatively small men, these Marines looked enormous! The colors gave me a thrill which I remember to this day. Serving with foreign troops and under another flag make one realize the love he holds for his own outfit."[17]

Shortly after Craig assumed command of the detachment, the post was attacked shortly after taps. "The bandits took up positions around the town and fired into our barracks. We had made plans for just such an emergency. I had my Guardias erect a six-foot, 10-strand barbed-wire fence in front of the cuartel. The back wall had guards with machine guns posted on it and other entrances had been barbed-wired, too. The signal for any emergency in the cuartel was a shot ... every man would go to his post. I also had doors or passageways made throughout, so that one could go from any part without going outside. We also stockpiled water, rations and ammunition in secure places. Certain Guardias manned defense positions while the bulk of my outfit formed an attack force."[18]

"We fanned out through the village and took the bandits under fire and they fled into the bush. Outside of a few hundred shells lying around we found nothing and returned to our barracks." A high-ranking officer of the Guardia inspected Craig's position and remarked, "There are no bandits in these parts so why all the barbed wire?" Craig explained why and the officer laughed it off. Upon leaving, he winked and remarked sarcastically, "Look out for bandits." "It was only a week after my detachment and departure that the bandits made a surprise attack in force, some 250 of them, armed with every weapon they had, including machine guns and grenades, and almost captured the place."[19]

Craig's detachment did not have a medical officer, not even a corpsman, so he was often called upon to treat injuries himself. "I remember my First Sergeant came down with an infected tooth. His whole face was swollen, and he was in great pain." Craig sent a message asking for assistance. They responded by sending him a pair of forceps. "I attempted to pull the tooth, but without any luck. The locals from the town gathered in the doorway while we were working on the poor man. Each time I would twist or yank on the tooth, he would pass out; and I'd have to bring him back again. I finally decided I couldn't do it and sent him to Jinotega where a local dentist extracted the abscessed tooth. Needless to say, my medical facilities were rather crude!"[20]

Craig found that the Guardias were good soldiers and loyal if they were treated like men and only punished when they understood that they had committed an offense. "If a Guardia knew he was guilty one could knock him down and he would not resist. However, punish one of them unjustly and your life was in danger. Being the only white man among fifty or a hundred of these local troops on patrol, with only a poor command of the Spanish language could be nerve wracking. The Guardias watched every movement or expression one made, and could pretty well tell how one was reacting." Most of Craig's men had an Indian background, so while the Spanish he learned in school helped quite a bit, he also had to learn many Indian words to be understood.[21]

Craig found that life in the Guardia was one crisis after another. He was in his small office one morning when a shot rang out and a bullet thudded into the wall beside his head. "Seems a Guardia who had just enlisted let his rifle to off while on guard in the tower. He deserted the next morning and I never did find out if the shot was accidental or intentional."[22]

The Guardias were tough and they had to be, according to Craig, in order to deal with the bandits and criminal elements. "I remember on one occasion, I gave orders to a Guardia to arrest a murderer. Later on in the day, I heard a loud thump outside my door. A Guardia came in and handed me a large pearl-handled .44 revolver, and told me the prisoner was outside. I said, 'Bring him in.'" The Guardia went outside and came back in, dragging a body by the legs. "It seems the man was armed and the Guardia, not wanting to take any chances, fired first. The thump I heard was the body being dropped from the Guardia's horse."[23]

Craig found that he had to be always on the alert for brutality. "In a country where killings, water cures, and hot pepper enemas were routine questioning techniques, one had to be on the watch to prevent excesses on the part of the Guardias." He had a burly Nicaraguan first sergeant who always seemed to be able to extract information from prisoners. "I was passing a small roof off the sallyport and found his method was to have a Guardia hold the prisoner while he grabbed his testicles and twisted. Being a powerful man, it seems only a few twists were necessary."[24]

"The government started a road-building program to support the economy and, at the same time, increase security in the remote areas by keeping potential bandits gainfully employed. I hired three hundred locals at fifty cents a day. They were issued picks and shovels and wheelbarrows, and that was the only road-building equipment they had." Craig laid out the route for a two-lane road with rather crude instruments. "I did not have a transit, so I constructed one out of field glasses and my marching compass, levels, and so forth. This jury-rigged system served the purpose."[25]

Craig laid the road out in long, straight stretches. "The locals got quite a kick out of seeing the roads go straight through fields and fences, rather than follow the old trails in a roundabout way. Blasting necessarily had to be done, and when we first got there, the only thing we had were cans of black powder, which was packed in on mules, minus fuses. We made our own using paper and black powder."[26]

At the end of each week, the men were paid. The money was dropped by plane, usually in large packs of one Cordova bills—a Cordova being one dollar in U.S. currency. "I had no place to keep these large packages of bills, which sometimes amounted to $3,000 to $4,000 at a drop. To reduce the size and be able to hide or carry this money, I contracted a German merchant to change it to U.S. dollars. I would stuff as many bills as I could in a money belt and put the rest in the walls of my room.

I naturally worried a great deal about the money ... but fortunately none of it ever disappeared."[27]

"Many of the men I employed were part-time bandits, and when most of them did not show up for work, I could always count on increased bandit activity while they were away." He never knew how to take his workers; sometimes they would be sullen and at other times smiling and contented. Craig sent out two of his men dressed and armed as bandits. "They encountered two of my workers on a side trail, and identified themselves as members of [guerrilla chief Augusto Cesar] Sandino's Army."* The undercover Guardias asked the workers to guide them in an attack on Craig's post. "The two immediately gave the information and stated they would help in the attack, if given rifles, as they hated the government and the Guardia." The two were arrested and Craig was surprised to find they were among his best workers.[28]

Normally, when Craig supervised the road gangs, he rode with four to five Guardia escorts. One day, however, he sent them on ahead, and almost immediately regretted the decision. "I was rounding a sharp curve. A deep valley dropped away on one side and a ridge overlooked me from across the valley. A bullet smacked against the stone cliff, missing me by inches, and I heard the report of a rifle." Craig put the spurs to his horse and bounded to cover before the hidden rifleman could fire another shot. On another occasion, while he was with the road gang, twelve bandits waved at him with their rifles. "They stood and watched us for some time but offered us no resistance and finally left. I had only two of my Guardias with me at the time and did not feel we should start a battle."[29]

A political leader urged Craig to take his brand-new Ford touring car to one of his outposts. Craig took two men and completed the first half of the tour without difficulty. On the way back, however, "We had no

---

* From May 1927 to December 1932, the Nicaraguan nationalist Augusto C. Sandino waged guerrilla war against the U.S. Marines and Guardia Nacional de Nicaragua to expel the "Yankee invaders" and achieve genuine national sovereignty. The war was centered in Las Segovias, the mountainous, sparsely populated northcentral region of Nicaragua bordering Honduras. Source: Digital Resources: The Sandino Rebellion Digital Historical Archive, Nicaragua, 1927–1934.

sooner started than a terrific storm came up. The further we went, the worse the road became. It was pitch dark and the rain was pouring down with much lightning and thunder." The car skidded off the road, rolled down a gully, and got stuck at the bottom. The driver knew the way to a ranch house. "It was after midnight when we reached the house. A sudden flash of lightening revealed a long porch where several men were asleep. Leaning against the wall behind them were rifles." Craig knew they could not be Guardia and signaled the others to hit the muddy ground. Quietly, they slithered back the way they had come, thanking their lucky stars the storm covered their getaway. "If the bandits had a sentry posted, the story might have had a different ending."[30]

Chinandega, A Political Quagmire

After being released from the hospital for the stomach ailment, Craig was ordered to Chinandega, which was on the railroad, partly between Managua and Corinto, the main port on the west coast. It is one of the largest departments in the country. Craig's duties included Guardia company commander, department commander and chief of police. As the chief of police, he was subject to the pressure of corrupt politicians. In one case, Craig was ordered by the President of Nicaragua to arrest and incarcerate his next-door neighbor, a wealthy businessman. No charges were brought and the man was released after several months by buying his way out of jail. "This was done in a number of cases," according to Craig.[31]

In another instance, the assistant warden killed a prisoner who was trying to escape. Craig conducted an investigation that found the Guardia innocent. However, an influential Liberal party politician friend influenced the President to incarcerate the man, who was Conservative. After several months, he was tried and sentenced to 50 years. Craig was distraught because he was one of the best Guardias he had and mentioned to his first sergeant, "I'll be very happy if that man disappears suddenly. I can't see him getting 50 years in prison for carrying out his duties. Two days later, a funny thing happened, he'd escaped during the night and received asylum in Honduras."[32]

"In the Department of Chinandega, we had an average of two or three machete-fight killings between civilians each month. The winner of the fight became a hunted man, and many joined the bandits or went over the border to Honduras." After one of the fights, the "winner" was arrested and incarcerated in the local hoosegow. Unfortunately, for the miscreant, the jailer was a relative of the victim. Craig was notified that a riot had developed after the prisoner was savagely murdered in his cell. "I found a milling crowd of some 2,000 Nicaraguans in front of the Cuartel [jail]. The body of the murdered man lay on the street, guarded by four Guardias. I could see a dangerous situation was in the making and ordered an interpreter [to] tell the mob that I would investigate ... and in the meantime stay calm." While the interpreter talked with the crowd, Craig telephoned for reinforcements. Just as the situation was turning critical, 10 Guardias carrying a machine gun roared up—in the best tradition of the cavalry. "When they had set it up, the mob began to disperse, and in twenty minutes the last one had disappeared."[33]

One of Craig's duties was to conduct a monthly inspection of all outposts. One of his main outposts was at Somotillo, near the Honduran border, a distance of 54 miles through thick jungle and scrub. "Mosquitoes were very thick, so thick in fact, they would swarm my horse and bring blood." Craig would leave Chinandega early in the morning and wouldn't arrive in Somotillo until after dark, a very tough ride. From there he would cross another mountain and inspect two other outposts, which sometime took him a week in the saddle.[34]

Craig decided to throw a big party as a way to develop a rapport with the locals. He was "rather nervous" about it because of the threat of bandit attack. "I asked my head man whether he thought the bandits would interfere. He laughed and put his arms around my shoulders and said, "Never worry, there are too many of them right here. You will have no trouble at all!"[35]

Craig noticed that after a few miles of the road had been constructed, the locals started coming in from outlying villages on Sundays to sell produce. "The road did much to open the country. I had about four or five miles constructed when I was ordered to other duty."[36]

Craig was always thankful for Marine aviation. "Each day one or two planes would come over to check and would not leave till they had observed an arrangement of air panels acknowledging that all was well." The planes would also deliver and pick up mail. "On patrol, if bandit information was hot, they would fly over to maintain contact for a certain period of the day, and if there was anything ahead, they would notify us with a message drop." The aircraft would also drop mail by means of drop sticks and pick up messages by means of a pick-up pole and string." The pilots were not averse to a little gallows humor. "One of the tricks they pulled on me was to drop colored advertisements taken from magazines of chocolate cakes, puddings, baked hams, etc. They knew we yearned for such things [which] were impossible to get. Rather a perverted sense of humor I thought at the time."[37]

After two and a half years in Nicaragua, Craig received orders to report to the embryonic 1st Marine Division at San Diego. The orders directed him to travel via Navy oil tanker. After all the hardships he had suffered, Craig requested to proceed at his own expense and come home in style. "Accordingly, I boarded the SS *Columbia* of the Panama Mail Steamship Line on September 2, 1931." After several stops along the coast, the ship docked at Mazatlan, Mexico, where the passengers went ashore for a celebration party. "Returning to the ship, we continued to party in the bar. The general air of festivities must have been catching, as I saw many trays of drinks going up to the ship's officers near the bridge." After getting under way, the ship encountered rough weather and high winds. Craig went below to his stateroom. "What a relief to have a clean cabin, a hot shower, and all the comforts of home. I lay down and relaxed on my bunk and thought how smart I had been to travel in this luxury."[38]

Craig dropped off to sleep. "I was awakened when I found myself on the deck. The ship was at an angle and the door to my stateroom was slanted over me. At first, I thought that it might be too many drinks." He soon realized the ship was in trouble and grabbed some personal articles and headed topside. "I could clearly see that we were aground. The ship was getting lower in the water and canted at quite an angle. The captain gave the orders to abandon ship." The lifeboats were swung out and all women and children were successfully loaded—but with great difficulty because of the canted deck. "When my turn came to leave, I had to climb down a Jacob's ladder. As I was about halfway down, crude oil spurted from a burst oil storage tank and covered us with crude oil, including everybody in the boat I was in. Craig manned an oar, along with some of the crew, and started to pull away from the ship. "The captain, known as 'Whispering Oakes' because of his name and loud voice, yelled down, 'Don't light any matches or it will burn up.' The engine room crew, who were not too fond of him, yelled back, 'Shut up you old son of bitch. We hope you go down with the ship!'"[39]

The lifeboats milled around for some time, as the various boat officers argued about the best course of action. It was quite rough and pitch dark; some of the ship's officers were still feeling pretty good, and they decided to row for shore. Craig was finally able to convince his still-tipsy officer to head for the open sea because of the jagged shoreline. "Sometime later we spotted a steamer on the horizon. We sent up rockets from most of the boats, but the steamer continued on its way." The bedraggled passengers quickly succumbed to mal de mar in the rough seas. "I could feel someone on the bottom of the boat every time I pulled on the oar. When daylight came, I found it was a German who was so sick that he would not even sit up." Late that morning, the SS *San Mateo* rescued them, ending their *Titanic*-like saga. An investigation revealed that *Columbia* had skirted the coast too close to Cape San Lucas and hit a submerged rock. Craig bemoaned his loss. "I lost all my clothing and personal gear, including a fine collection of some thirty-five beautiful revolvers. The only things I saved were my Zeiss field glasses, my Colt pistol, and my wallet. I landed in a pair of dungarees."[40]

His wife, Elizabeth "Betty" met him at San Pedro, "with a new car and a suitcase full of clothes. I got dressed and reported to the commandant of the district in civilian clothes. He sarcastically informed me it was the first time that any officer had reported in civilian clothes."[41]

Electoral Commission, June–November 1932

Craig was assigned for a short time to the 1st Marine Division, which was then forming at Camp Pendleton. After participating in a training exercise in Hawaii, he was reassigned to the Recruit Depot, San Diego as executive officer. In June 1932, he received orders to organize an electoral detachment under the State Department for duty in Nicaragua to conduct elections.

"I was assigned duty as president of the electoral board in Chinandega department, which I had previously served in, and which helped quite a bit because I knew the people and the political situation." Craig ran into so many difficulties from bandit interference that he requested permission to "use my own discretion in changing electoral laws and procedures as necessary to fit the situation." He received approval. "Due to a very rainy season, making the trails and rivers almost impassable, and the bandit situation, we had a terrific time putting this election over, but it went over very fine in the end...."[42] After six months, he returned to the United States in November 1932.

In a letter to the author in 1985 after reading a Vietnam article about small unit operations, Craig pointed out similarities with his experiences in Haiti, Nicaragua, and Santo Domingo:

> There our forces were smaller of course, but [our] base camps were set up at critical points and squad and platoon-size units operated against the enemy. Main bases were used by regiments and the Brigade, and these were more or less permanent during the entire campaign. Many platoon-size outposts were maintained which gave junior officers valuable leadership experience. Usually, guerrilla activity was confined to a small part of the country, but security had to be maintained over other areas too. I must say, that due to a lack of adequate communications, poor planning in coordinating in the operations of patrols, and inexperience of some commanders, there was much to be desired. However, where regimental commanders really took charge and showed leadership, much was accomplished ... Sorry to say, none of the brigade commanders ever visited my outfit ... and visits by battalion commanders were infrequent.[43]

CHAPTER 10

Oriental Adventures 1924–26

USS *Huron*

Upon return to the United States, "I went to the detail officer in Washington, D.C. and requested duty in San Diego. He told me that funds for transportation were quite low, but if I wanted to pay my own way ... I agreed, and was told to report to the Department of the Pacific in San Francisco for further assignment to San Diego." It was not to be. Upon reporting, instead of San Diego, he was ordered to the Naval Ammunition Depot at Puget Sound, Washington. "Perhaps later on I could be transferred to San Diego."[1]

"I arrived in Puget Sound with no money and minus a couple of meals on the way up. I went to the Marine Barracks Navy Yard and saw the mess sergeant, who gave me a free meal. The next day I took over as the Commanding Officer of the ammunition depot." For the next year and a half, Craig enjoyed the comfort of a fully furnished house and the benefits of his rank. He was able to make changes that benefited the enlisted men, but he was a "bachelor at the time and in a rather isolated position and requested a change of duty."[2]

His request for transfer was approved and he received orders to Olongapo, Philippine Islands, where "I found there were many [illegal] things that were not going as they should. I suspected that my commanding officer was involved in various shady deals, and although I could not put my hands directly on them, I decided that I wanted a transfer as soon as I could." Craig's suspicions were confirmed "a few months later when the officer was brought to trial by general courts martial and discharged from the service."[3]

It just so happened that the USS *Huron*, an armored cruiser, flagship of the Asiatic Fleet, arrived for repairs. Craig was able to work out a trade with the *Huron*'s detachment commander and soon found himself on a two-year cruise, "One of the most enjoyable tours of duty that I ever had. We spent the best season of each year in China and the Philippines and touched at every port of importance from Vladivostok to Batavia, Java."[4]

"The admiral had it all figured out where the best weather would be at certain times, and I think he must have scheduled his ships accordingly. The admiral lived on a converted yacht with his family, and even an orchestra. He lashed a Cadillac on the boat deck, and in Manila he had a special barge at his disposal."[5]

"I took part in three landing force operations and spent some six months ashore in China. The first landing was in Shanghai shortly after I joined *Huron*. Rival Chinese armies were fighting outside the city and the [Shanghai] City Council was afraid that they would retreat into the city. The Marines were landed to protect the foreign nationals in the International Settlement, together with the British Marines, Italian, and Japanese troops, for about a month.[6]

"The Marines' main duty on the *Huron* was furnishing the guards, manning the four 6-inch guns and controlling them, acting as the captain's and admiral's orderlies. As a flagship, we made cruises up and down the coast from Vladivostok all the way down to Java. At every port, of course, there were many functions for the officers and crew; so, it was a very pleasant two years, interspersed with various landings."[7]

Expeditionary Duty Peking

The political and military situation in North China was rapidly worsening. Heavy fighting was taking place between rival warlords and because of the danger to United States citizens, their property, and American interests, Marines were often called upon to intervene.

"Emergency orders arrived on the *Huron* at Chefoo directing the Marine detachment, 3 officers and 135 men, to disembark ... in destroyers and proceed to Tientsin where we would take a train and go to Peking to reinforce the Legation Guard there, with all haste. Chiang Tso-lin and Wu Pei-fu were battling in the area. Chiang was holding Peking and Wu's armies were coming up the railroads ... from a place called Shanhaikwan. The situation in the city was 'approaching pandemonium.' Chinese ships choked the river, Chinese deserters were looting the local quarter, and all foreigners had been called into the International Settlement for protection by the U.S. Army's 15th Infantry Regiment. The fact that we had to pass between the fighting lines of two rival armies to get to Peking seemed not to concern the headquarters that issued the order!"[8]

"The *Huron* arrived at the Taku Bar where tugs and barges took aboard the detachment and transported it to the quay at Tientsin. As no trains were running and the rival Chinese armies were by now deployed across the railroad tracks leading to Peking, we were at a loss as to how to proceed further." A British civilian, an old China hand who spoke Mandarin, helped get a train together. "Before long we had an engine and four cars attached. We quickly got underway, even though we didn't have written orders."[9]

"We draped a huge American flag over the front of the engine and slowly steamed out of the station. Eight or ten miles out of Tientsin, we ran into our first trouble. Troop trains, filled with thousands of Chinese troops, artillery, and even mules and camels, completely blocked the tracks. We located the local Chinese general and, after some argument by the old China hand, persuaded him to shunt his troop train onto a siding. We finally got underway. Dead soldiers lay about attesting to the fighting. We could also see soldiers, in hastily dug trenches, on both sides of the track."[10]

"The armies maintained by the warlords were huge, and I found that a large percentage were professionals who had been soldiering all their lives. The officers in many cases were trained at the Whampoa Military Academy in Canton, and at many foreign schools. I was later to see first-hand a close up of a Chinese Army in action [Korea, 1950]."[11]

"It was only the first of several stops before we arrived outside Peking. At another stop I noted a long train containing White Russian soldiers in regular Russian uniforms, who had fled Russia and were fighting for one of the warlords. Their equipment looked good, and they even had Russian nurses. Later I heard that this brigade had been put in a position where they were practically annihilated because their officers were negotiating to switch sides."[12]

"At Peking, a Chinese officer came into our freezing compartment—all the windows had been knocked out and the Marines were in khaki shirts and trousers—and demanded our written authority for entering the city. We had none, so we attempted to argue, but to no avail. Finally, Marine Gunner E. Kellison pulled out an old set of travel orders authorizing travel from Cavite to Shanghai and pushed them under the Chinese officers' face. The official looking document—it had a good heading and a signature—convinced him and we were allowed to proceed."[13]

"I had orders to reserve a state room for a British general but when I got aboard, I found the room was occupied by officials from the Soviet Embassy. I explained the situation to them—one of them spoke English—and they informed me that they were as good as anybody's general ... and they wouldn't move. There was a squad of British soldiers right near the entrance to the car. I told the sergeant to clear the room ... and before I hardly gave the order, he was in there with three or four men; and they had the Russians out in the aisle!

"The trip to Peking gave me my first real look at a Chinese Army in the field. I was amazed at the organization and equipment of the various units. While transport was crude, consisting of mostly dated trucks, mule carts, pack mules and even camels, it seemed to be sufficient to support operations. At one of the stops, I had the opportunity of looking at a military school. It was set up on a train complete with classrooms and sleeping cars for the students and instructors. The train would remain well in the rear of the fighting lines but the students, consisting of young boys aged about 16 to 19 would be given the opportunity between classes to observe the fighting."[14]

One of the Marines' main duties was to disarm any Chinese troops that came into the International Settlement. "One time they disarmed so many, that we had a pile 10 feet high of Mauser automatic pistols and thousands of rifles, which we turned over to the Municipal Council and melted." "Each legation would furnish a guard," Craig said, "normally 10 to 12 men armed with rifles and BARs. However, the Japanese would often exceed this number and instead provide a full platoon of forty to fifty men, which caused some concern in the diplomatic community as the Western diplomats attempted to remain neutral as possible in the fighting that had been ongoing since 1911.[15]

"After several weeks of duty in Peking, I was ordered to rejoin the *Huron* at Chefoo, where the Marine detachment was 'coaling' the ship in a heavy rain. The Marines were filthy and completely disillusioned with sea duty. We normally coaled once a month. It was an all-hands operation and commenced before daylight. The band played while everyone shoveled. Sometimes we coaled from Chinese junks or Japanese colliers, but usually from four large barges which would be tied up, two to a side."[16]

The call, "Rig ship for coaling" was hated by all hands. It was a backbreaking dirty business, which left the ship and crew covered with thick, black coal dust, which was very difficult to clean off. The coal would be shoveled into canvas bags and carried aboard the ship and then shoveled into the ship's bunkers.

Saigon: Pearl of the Far East

"The *Huron* threaded its way past numerous small islands and inlets as the city of Saigon came into view and we soon tied up to the dock. Saigon was one of the best liberty ports that we visited. However, our mission was diplomatic, to show the flag and make friends. At the time, I was treasurer of the Wardroom mess and it fell on my lot to go out in town and purchase certain special food and drinks for a huge party that the ship's officers were giving for the townspeople. We solved the problem of drinks on a Navy ship by having certain staterooms well stocked with Cognac—the national drink in Indo China—and invite a few guests at a time to sample the stock. The party was a huge success."[17]

"Between official parties, we roamed the city. One of the points of interest was the government-operated opium house which we visited. I saw hundreds of locals and foreigners smoking opium or sleeping off its effects. Each of our party tried a puff or two from an opium pipe. I felt no effects whatever but some of our party carried on the appearance of having got a kick from it and insisted on pulling the rickshaws with the drivers in the seat! I did note that at a couple of parties we attended in private homes that the French smoked opium openly and apparently nothing was thought of it. We left Saigon for China with regrets as the people were friendly and full of fun. I found my mess account was $250 short. I laid it to lose shopping ashore and paid the shortage out of my own pocket. It was not until some years later that I was going through some books and papers in my trunk that I found receipts covering my shortage."[18]

Shanghai: Pearl of the Orient

"On 30 May 1925, we arrived in Chefoo, China, and had just completed night battle practice with the 6-inch guns when a message arrived directing the Marine detachment to embark on two destroyers, USS *Stewart* and USS *Hart*, for transfer to Shanghai. An Allied landing force was being assembled post haste to protect the International Settlement."[19] The Chinese were in one of their unending civil wars and anti-foreign uprisings. On June 1, 1925, consular representatives at an international conference at Shanghai requested an international naval force sufficient to land 2,000 men; on June 5, there was due to arrive at Shanghai the destroyers *Hart* and *Stewart*, transporting the Flagship *Huron*'s Marines.[20]

"As we left Chefoo harbor, storm warnings were flying, and a few hours out, we were hit by a typical Asiatic typhoon. I had never been in a 'tin can' during rough weather before and it seemed at times we were literally sliding along on the sides of the ship. At other times the bow would be in the air and then come crashing down with a big slap ... with the propellers whirling and shaking the ship as they spun in the air. At two in the morning, I decided to see how my men were faring. I had a terrific time finding them. Most of them were lying in the passageways or the fireroom and deathly seasick! Many of the officers and crew were also affected. I was congratulating myself on my sea legs when I arrived back in the wardroom where I found a terrific odor of alcohol permeating it. That did it! I became seasick immediately."[21]

"We finally arrived off the mouth of the Whangpoo. I was detailed to go ashore and determine the situation and confer with the senior officer ashore as to our disposition. As I went up Nanking Road I noticed that all shops and windows were barricaded and there were very few people in the streets. There had been rioting and the police station had been attacked by communist-inspired students. Even in 1925 the communists were starting to work on the people in preparation to finally taking over. I found that we were to take over the Shanghai College for billets and patrol a designated sector of the city in conjunction with British, Italian, French and Japanese landing forces."[22]

"By noon the Marines were starting to land in a driving rain and we marched through the city to the College. The place was literally packed with printing presses and piles of communist propaganda books and leaflets. Huge bonfires took care of the situation, and we were soon billeted and patrols dispatched. We spent over two months on this duty, and as things finally calmed down we found time for a little liberty."[23]

"I was returning to my billet late one night after having dinner with friends, and in order to save time, I decided to take a short cut through a long dark alley in the French Concession. I had my pistol wrapped inside a folded newspaper as I did not want to carry it openly while on liberty. As I was about to emerge from the alley into a lighted street, I could hear a commotion and shots. At that moment a man ran into the alley towards me. Suddenly another man appeared and fired a number of shots at the first man, who dropped dead at my feet! I was by this time fumbling to get my pistol out of the newspaper. I finally recognized the man with a carbine as an Annamite policeman employed by the French Concession. As he came up to me, he pumped two more shots into the prostrate form at my feet."[24]

"Before I knew it, the alley was filled with Chinese. They were in a hostile mood and shouting at both the policeman and me. Anti-foreign feeling was still high in Shanghai and a mob would not understand who had killed the man lying in the alley. The policeman and I finally pushed and fought our way to the street where we found a big private limousine stalled in the crowd. I got in and the policeman followed still clutching the dead man. He dragged him inside, closed the door, and poking his carbine in the back of the Chinese chauffeur who was protesting loudly about the blood on the seats, ordered him to drive on through the mob. Finally, after much shouting and threats we were able to get away."[25]

"Armed robbery was at that time always punished by death, and it was not unusual to see trucks loaded with four or five Chinese convicted of armed robbery being paraded through the streets with signs telling of their sentence. I went out one time to see the sentences carried out. They were bound hand and foot. Hands behind their backs. Then made to kneel and an executioner with a huge sword chopped off each head in turn. The blood would shoot high in the air as the headless corpse fell over. The prisoners never seemed to make any resistance and usually uttered no word during the whole proceedings."[26]

"More trouble started to brew along the waterfront in the Hongkew Wharf area and we were ordered to move our billets as a result. We were assigned to the Shanghai Shipbuilding compound and I have never had to live in a dirtier, filthier place in my career. Cholera had broken out in the city and many were dying each day of it, so when I found the situation existing at our new billets I was deeply concerned. The Chinese had been using the rooms as toilets and they were deep in filth. The courtyard was a foot deep in filth which had collected over a long period and the surface could be seen moving with maggots. Flies were thick and a terrible odor hung over the whole place. I convinced the health authorities to send a clean-up squad to help us out. They arrived with rubber suits, masks and disinfectant. Fortunately, we only had to stay in the place for two weeks and I had no cases of cholera occur. It was a relief when orders came for us to embark on the destroyers and rejoin the *Huron* anchored off the Bund."[27]

"I received orders to take eight Marines and proceed to the foreign cemetery to take charge of the body of the American Foreign Minister, who had died in Peking, and escort the remains to the USS *Chaumont*. We proceeded to the cemetery in full blue dress uniforms. I was most surprised when the funeral director turned over a little square box—the minister had been cremated—which upset all the planning centered on a coffin."[28]

While in Shanghai, Craig met a young woman who would become his wife, Elizabeth "Betty" Newton.

I first met Betty in Shanghai in 1925. She was an orphan living in a convent in Yokohama, when an earthquake struck. She was one of the few survivors. Old friends of her family, who lived in Shanghai, were appointed guardians. In 1929, she moved to Washington, D.C., where we were married. She was a beautiful and wonderful person and we were very close.[29]

Crossing the Equator—Pollywog to Shellback

"I had never crossed the equator and those of us who were still pollywogs [uninitiated shellbacks] finally found the *Huron* headed south from Singapore to Surabaya, Java in the Dutch East Indies. As we neared the imaginary line of the equator, subpoenas to appear before Neptune's Court were given to us. I was charged with being a Marine, the most dangerous criminal."[30]

"The night before we crossed the line, Neptune's policemen—the biggest, roughest members of the crew were equipped with truncheons— long canvas bags filled with sand—and handcuffs. I was handcuffed to a stanchion in the junior officer's stateroom, while others were locked below decks in empty compartments for the night. Early the next morning we were taken to see King Neptune climb over the bow. A huge platform and tank of water had been constructed on the forecastle. Two chairs, arranged with their backs to the water made for easy tipping."[31]

"The pollywogs were brought before the court, their charges read, and sentence pronounced and executed, with great dispatch. If it was a Marine, all the Shellbacks would yell, 'Treat him easy, he's a Marine,' and, of course he would get the works. Pills made from soap, putty and quinine and a haircut. The royal barber clipped a path through their hair, down to their scalp. They were then lathered with fuel oil; the chair was tipped and into the tank they went. The 'bear,' a huge sailor, grabbed them and held them underwater, raising and lowering them, until dazed, they were put over the side to face a double line 'policemen' with the canvas clubs. The unfortunates then ran the gauntlet."[32]

"A number of officers and enlisted men, including myself had sneaked away, but I was discovered and punished! As I cleared the gauntlet, half drowned, my mouth full of vile tasting 'pills' and what hair I had left saturated with fuel oil, I headed for the showers ... I was now a full-fledged Shellback, but I still felt shaky! I soon found how hard it is to get fuel oil off and the taste of raw quinine and soap out of your mouth. The royal barbers had ruined my hair, made me a sorry sight to court the girls of the various ports we were to visit."[33]

"Little did I think that my next crossing the equator would be on the SS *Bloemfontein*, code name 'Burp', a Dutch liner taking me to World War II in the Pacific, nor that my certificate of crossing would be lost in the sinking of the SS *Columbia* off Cape San Lucas, Mexico."[34]

Stateside Duty 1926–28

Upon returning to the United States, Craig joined the truncated 4th Marine Regiment at the Marine Corps Base, San Diego, as a company officer. "I had been placed in command of Company 'A' with orders to embark aboard the USS *Utah** for an amphibious landing on San Clemente Island. That evening, I watched the old battleship back slowly away from the pier and saw that the USS *Holland* was directly in her path. In seconds, her clipper bow cut along the quarterdeck taking off stanchions and lifelines. The *Utah* finally stopped and continued out of the harbor."[35]

"Shortly after daylight the following morning we debarked over the side into small boats. Many of the men in my boat were seasick. I had a sergeant who considered himself quite salty. He spent much of the time berating the seasick men, calling them recruits and softies. It was just before we hit the beach, we were ordered to turn around, but we got lost in the fog. For hours we pitched and tossed in the heavy seas. Almost every man was seasick, and the sergeant still berated them. Finally, one very sick Marine pulled out a corned beef sandwich from his pack and offered it to the hazer: 'Here, if you are so salty eat this!' The sergeant

---

* In 1931, *Utah* was demilitarized and converted into a target ship. At Pearl Harbor on the morning of December 7, 1941, she was hit by two Japanese torpedoes, which caused serious flooding. *Utah* quickly rolled over and sank; 58 men were killed, but the vast majority of her crew were able to escape. The wreck remains in the harbor.

took one bite and promptly heaved over the side. A great cheer went up from the men. Late afternoon, we finally made it back to the ship."[36]

"Sometime later, I was again aboard the *Utah* for a landing on Midway, as part of a fleet problem VII, to test amphibious doctrines and equipment. Debarking in heavy seas was hazardous and a cruiser was brought alongside to make calmer water. Even then the landing boats bobbed up and down on the swells and one had to hang to the net and jump into the boat as it came up on the swell. Several men were injured after jumping at the wrong time."[37]

"Our landing craft formed a column to pass through the entrance to the reef and land on the beach. We ran for 300 yards across the soft white coral sand in a terrific heat toward the cover of the sand dunes and dwarf Magnolia, which grew thick across the island. Imagine our surprise when we entered the trees and found literally thousands of huge gooney birds [albatross] nested among the bushes. They did not run but simply snapped their beaks at us and refused to budge.* We stayed on the island for two weeks laying out defenses and carrying out various exercises, and then we returned to Pearl Harbor."[38]

"Relations with the Japanese were not too good at the time, and we had been practically on their front door on this maneuver. Full wartime conditions were observed and for the first time the entire U.S. Fleet was to be based in Pearl Harbor as a unit.† Great security precautions were taken ... all cameras were required to be turned in so that any pictures of the fleet berthed there would never get to the Japs. As our ship steamed into a berth through the narrow channel, we discussed the foolishness of putting all the ships of the fleet in a place that could be so easily blocked up or attacked by air. Little did we think however that the good ship

---

* Gooney birds still inhabit the island, as the author found during a tour of the island. The birds cover the island and dare a trespasser to come within "snapping" distance.

† President Roosevelt ordered the fleet to Pearl Harbor over the objections of Admiral James O. Richardson, commander in chief of the United States Fleet, who believed basing the fleet at Pearl Harbor would pose an irresistible target for the Japanese. After a heated meeting with the President, Richardson was relieved because he "hurt the President's feelings," according to the Secretary of the Navy.

Utah would someday lie on the bottom of Pearl Harbor, the victim of a Japanese bomb."[39]

"Liberty was granted and in Honolulu we found that practically every Japanese photo shop had pictures of the fleet. The photographs had been taken from the heights above Pearl Harbor, developed and printed the day we arrived, and were for sale the next day. The cameras we had turned in were not returned to us until after we had left Hawaii a week later."[40]

Craig was ordered to the senior course at Quantico in 1937. He thought the course was excellent and that it helped prepare him to handle the increased responsibilities as he advanced in rank. The course taught the "Guam Problem," dealing with the capture of Guam, which turned out to be far-sighted seven years later when Craig led the 9th Marines attacking the same locations on the island he had studied. The school year was difficult for him. "My wife was ill and under treatment for tuberculosis, and I could not take her with me and I had to leave her in San Diego. I rented a home there and hired a practical nurse to care for her. I did not see her again till the end of the school year. We wrote each other each day and telephoned frequently. I lived in the Bachelor Officers' Quarters. Weekends were really lonesome ... I rode horseback, shot on the range, visited Civil War battlefields ... money was really scarce."[41]

PART III

World War II 1941–45

CHAPTER II

Staff, Aircraft Battle Force

Upon completing the senior course, Craig was ordered back to San Diego where he was able to care for his wife. He remained there for six months before being assigned as the Marine Intelligence Officer on the staff of Admiral King, Commander, Aircraft Battle Force, aboard the USS *Yorktown*.* He and his wife were separated for long stretches. "The ship was in and out of San Diego, and back and forth to Hawaii and Bremerton, and long stretches at sea on maneuvers," which posed a hardship in caring for his sick wife.[1]

Professionally, Craig was proud of his time on the *Yorktown*. He organized the Battle Force's Intelligence Procedure Order and the Combat Intelligence Section, which operated on the flagship bridge during maneuvers. "I was also connected with quite a number of intelligence activities going on around Pearl Harbor, which at that time was getting to be a hot place."

---

* Admiral Halsey placed Craig on a special board to develop an incendiary bomb, the forerunner of napalm, "that could be made from local materials at Pearl Harbor, and which would be suitable for dropping from an airplane in quantities." Admiral Halsey explained that neither the Army or the Navy had a real incendiary bomb that was available in case of emergency such as war with Japan, which might develop at any time and at short notice. He wanted something that he could drop on such places as Tokyo and Yokohama in case such a war should come. "We built a small wooden village, and a section of planes dropped the bombs on it and completely burned up the village." A type of these incendiary bombs was later used during Operation *Meetinghouse*, the bombing of Tokyo in which conservative estimates placed the number of Japanese killed to 80,000 to 100,000 people. Craig, interview, 115.

He served under Admirals King and Halsey. He characterized King as "a real work horse and required everybody under him to be the same. I noticed that a good many officers on his staff had developed ulcers ... but Admiral King nevertheless got results, and he had that Aircraft Battle Force ready for war when he left. He was a good commander." Admiral Halsey he characterized as a very calm, very quiet, and very kindly officer. "I was greatly surprised during the war when I heard him called 'Bull' Halsey, because while I served with him, he was a most considerate, very quiet officer, who demanded results but did not get them in a loud way. We knew we had to put out, and if you didn't, you would get a negative report or get transferred; he had a very fine outfit."[2]

Second Marine Division

On February 24, 1942, Craig was transferred to the 2nd Marine Division that was forming at Camp Pendleton and assigned as Commanding Officer, 2nd Pioneer Battalion, 2nd Marine Division. "I was not too happy to be assigned to service troops. I wanted to stay with the infantry, but I realized that my rank precluded it. Only so many colonels in the division could have a command of that type. I talked to General Barrett, my division commander, and told him that I would do what I possibly could to make service troops what he wanted, but I would like to get an infantry outfit if I possibly could, and he promised me at that time that the first vacancy that came up I would have. At this time, I did not know what a pioneer battalion was." However, he began an intense period of infantry and engineer tactics and landing operations training. "Knowing the CO of the Recruit Depot, I made arrangements to have some very fine and highly qualified men transferred to my battalion, and before long, I had a well-trained outfit of which I was very proud."

Three months later, Craig was transferred to the 9th Marines and assigned as executive officer under his old friend Colonel Lemuel Shepherd, Jr. (later Commandant of the Marine Corps). "One day Colonel Shepherd stopped by to see me and I took him out to watch my men train. They put on a good show and soon after I was transferred to the 9th Marines as regimental executive officer." Craig found out later that as soon as Shepherd left the training area, he had gone to the division commander and asked for his transfer to the 9th Marines.[3]

Shortly after Craig joined the regiment, it was transferred to the new base at Camp Pendleton, 40 miles north of San Diego. "We marched early one morning under full combat equipment and with all motor transport. Colonel Shepherd believed in having a complete CP set-up, including a folding head [toilet] for his personal use. His idiosyncrasy was "a folding 'one seater' head made of plywood, painted Marine Corps green reserved for his personal use. It was rather a huge thing. I had detailed an old time sergeant to make sure this head was moved and set up at each camp site and promptly forgot the matter." At one site, the head was not there. "I jumped in a jeep and drove back over our route to check. I soon located the sergeant standing with the folded head trying to thumb a ride. It seemed that his detail failed to show up and he dragged the head to the highway and thumbed a ride for a couple of miles until the car turned off the road and he had to get out and wait for another car. Cars in wartime were few and after struggling a half-mile with the thing, he had given up and just waited. What a sight he was—a very military-looking old timer complete with handle-bar moustache and full field equipment and a folding head waiting by the side of the road! We both got a good laugh out of it." By darkness the portable head was set up and ready for the regimental commander's business.[4]

Craig admired Shepherd. "Colonel Shepherd was a fine officer, who was always on the job and demanded perfection in training." He was particularly keen on all types of field training. "I'll never forget the first field problem we had. We were about to go home at 5 o'clock in the afternoon when he announced that we would leave at six that night for a field problem." Promptly at six, the entire reinforced regiment jumped off, more than three thousand men, and marched to the field. That night, orders were prepared to seize the Camp Pendleton airfield. "At daylight, the regiment jumped off, hauling everything over those hills, including their machine gun carts and everything else, and took the airfield as scheduled. I was just about whipped, but the training was thorough, and it paid off later on when we got into combat."[5]

Heartrending Farewell

Craig was due to ship out on board the SS *Bloemfontein* for combat duty overseas when his wife, "Betty" was hospitalized with an advanced case of tuberculosis. "We both knew that a cure would be a miracle and the doctor gave me little hope."[6]

Major General Charles D. Barrett, the division commander, was aware that Craig's wife was all alone and offered to transfer him to another unit so he could stay behind with her. He even went to the hospital to talk with her. She told him, "Her husband was a Marine, that he had trained many years for just this occasion to go to war, that it was his duty to his country, and her duty as an American to send him ... the effect on her as an individual was small compared to the needs of her country and that she would not hear of him being transferred."[7]

The night before shipping out, Craig spent the night with her at the hospital. "We talked all night—of our life together which had been happy despite her sickness. At five thirty the next morning a car was waiting for me. Betty maintained her composure till the very end. As I closed the door to her room, she had a smile on her face as she said her last goodbye. I walked a few steps down the hall but felt that I must see her once again. I turned, went back and softly opened the door to her room. She had broken down completely and lay sobbing on her bed. She would not have wanted me to see her in that condition and I did not make my presence known. I turned and left. I will never forget that moment."[8]

In New Zealand, Craig received a letter from his wife's doctor advising him of her worsening condition and suggested flying back, if possible. The division commander approved the request saying, "There was no reason Craig should not go for a short visit, as the division would not go into combat for some months." However, the request had to be approved by the corps commander, General Barney Vogel. "This he refused to do, stating, 'there was a war on, that he could not see why a trip was necessary and that in any event there was no transportation available by air.' I did not go. I found out later that Vogel dispatched a plane to the United States two days later with orders to pick up a load of liquor and a portable bar. Some of his staff went in it to see their families. This made me sick to my stomach."[9]

General Vogel was relieved of command shortly afterward because he failed as a leader. Craig said, "he was one of the very few Marines who I could not respect or like." This was the second time Vogel had been in trouble. "As Chief of Staff of the Guardia, he was relieved because of drunkenness and disgraceful conduct," Craig reported.[10]

Craig was on Guadalcanal when he received a note from Mrs. Shepherd. "She had just been to my dear Betty's funeral. This was the first word that I received of her death." He later received a letter from a Navy chaplain with the official notification. "My wife had written every day up till the time she passed. I continued to receive letters from her for many days after, due to the slowness of the mail. In her last letter she indicated that she thought the end was near ... It was still a very brave and cheerful letter. I was choked with emotion and went to my jeep and drove off to be by myself and tried to compose myself. I finally ended up at the end of a trail. I got out and walked up and down the beach for hours, trying to compose myself and make some sense out of things. I finally realized what Betty would expect of me and how in her last letter she told me to carry on no matter what happened. She had placed her faith in God."[11]

Some months later he wrote a letter to his beloved mother and father. "I feel very alone without Betty. God did not see fit to give us much time together, but what short periods together that we did have were very happy and the memory is very precious to me."[12]

Guadalcanal Command

On July 19, 1943, Craig relieved Colonel Shepherd, who said that Craig was "a very fine officer, of the highest type," during a regimental review in a large field on Guadalcanal. He pledged to "Carry on the traditions of the Ninth Regiment which I know, in the days to come, will defeat the Japs." Shepherd was promoted to Brigadier General and assigned as Assistant Division Commander (ADC), 1st Marine Division. "Training was most intensive [and realistic]. We had patrols out most of the time in the jungle searching for Japanese that had been left behind after we took the island. During the time we were there, the Japs were still coming over once in a while and bombing various units on the island. One bomb landed in our camp and wounded a number of men."[13]

Shortly after taking over the regiment, Craig received orders to fly to New Georgia to observe the Army and report his observations to the division commander. "I was most happy to do this as it would give me an opportunity to familiarize myself with the tactics employed by the Japanese as well as our own forces." On August 17, he boarded an Army plane which was to rendezvous with a fighter escort, because Japanese planes were still active. "We began to worry when we arrived at the appointed place and the escort failed to show. The pilot circled while we waited until finally four fighters finally arrived and escorted us to Munda."[14]

Craig met with the Army corps commander and was given permission to go anywhere he wanted in the area controlled by the U.S. Army. He was given a jeep and driver to facilitate his visits. "I spent about 10 days there—constantly on the move—and I was able to go to all their units that were in contact with the Japanese and gather much data and information which proved of great value." Craig quickly learned that being around the corps and division headquarters near the beach was hazardous to one's health. "I found that sleeping near the front lines at night was far better than staying at these places. They were bombed by Japanese planes each night with regularity. Few casualties resulted but it was annoying to have red alerts sounded many times each night ... and then have to wait for the bombs to fall. Most of the artillery was concentrated near the beach also and they would keep up a continual barrage most of the night. The front lines were peaceful in comparison with only occasional shots and the sound of artillery exploding far away."[15]

On one of his trips to the front he was caught in a barrage and had to take cover in a swamp, and by the time he got out of it he was covered in mud. On another occasion, he took an engineer boat to an island off the coast where a battalion was in the process of clearing out a pocket of Japanese. "I took an engineer type boat with an outboard motor, with a sergeant, and as we got near the island, mortar shells started falling all around the boat. The motor stopped. I picked up the oars and rowed [like hell]. We finally got to shore and found that we were in front of the line instead of in the back of it. We landed in a tangle of mangroves and swamp mud, dove into the jungle, and headed toward where we thought the Army lines were. The jungle was thick, covered with huge vines, with roots growing out of the swamp. We had tough going!"[16]

Craig and the sergeant stumbled through the jungle until they finally reached a trail that led into the Army lines. "The men looked thin and white and demoralized. I saw the first so-called shell shock cases—15 or 20 of them—apparently, they hadn't been able to take it—it was a pretty bad situation." Craig caught a boat back to Munda. At dinner that night at the Corps Headquarters, he discovered just how much the gap was between the infantry and the staff. "Dinner was excellent. I had the first fresh meat since leaving New Zealand. I took very little enjoyment in eating however, as I could not get out of my mind the thought of all the poor devils out in the rain who had to eat C rations. I made up my mind that no organization which I commanded would ever live this way. I always prided myself that I would eat at my mess only what the enlisted men had to eat."[17]

Craig had the opportunity to observe the Army's approach to using fire support on a heavily defended Japanese ridge. The position lay in thick jungle and had proven to be a tough nut to crack. After taking quite a few casualties, the Army concentrated several battalions of artillery fire on one end of the ridge and working it back and forth until the Japanese were wiped out. Craig walked into the devastated position. "No living thing was left. Arms, legs, torsos and weapons lay scattered over an area which looked like it had been plowed and human remains mixed in with the red clay. I often wondered how many rounds of 105s and 155s it took to do this. However, it saved American lives and reduced a very strong defense position."[18]

Upon Craig's return from New Georgia, he instituted a stiff regimental training schedule to get ready for the next operation. Unfortunately, it was interrupted when his men were yanked to unload cargo ships for three months, a menial job considering his men were trained combat troops. Craig said the assignment greatly upset him.

On October 9, 1943, he wrote to his parents from Guadalcanal:

Dear Mother and Father,

The past week has been one of the most strenuous in my service I believe. We had continuous regimental problems all week, including overhead fire with all types of weapons. It is really tough going in these jungles. One cannot really appreciate the difficulties of fighting in this terrain ... It makes me proud to command this outfit ... they are the finest group of men that I have ever seen together. I know that they will acquit themselves well in combat ...

Your loving son, Ned.

Craig suffered a near death experience while returning from a conference. About a half-mile from the regiment's camp, all the Japanese ammunition had been collected, as well as excess American ammunition, and placed in a huge unguarded dump. "I was driving alongside the ammunition dump when without warning a terrific explosion occurred. Debris showered all over the road. I stopped my jeep, dived into a two-foot-deep ditch, and lay there as explosion after explosion occurred. Palm trees alongside the road were flattened, and huge pieces of debris flew over the ditch. The air was thick with dust and the smoke was so thick, I could hardly breathe. I pulled my helmet down and lay with my face in the mud praying that nothing would hit me. To say that I was afraid would be putting it mildly. The earth shook with each explosion, and I could hear things hitting all around."[19]

Craig lay there for an hour before it was over. His jeep was peppered with shrapnel holes and covered with a layer of thick black dirt ... but it started. He hurried back to camp because he thought there may have been casualties and damage, but "their experience was better than mine. A few punctured tents but the men had taken cover in foxholes and escaped injury. I went to the galley for a cup of black coffee and it never tasted better as I was a little shaken. At any rate, the problem of what to do with all the Jap ammo was solved."[20]

CHAPTER 12

Operation *Cherry Blossom* (Bougainville)

After "live-fire" training for three months against Japanese holdouts in the jungles of Guadalcanal, Craig, his headquarters, and one infantry battalion embarked on the USS *American Legion* (APA-17). The rest of the regiment and supporting units, a total of 5,500 men, were embarked on three other attack transports for "Operation *Cherry Blossom*," the amphibious assault of Bougainville, the northernmost island in the Solomons. The island was selected as the next target because of its strategic location in relation to the Japanese-held island of Rabaul, a major Imperial naval fleet base that supported their offense operations against New Guinea, Australia and New Zealand. Allied airfields on Bougainville would enable light bombers and escort aircraft to be used to neutralize Rabaul, 210 air miles to the north.

Bougainville is the largest island in the Solomon Islands, nearly 30 miles wide and 125 miles in length, populated by 40,000 locals.* The island is a tropical forest, with an average rainfall of 15 inches a month.

---

* It was reported by the 3rd Marine Division history that, "[Bougainville] was inhabited by a wild, uncultured race of people reported to be head hunters." First Lieutenant Robert A. Arthur, USMCR and First Lieutenant Kenneth Cohlmia, USMCR, *The Third Marine Division* (Washington, D.C.: Infantry Journal Press, 1948) 51. An unfriendly local assisted Japanese patrols in forcing Australian Coastwatchers to constantly be on the move—several were captured and executed. The local responsible for the capture of Allied personnel was seized and shot after the island was captured. Henry I. Shaw, jr., and Major Douglas T. Kane, USMC. *Isolation of Rabaul: History of U.S. Marine Corps Operations in World War II, Vol.2.* (Washington, D.C.: Historical Branch, G-3, Headquarters U.S. Marine Corps, 1963) 172.

Intelligence estimates placed the strength of the Japanese garrison at 35,000–44,000 troops of the Seventeenth Army built around the 6th Division (Bright Division) and the 4th South Seas Garrison Unit—three battalions, plus a naval detachment.[1] The biggest concentration of defenders was in the southern part of the island, where an estimated 17,000 men of the 17th Army were headquartered. However, the total defenders of Cape Torokina area of Empress Augusta Bay, the division landing beach, consisted of the 2nd Company, 1st Battalion, 23rd Infantry plus 30 men from the Regimental Gun Company, a total of 270 men with one casemated Type 41, 75mm gun. They were positioned in 18 pillboxes, solidly constructed with coconut logs and dirt, with connecting trenches and rifle pits.[2]

Underway

"We sailed for Éfaté first, where we carried out a practice landing simulating the one we were to make later on Bougainville. It was the first night ashore and the rain was pouring down. I had made visits to all my units along the line we had established in the jungle and was dog tired when I returned to my CP. I lashed my jungle hammock, which I had been issued in Guadalcanal, to two trees, and with a big leap jumped into it as best I could. It no sooner took my weight than the hammock ring parted and I landed on my back on a tree stump which was some three feet below. I thought for a moment that I had broken my back … but after lying on the ground in the rain for some time I finally snapped out of it and decided I was alright. I spent the rest of the night on the ground under my poncho lying on the downed hammock. I never again tried to use a so-called jungle hammock."[3]

The next morning the transports sailed for Bougainville. "The trip was uneventful except for one attack on the convoy which did no damage … most of the Japanese planes were shot down by our air cover. Life aboard the USS *American Legion* was not good. The Navy did little to help us out. It was the first Navy ship that I had been on which did not try to make things comfortable. We were glad when we finally arrived at Empress Augusta Bay and began to debark for the landing."[4]

In a letter to his parents before the landing, Craig wrote:

> Dear Mother and Father,
> I have a very large task unit which includes my regiment and the responsibility is great. I only pray to God that I can be worthy of the trust placed in me, and that I may bring my men through ... they are the finest group of fighting men that I have ever seen in one unit. They are hard, bronzed, and tough. What a pity to think what is in store for many of them. It makes me hate our enemy the more to think of the hardships and suffering they are causing....
> As ever, your loving son, Ned.

The landing plan called for the simultaneous landing of two regiments abreast on numbered beaches—Red Beach 1 through 3, and Yellow 2 and 3 in the Cape Torokina area, located on the west coast of the island. The landing was scheduled for 0730 on November 1, 1943. The 9th Marines, reinforced by the attached 3rd Raider Battalion, would assault over five beaches on the left flank of the beachhead, the 3rd Marines on their right, while the 21st Marines still in Guadalcanal were to be brought up later. Craig related that, "the 9th Regiment consisted of some 5,500 men counting the attached units—2nd Raider Regiment was attached soon after landing. The regiment was combat loaded and sailed for Efate, where it carried out a practice landing, simulating the one we were to make on Bougainville, except for the difficult surf conditions."[5]

"The men of the 9th Marine Regiment knew their job! They had rehearsed every step; they had been shown the maps with all terrain features; they knew approximately where the enemy was, and they knew how to meet and kill him. They were confident of their ability."[6]

Eight APAs (attack personnel transport) and four AKAs (attack cargo transports) carried the Marines to the objective area. "It was a rather unusual landing in that more emphasis was put on the logistical part of it, I think, than on the landing itself. As a consequence, we landed three battalions abreast in each regiment on a very narrow beach; and my regimental zone, due to the high waves, lost some eighty landing craft of various descriptions," Craig reported.[7]

On D-day, November 1, 1943, the 12 attack transports and cargo ships followed the minesweepers into Empress Augusta Bay and anchored in line, about 3,000 yards from the beach. General Quarters was sounded at 5am, two and a half hours before H-hour. After the traditional steak and eggs breakfast, many of the embarked troops lined the rails and watched as dawn broke bright and clear, in a beautiful sunrise. An hour later, they mustered on deck at their debarkation stations. At 0645, three destroyers and the APAs commenced preparatory fire on Japanese positions on Cape Torokina and Puruata Island, the Raider objectives, with their 3-inch, 5-inch, and 40mm guns. The ships' performance left much to be desired. Their salvos landed in the water and it took some time to correct their aim. One Raider officer commented, "… some, if not most of [our] deaths could have been averted had the pre-landing naval bombardment been more effective."[8]

At 06:45, the command "land the landing force" was signaled, and the Marines, in their camouflaged jungle suits, clambered over the sides down cargo nets into Higgins boats. "At this moment," Craig reported, "Jap planes came in to bomb us. Our air cover [a New Zealand fighter squadron] made short work of them. Only one bomb dropped near our ship." The attack began at 0735 and consisted of between seven and nine Val dive-bombers escorted by 44 Zero fighters. Early warning, effective defense by land-based Allied aircraft, intense anti-aircraft fire, and well-rehearsed maneuvering by the transports resulted in all but 12 of the aircraft being driven off or shot down, with only one near miss on a destroyer-transport. "Fighter cover succeeded in breaking up most of the Japanese formations, but about 12 Val dive-bombers were able to break through. Two men were killed and five others wounded."[9] While there were few casualties, the most serious consequence was on the resultant delay in unloading. Twice during the day all ships were required to withdraw from the transport area for defensive maneuvering.[10]

The next air attack, coming in at noon, was more formidable, consisting of 100 Japanese carrier aircraft (operating from Rabaul), but these were driven off by effective opposition from 34 land-based Allied fighters. "On our way to the beach another air attack hit us and it was at this time that the regiment had our first casualties," Craig recounted. "I lost an officer and two men." The attack was driven off by Marine fighters from VMF-215 and VMF-221.[11] Several more serious attempts to attack the ships were made within the next few hours. During this period three enemy Zeros ineffectually strafed the beaches." One observer noted: "... each time a Jap plane strafed there usually was an F4U [Corsair] on his tail ... we could see puffs from the Corsair's machine guns as it fired on the Jap plane. I remember at least two of the Jap planes smoking as they pulled up attempting to shake off the Marine fighter."[12]

Craig's landing craft reached a line of amphibious tractors and transferred to one in order to climb over the reef that surrounded the island. As Craig's tractor made its run for the beach, he observed that "Bougainville looked beautiful but sinister in the distance with a large volcano lying among the low hills and mountains. On the way to the beach another air attack hit us. As our landing boats rounded Puruata Island, we were taken under a crossfire by machine guns and a 75mm gun on the Cape. Three boats were sunk and three damaged. Looking ahead, I could see a steep and narrow sand beach, with the jungle coming right down to the edge, and the surf piling up on it. I knew we were in for trouble. The rolling surf played havoc with the unwieldly landing craft." More than eighty of the valuable craft broached and were left stranded on the beach, which caused severe problems in the general unloading phase of the operation.[13]

D-day Landings: Cape Torokina—Puruata Island

Craig's assault battalions pushed rapidly inland against light resistance from the Japanese 1st Battalion, 23rd Infantry, and one 75mm gun; a total strength of 270 men. The Cape itself was fortified with 18 solidly constructed coconut log and dirt pillboxes. Nevertheless, his men pushed rapidly inland to establish a night perimeter. The 3rd Marines on his right "ran head on into machine gun emplacements and took some casualties. My flank patrols were engaged during the night, but my main line of resistance was not hit. We were well dug in from 300 to 400 yards off the beach."[14] As nightfall approached, the frontline units sited all weapons along fixed lines to coordinate their fire with adjacent units, and all companies set up an all-around defense. The word was passed that there was to be no unnecessary firing and no movement. "Marines were to resort to bayonets and knives when needed...."[15]

Puruata Island

"The [3rd] Raider Battalion [I and K Companies] which was attached to my regiment landed on the north side of Puruata Island," Craig pointed out.[16] The landing on Beach Green 1 was opposed with small arms and automatic weapons from a reinforced rifle platoon. By 0930, the Raiders had established a secure perimeter around 125 yards deep. They were facing snipers, machine guns and mortars. Private Elmer Mapes recalled: "We encountered what the historians noted as 'light opposition.' We didn't actually lose many men, but our C.O. was killed for one. My most vivid memory of getting to the beach was the strafing by five or six Jap Zeros where, as you might imagine, I 'climbed into my helmet,' or at least as far as I could! Our first problem was the fact that we landed where the beach must have been only about 15 yards deep. Swampy ground behind it forced us to detour." And so, at 1:30pm the rest of the battalion joined the attack, supported by some self-propelled 75mm guns. The battalion then launched an attack that saw them occupy half of the island by the end of the day. The next day, the Raiders launched a two-pronged attack on the Japanese half of the island. This time they only faced rifle fire, and by 3:30pm the island was secure. Twenty-nine Japanese bodies were found, but the rest of the garrison appears to have escaped to Bougainville. The Marines lost five dead and 32 wounded.[17]

Japanese Counter landing–Koromokina Lagoon

Shortly before 0600 on the morning of November 7, four Japanese destroyers, screened by two cruisers and seven destroyers, hove to in Atsinima Bay, on the western flank of the perimeter. In the half-light of dawn, a provisional battalion, some 500 men, mainly from the 54th Infantry Battalion, landed by small landing craft and barges at scattered points along the shoreline. Their craft looked like American boats in the dim light, and they were not immediately taken under fire. "Fortunately, because they landed over such a large area, its commander, Major Miwa Mitsuhiro, unable to reassemble quickly, was forced to attack in small numbers."[18]

Craig's Company K, 9th Marines and 3rd Platoon, 9th Marines Weapons Company were in position to stop them. "There were some 500 men in the landing force, and there was quite a hot fight there for a while." The Japanese were taken under fire by a 37mm antitank gun with canister and high explosive, wiping out the advance party. Scattered fighting continued as the Japanese attempted to determine the extent of the resistance.[19]

In the confused fighting, a platoon from Company K, which happened to be on patrol, ambushed a pursuing Japanese unit several times before escaping into the interior. It slipped through the jungle, bypassing other enemy forces without being observed. Instead of heading to the interior and risk being observed, the platoon worked its way through the jungle to the coast and holed up for the night. The next morning, it attracted the attention of an Allied plane and within an hour the platoon was picked up by two tank lighters and returned to the main lines. Another isolated unit, a patrol from Company B, was cut off from the rest of the battalion during the fighting and spent the night of November 7/8 behind Japanese lines without being detected.[20]

The platoon returned to the Marine lines 30 hours later, with one man wounded and one man missing, after inflicting a number of casualties on the Japanese landing force. Another patrol from Company M, 3rd Battalion, 9th Marine Regiment was cut off on the beach between two enemy forces, and when the radio of the artillery officer with the patrol failed, he headed back to the main lines where he directed an artillery barrage that landed on the Japanese position to the left of the patrol from Company M. The patrol then moved toward the Marine lines, only to find the beach blocked by Japanese forces opposing Company K. The patrol scratched an SOS message in the sand of the beach. It was seen by an air spotter who guided two landing craft to the scene and successfully evacuated the 60-man patrol. It was estimated that 35 Japanese had been killed, while only two Marines were wounded and one missing.[21]

Company K was ordered to attack. About 150 yards from the perimeter, the company hit the dug-in Japanese. Heavy fighting broke out, with the Japanese using light machine guns from well-concealed fortifications and snipers hidden in the trees. The Japanese brought up reinforcements and the Marine attack stalled. Craig requested to bring in another battalion, which was approved, and then he coordinated the difficult deployment in the face of heavy Japanese fire.

The 1st Battalion, 3rd Marines passed through the 3rd Battalion and continued the attack but soon found itself under heavy machine gun and automatic weapons fire as it tried to dislodge the Japanese. The battalion's attack was halted to avoid casualties and to bring in a heavy artillery barrage.

The next morning, the 1st Battalion, 21st Marines, and the 9th Marines regimental reserve renewed the attack. After a 20-minute preparatory barrage by five batteries of artillery together with machine gun, mortar and antitank-gun fire, the 1st Battalion renewed its attack. This combination of fire support completely broke up and disintegrated the enemy counter landing. Five hundred and fifty-one bodies were counted on the battlefield. The Marines lost 17. "It was later determined that the Japanese area commander planned to put 3,000 men ashore in three echelons, however he failed to follow through when the first echelon was wiped out."[22]

The three-day action on the left flank of the perimeter ended enemy activity, and on the morning of the 8th, the U.S. Army's 148th Infantry Regiment of the 37th Division took over for the Marine units.

Piva Trail Road Block

"Shortly after we landed, the 2nd Raider Regiment was attached to my regiment," Craig reported. "Its 3rd Battalion, supported by my Regimental Weapons Company and two light tanks, was holding a roadblock on the Piva Trail on November 8, when elements of the Japanese 23rd Infantry Regiment attacked the next day and a hot fight ensued." The Raiders counterattacked and drove the Japanese back, but after suffering heavy casualties, they were forced to withdraw to the roadblock for the night." Craig launched a coordinated air, artillery and infantry attack with two companies abreast astride the Piva Trail. In the confused fighting that followed, the Japanese attempted to flank the Raider advance. Craig deployed his weapons company which stopped the Japanese.[23]

The Raider advance slowly continued until early afternoon when the Japanese resistance suddenly collapsed and the Marines established a night defense position. Over 100 enemy dead were counted on the field. The Marines lost 12 killed and 30 wounded. That night Craig once again planned an attack for the following day.[24]

The attack on the 9th jumped off at mid-morning and found no resistance. The Japanese had withdrawn, leaving equipment, ammunition, and weapons behind. The 1st Battalion, 9th Marines moved north on the Numa Numa trail and dug in. The battle for the Piva Road Bock was over.[25] Enemy casualties amounted to over 550 dead compared to 19 Marines killed and 32 wounded.

Craig received orders to prepare to cross the Piva River. "To carry this out, I issued orders to my scout platoon to reconnoiter the other side of the river and find routes for possible bridge sites through the swamps that covered most of the area on the far side. The patrol brought back the information and I had my attached engineer company start building temporary bridges." His engineers worked hard and practically had them completed when they were called back to their engineer regiment. "I immediately protested but I was informed that the engineer regimental commander would take control."[26]

The engineer soon arrived with members of his staff and told Craig that his site would not be used ... and instead new sites were picked. Craig checked the sites and found "they would lead directly into impassable swamps ... and my tanks and heavy equipment would get bogged down." The engineer officer would not listen to Craig's pleas and insisted on the new sites. Craig felt justified in going directly to the division commander with the issue. The end result was that Craig's bridges were used. The engineer was relieved and transferred. "One man's stubbornness had almost disrupted the attack of a division and I could never figure out the reasons for that engineer's actions. It was one of the most frustrating incidents of the campaign."[27]

The next morning, Craig left his CP to visit the heavily engaged Raider Battalion. He could not use his jeep because of the deep mud and was forced to walk. "After a tiring hike through the mud and jungle, I finally reached the front lines and talked with Lieutenant Colonel Fred

Beans, the battalion commander." After giving him instructions for the next day's advance, Craig started back to his CP. "I passed what I have always thought was the most gruesome sight that I witnessed during the war. A light tank going to the rear with wounded strapped to the outside was mired down in a swamp off the trail. It could not move, and I could see the bandaged men with blood dripping down the side of the tank lying there helpless. To make matters worse, snipers in the vicinity had pinned the crew inside unable to help the wounded who were lying in the open unable to help themselves. It was a most pitiful sight. I notified the Raiders and had them send out a platoon to rescue the tank and the wounded."[28] In the meantime, Craig talked the division commander into assigning "sufficient LVTs [amphibious vehicle tracked] to handle casualty evacuation and resupply at the front ... it was the only vehicle that could operate over most of the thick, swampy jungle terrain."[29]

One night after checking the lines, Craig returned to his CP. "I had just opened a can of 'C' rations when I received a radio call from the division commander directing me to report to headquarters for a conference. I thought it was rather unusual that I should be called all the way to division and presumed that there must be something in the wind."[30]

Craig started out on the hazardous trip just as it was getting dark, which could not have been worse timing. The men were "trigger happy and had orders to shoot anything moving during darkness. There were no roads or trails through the jungle and I did not know exactly where the division headquarters was." Somehow, he made it to the beach and flagged down an LVT, which took him along the coast to an opening in the jungle where he was supposed to meet a guide. "I proceeded into the jungle and walked blindly toward what I hoped was the CP. I had several close calls but finally found the general." After exchanging pleasantries, "The general was a kindly man and just wanted to know how the day had gone! He did not realize the difficulties in getting to his CP and I did not tell him. The aide conducted me to the beach and we finally found the LVT. The ride back was hectic. Shots were fired at us a number of times and the surf was running high. We finally landed near the trail leading toward my CP. A shot rang out and I yelled at the top of my voice 'Colonel Craig coming through.' Fortunately, the Marines recognized my voice and I finally reached my CP. I was a little shaken to tell the truth and decided then and there to never call a subordinate to my CP under conditions of darkness and confusion if I could ever help it." Little did Craig know that he would have a repeat performance in Korea in 1950 when he was called back to an Army division CP as darkness was setting in and he had to return by helicopter to his CP without proper navigational equipment.[31]

Craig always established his CP close to the front lines, relying on headquarters personnel for close-in security. One night they made the mistake of setting in at a well-known trail junction and were bombed. "I took shelter under one of the LVTs with my executive officer and orderly. As I lay there, I thought, 'here we are lying under an LVT loaded with hundreds of gallons of gasoline. I wonder what will happen if we get hit?" The Raiders had buried several Japanese in shallow graves that had been unearthed. "I will always remember one huge looking Jap who was sitting right up in the mud with his face turned our way. Early the next morning, my orderly brought me a helmet full of water. I splashed some on my face and immediately smelled a terrific odor of dead Jap. He had unknowingly dipped the water from a pool full of dead Japanese without knowing it. I rushed to my medical officer and got some alcohol and washed my face with it. Even with that it took some time to get rid of the smell."[32]

Two nights later, Craig had just turned in when the Japanese bombed the perimeter. "I could hear the whistle of the bomb and knew it was going to hit close. My fox hole was on the other side of a pile of equipment. I gave one dive over the pile and landed on my right wrist in a foot of water in the foxhole. I was sure I had broken my wrist as I lay wet and muddy in the hole and the bombs bursting very close. One of them almost wiped out the aid station nearby."[33]

Several days later, Craig was returning from the front lines on foot, when an LVT came up behind him. "I stopped it for a lift. On climbing up the side, I found it filled with 14 dead Marines piled on top of one another from the battle of the 21st Marines at the Coconut Grove. They were in complete equipment even to their helmets in some cases. The odor was terrific but the LVT had gotten underway and I was afraid to jump down, so I sat on the side and held on. I wasn't looking and a huge branch swept back and hit me on the shoulder knocking me down among the rotting corpses ... I was well acquainted with them by the time I debarked! I only suffered from a very sore and black and blue shoulder."[34]

"After attacking through almost impenetrable jungle and swamp, the 9th Marines finally reached the Force Beachhead Line. "It was deep in the jungle and contact between units was most difficult. The right flank of my regiment was resting in the vicinity of what was later known as Hellzapopping Ridge, and was supposed to be in contact with the 3rd Parachute Battalion. However, my battalion commander reported that he was unable to locate the parachute outfit and that there was a gap in the line. I decided to go on foot with my bodyguard and try to locate the missing commander. When I finally located him, he told me that his flank was resting on the spot designated. This was great news to me and I asked for a guide to go to the spot and talk with my battalion commander."[35]

"The Parachute Battalion had been in some rough fighting and their CP looked rather disorganized but I thought nothing about it at the time. However, as I proceeded through the jungle and found little evidence of a coordinated front, I began to suspect that the parachutists were a little overextended. Actually, they were covering about 1,500 yards of front with some 800 men, which should have been sufficient. However, due to the heavy jungle, many steep ravines and hills, and lack of a definitive line, I found that they were poorly set up to repel an attack or prevent the Japs from infiltrating their lines."[36]

"To add insult to injury, my guide finally admitted that he was lost and did not know where the left flank of the Parachute Battalion was. Trails were by now non-existent and I pictured myself running into the enemy and being captured or killed. What a sorry thing to happen to a regimental commander who should have been with his unit. Little did I think that when I started out I would become separated from my men in combat!"[37]

"Pushing through the dense jungle, climbing steep muddy hills and sliding down others, we walked and walked in the humid heat. My field equipment became heavy and my boots weighed a ton. I checked my map, which was very poor, and with the aid of my compass and the sound of occasional firing, we finally reached a dug-in patrol of the Parachute Battalion. We first noticed their presence when we were fired on and only avoided becoming casualties by shouting our identity."[38] "I found that the patrol leader had no idea where the 9th Marines were, nor did he know exactly how to get back to his own battalion CP. It was only after a number of hours of such incidents that I arrived completely exhausted at the right flank of my regiment. I telephoned the situation to division and the next day the 21st Marines moved in to relieve the Parachute Battalion and prevent further infiltration of the Japs."[39]

"One of the great difficulties we had in Bougainville was with our maps. The map furnished for our landing was a very rough, inaccurate affair. When we got ashore, we found that many points were incorrect. During our advance through the jungle, it was very difficult for me to find where my troops were actually located on the map. To remedy this situation, I had an aerial photograph taken of the area after I had each platoon raise a small weather balloon above the jungle foliage; and from spotting these various balloons on the photo I could tell approximately where my front lines were at the time. This worked out very well in the absence of an accurate map."[40]

A Christmas Miracle

Toward the end of the campaign, Craig received orders to launch a final attack on Christmas day against a strongly held position in a steep thickly wooded hill on which a company of Japanese infantry reinforced with one heavy machine gun, three light machine guns, as well as 50mm mortars were well dug-in. "I felt very deeply that my men should not be killed or wounded on that day. The matter worried me considerably." He planned for massive artillery preparation fires, "as I wanted to save lives on this Christmas day; that is, the lives of my men." After doing all he could to prepare, Craig issued the orders and the men moved out to their assault positions. "I went to my tent and sat down and worried. The whole thing just did not seem right. We were scheduled to go back aboard ship in a few days, and on Christmas day, I must lose men, the men I had lived, trained, and fought with for so long. On an impulse, I got down on my knees and prayed to God that none of my men would be killed or seriously wounded." After some time, he lay down, feeling that he had done all he could. "Sometime around three in the morning, my telephone rang and division informed me that forward patrols had reported that Japanese fire had ceased and they were pulling off the hill." The attack was canceled. "I closed my eyes and thanked God for a seeming miracle."[41]

On December 27, Craig's regiment was relieved on the lines by the Army's 164th Infantry Regiment and immediately embarked on shipping for transport to Guadalcanal, its old stomping ground, to rest and refit for Operation *Stevedore*, the amphibious assault of Guam. "We returned to Guadalcanal and spent two months there training in the type of operation we would carry out," Craig said.[42]

CHAPTER 13

Operation *Stevedore* (Guam)

In the summer of 1944, the United States had advanced across the Pacific in a two-pronged attack toward the Japanese home islands. The recapture of Guam, Operation *Stevedore*, was the last of the objectives in the Marianas and, from the standpoint of national pride, was the most important. Major General Roy S. Geiger's III Amphibious Corps was tasked to recapture the island. His force consisted of the 3rd Marine Division, composed of the 3rd, 9th, and 19th (engineers and pioneers) and 21st Marines, totaling approximately 20,000 men, and the 1st Provisional Marine Brigade, composed of the 4th and 2nd Marines and supporting units with 9,886 men, as well as the U.S. Army's 77th Infantry Division.

The island of Guam is 35 miles long and nine miles at its widest. It is rugged and mountainous in the south, while the north is more rolling, and jungle covered. The most approachable landing beaches are located along the west coast but pose a special tactical problem because they are backed by ridges that gradually rise to form mountains. This high ground, properly defended, could be murder for assault troops. With only 15 miles of usable beaches available to the Americans, the Japanese quickly decided to orient their formidable defenses toward the west.

Guam became a territorial possession of the United States in 1898, as a result of the Spanish-American War. The island was considered strategically important, because it was located in the Japanese Central Pacific defensive cordon. Unfortunately, at the start of the war, it was practically undefended. On December 8, 1941, Japanese planes bombed the Marine Barracks. Corporal Martin Boyle described the island's air defense: "We soon learned that a rifle is useless as tits on a boar hog when pitted against even the slowest moving airplanes. It takes a damn lucky shot to do any good, and we weren't very lucky that day." Two days later, a Japanese force of 6,000 men landed and quickly overwhelmed the garrison of only 153 Marines and the 80-man Insular Force Guard, local Chamorros led by Marine NCOs. The population of 20,000 Guamanians, all loyal American nationals, found themselves in the tender mercies of the Japanese Army.[1]

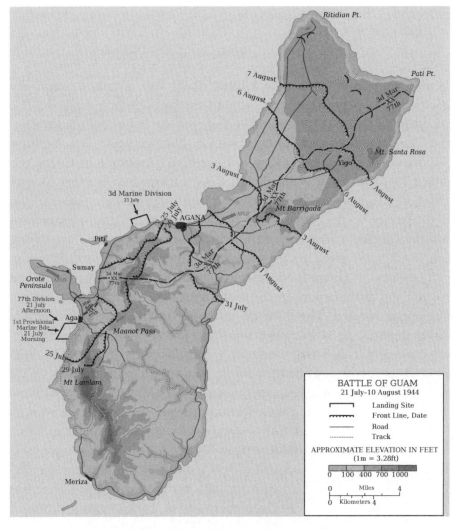

Battle of Guam, 21 July–19 August 1944

The recapture of Guam had been a long-standing student exercise at Marine Corps School, Quantico. Generations of Marine officers had passed through the demanding course—and many were now heading for Guam and the "final graduation exercise." One of the school's instructors noted: "I had prepared a study for a landing on Guam at the Naval War College and so I knew the island pretty well. I wrote an estimate of the situation on this island. At that time the only place you could land without crossing the reef was at Talofofo."[2]

However, the school solution they had spent so much time teaching was not used. The landing occurred on the side of the island that was considered unsatisfactory by the instructors—resulting in a grade of "U" if the student chose the incorrect beach. It was obviously not a suitable place to land due to the limited width of the passage through the reef and the ease with which the Japanese could defend. The introduction of the amphibious tractor (amtrac), which could cross the fringing reefs, made the old plan obsolete. Unfortunately, there were only enough amtracs to boat the first few waves. After landing the troops on the beach, the tractors which had not been knocked out by Japanese gunfire returned to the seaward edge of the fringing reef, where they met boats from the ships on what were called the "transfer line."[3]

The Japanese 29th Division and various naval base and defense troops, some nineteen thousand men, garrisoned the island. They were well supplied with coast defense artillery, antiaircraft guns, and field artillery, which were heavily camouflaged and cleverly emplaced to disrupt and destroy an enemy landing. The western beaches were studded with mines and anti-boat obstacles. Machine guns and mortars were sited to provide covering fire. The Japanese commander knew the Americans were coming and pushed his men hard to prepare. "We have an excellent opportunity to annihilate him on the beaches," he said.[4]

Death is Lighter Than a Feather

The Japanese believed in the military code of Bushido, or the way of the warrior. Article 2 of the Japanese Imperial Army Military Training regulation stated: "The duty of the military is to sacrifice their lives for the emperor's country." The individual Japanese soldier believed that if he surrendered, he lost all honor and brought disgrace to his family. His paramount duty was loyalty unto death: "Duty is weightier than a mountain, while death is lighter than a feather." "Faith is strength," was his credo, and for the most part, the Japanese soldier carried out his duty without reservation—even in the face of certain death. The infamous banzai charge was perhaps the embodiment of this self-sacrifice.[5]

American researchers concluded that the banzai was a "mutual exhortation which started between unit members and increased to the point of much hysteria. But this was a spontaneous affair and not maneuvered by the commanding officers, who merely explained the tactical situation and placed the challenge before the men." Colonel Hiromichi Yahara, senior staff officer, Japanese 32nd Army, described the assault as "Masses of Japanese soldiers wearing frantic, weird expressions, brandishing swords, throwing grenades, and stabbing with bayonets, charge ceaselessly, jumping over the dead bodies of their fallen comrades while screaming 'banzai.'" One Marine who observed one of these attacks said "it sounded like New Year's Eve in the zoo."[6]

Japanese Myth

Japanese victories after Pearl Harbor earned them a superhuman reputation as jungle fighters. A Marine officer who was familiar with this common perception observed: "I think that at the beginning of the war, the Japs made very remarkable advances—down the Malay Peninsula, Singapore, and all through the Southwest Pacific islands—and they built a reputation of being wonderful jungle fighters. It became something of a bugaboo to all of us, I mean, we just thought Japs could swing from tree to tree in the jungle." However, he did not believe it. "I found in my experience that our Marines were better jungle fighters than the Japs were. They were cunning; they were determined. And they were painstaking in their digging—you know, they loved to bore, they were always digging and organizing the ground, but they certainly didn't have much imagination, and I don't think that their units were too effective. But they were good fighters; there wasn't any question about that."

However, he did not think the Japanese were as good as "the more intelligent European." "Where the Europeans saw that they were going to be defeated, they gave up. But the Jap was so imbued with the idea that he must never give up, he must fight until the last drop of blood for the emperor...."[7]

Landing Plan

The landing plan called for the 20,000-man 3rd Marine Division to land three regiments abreast on Asan Point, to capture the high ground immediately inland. The 1st Marine Brigade's 19,000 men were tasked with establishing a beachhead in the vicinity of Agat, and then drive north to cut off the Orote Peninsula. The Army's 77th Infantry Division would follow up the Marine brigade's initial landings and fight alongside them in the drive north. The three infantry elements were to be backed up by the heavy guns of the Corps artillery and the Navy's gunfire support ships. Rear Admiral Richard L. Connolly said: "My aim is to get the troops ashore standing up." As a result, Guam received the most devastating preliminary bombardment of the war.[8]

On July 20, Craig wrote to his mother and father. Written the day prior to the assault landing on Guam, the tenor of the letter suggests he was preparing them for the worst:

> Dear Mother and Father,
> You will probably wonder where I am ... but think that you can guess. I am so thankful that I have been blessed with two wonderful parents. I will always be grateful to you for all you have done for me and the inspiration that you have been. I love you both dearly and only pray that God will permit me to return to you soon and in good health.
> Your loving son, Ned.

Under Fire Again

On July 21, 1944, the 9th Marines landed in a column of battalions—3rd Battalion, 2nd Battalion, and 1st Battalion in reserve—over Blue Beach on the division's right flank. "My mission was to capture Asan Point and the low hills just to the left of that, situated across a very flat area which at one time had been rice paddies." Craig's 3rd Battalion came under a deluge of Japanese small arms, mortar, and artillery fire as soon as it came within range. "I saw two tractors hit," Craig said. "It was at this moment that mortar shells started to fall around us. I was in a 'free boat' and able to see the progress of the initial landing." Craig directed his boat to land immediately. "My boat officer, a brand new ensign, had a hard time understanding this however, and insisted that he was assigned to a certain wave, which was then coming in, and he could not change his orders. I told him that if he didn't carry out my orders, he'd be over the side; and about that time one of my sergeants jumped up and said, 'I'd be delighted.' So, this ensign decided to change his orders and go in."[9]

At the reef line, Craig and his command group transferred to an amphibious tractor for the final run to the beach. "It was a great feeling of relief when the tractor started to crawl along the coral toward the sandy beach. It was just at this moment that mortar shells started to fall around us, some of them too close for comfort. Fire was also coming from the right flank at Asan Point ... I saw two more tractors hit and we decided to keep our heads down."* Craig made a mental note to check the area of the Japanese fire when he had a spare moment.[10]

The tractor reached the beach and the command group piled out and dashed forward through a tangle of fallen palm trees and demolished houses to several bomb craters, where they set up the CP. "It was just inland that we had a bad time. Asan Point was a real strongpoint. It gave the Japs great enfilading fire down the beach on our right. I had one battalion assigned to take the position. However there so many concealed Jap positions that some were not immediately discovered. We were lucky as the beach on the opposite of Asan Point was covered by two concealed 8-inch guns. It also had a great deal of barbed wire and obstacles."[11]

---

* While visiting Guam in the late 1990s, the author came across the Japanese gun emplacement carved out of a huge boulder facing the 9th Marines landing beaches. It was beautifully placed to enfilade the beach. I mentioned it to General Craig upon my return and he immediately remembered the emplacement. He recalled that it housed an anti-boat gun that knocked out several LVTs and wasn't destroyed until the assault troops were able to come in behind it.

"I landed just behind the assault battalion. Ahead of us was a flat area of old paddies with a low-lying hill dominating the area. It ran directly across our zone of action. The ridge was in our hands but there were some cave positions that were still occupied by the Japs. I picked a group of shell holes for a temporary CP. Antitank and rifle fire was mostly from our right. The battalions were laying comm wire as they advanced, so I had radio communication with them."[12]

Time, the weekly newsmagazine reported:

> An officer who fought with Craig related: After I ran ashore, the bullets were raining in from pillboxes, so I dived into the nearest foxhole. Who was in there but Eddie Craig. He was lying there with a phone and a notebook, talking to a runner. He was so quiet and collected he could have been at a desk in the Pentagon. "We got to get those pillboxes!" I yelled at him. "Now sit down there a minute," Craig says, "we'll get to 'em." He just looked at me and smiled. In a few we had [knocked out] the pillboxes. There's one thing about going to war with that man: there's no need to worry about who's running the show.[13]

Craig went forward with his adjutant, Captain Charlie Henderson, to find the battalion commander, Lieutenant Colonel Walter Asmuth. Heavy small arms and automatic weapons fire swept the area, forcing the two to take cover behind a low mound. "I was looking through my glasses at the ridge ahead when he [Henderson] suddenly toppled over across my knees, shot through the throat. I lay him out behind the mound and yelled for corpsman." Craig continued forward after the severely wounded adjutant was evacuated and "found Asmuth had just been wounded in the arm." As he returned to his CP, "Some stretcher bearers passed me and I recognized Captain Harry Barker, one of my best company commanders, lying on one of them dead. Waiting for me at the CP was my runner, who reported that my good friend Jaime Sabater [executive officer] had been wounded a moment after he landed and had been evacuated."[14]

During a short lull, Craig remembered the Japanese gun that had hit the two amphibious tractors as they came over the reef. "I was sure it was from a hidden gun emplacement on the ridge ... Sure enough, I saw a light puff of smoke on the side of the ridge, and it came from a spot which looked like a natural hillside, not over 150 yards away." He spotted two 75mm half-tracks and pointed out the camouflaged position. "The second and third rounds hit the target exactly and I could momentarily see parts of the gun and Japs intermingled in a depression on the side of the ridge. Another round hit above the position, causing a small landslide that covered the site." Two months later, Craig happened to be in the area and noted a large group of men gathered around an old Japanese position that had been uncovered. "There in front of me was what remained of a very modern anti-tank gun together with four or five very ripe Japs well mixed up with it. I wondered how many good Marines these dead Japanese soldiers had accounted for before the position was knocked out."[15]

Two Marines accompanied Craig as bodyguards on his tours of the front lines. "I have always been most fortunate in picking drivers and runners. They were both fearless and outstanding Marines." One, Private First Class Arthur Highsaw, always positioned himself in front of Craig, using his body as a shield. "Highsaw was standing by me when he suddenly dropped his automatic rifle and spun around. He had been hit in the upper arm by a Jap sniper. As we carried him away, he said, "I'm sorry I crapped out on you like this, Colonel." Highsaw was evacuated to a hospital ship and Craig did not expect to see him again. "However, the next morning, he appeared with his automatic rifle ready to accompany me on my rounds of the units. He had escaped from the hospital ship. He looked white and drawn and, as I spoke to him, he fell over in a dead faint." Highsaw was evacuated a second time, and that was the last time Craig saw him.[16]

Craig was down to one bodyguard, Corporal Walter Lamka, his runner. "Lamka and I were on our way from a company CP towards one of the platoons. Suddenly a machine gun opened up on us and we both hit the ground and rolled into a shallow depression. Every time we moved, the machine gun would fire at us, and the bullets were just grazing us." A Marine patrol happened by and attacked the Japanese position from another angle. "We rolled, got up, and ran into the jungle. We jumped into a Japanese gun pit and landed right on top several Jap bodies. When the firing stopped, we got quickly out of the mess."[17]

The 77th Infantry Division was deployed on the 9th Marines' right flank. Craig was anxious to ensure that his troops were in the right position, so he went forward on a personal reconnaissance.

"I started out in a jeep with Corporal Lamka and proceeded over a fairly good Carabao cart trail to the northwest. We had just entered a broad valley and were driving along over smooth ground when I happened to look down and just ahead of the jeep ... [and] I saw many low mounds. I suddenly realized that they were land mines and yelled at the top of my voice, 'STOP!'" Lamka slammed on the brakes and the two looked around. They had driven into the middle of a mine field. "There was nothing to do but back out over our own tire tracks. We were lucky to get out alive."[18]

After extricating themselves, the two drove on until reaching a former Japanese first aid site. "We ran across some 25 dead Japanese soldiers on litters. Most of them had a big hole in their chests, indicating they had blown themselves up with hand grenades, even though wounded. Craig had seen other examples of the Japanese penchant for suicide rather than surrender. "It was hard to believe that men in a wounded condition would choose death to capture." He did not feel sorry for them, however. "I was shown a group of Guamanian Chamorros which one of the patrols had overrun. Every man had been beheaded by the Japs.... They lay in the jungle with their hands tightly bound behind their backs, flies crawling over them and their heads lying about among the bodies. This had been a cold-blooded massacre without reason."[19]

The Japanese did not intend to release captured Guamanians. Lieutenant Wilcie O'Bannon related: "It appeared that the Japanese had practiced their samurai sword action, just chopped across the body horizontally."[20]

Perils of Command

Craig learned that his right flank was being held up and went forward to see what he could do. "I always felt that a command should be where his troops are held up and cannot advance. Being there he can take any required action on the spot and his presence sometimes steadies the situation." He caught up with the right flank platoon and was advancing with it when "we received intense machine gun fire from Asan ridge, which was then to our right rear. Taking cover, we located the position, a concrete machine gun emplacement not over 25 yards away and took it out."[21]

After watching the unit take its objective, Craig started back to his CP. "As I was walking along the road with Captain George Percy and a runner, I was surprised to look to my left and see a couple Japanese soldiers who had just come out of a cave. One of them raised a square package in his hand and threw it at me. It landed some distance away and exploded with a terrific roar, knocking me off the road into a ditch filled with sharp stones." Craig's companions were farther from the explosion and did not get its full effect. Several Marines came to the rescue, including a crew with a jeep mounted antitank gun, which blasted the cave, killing the inhabitants. Craig was unhurt, but "was severely bruised from the concussion, which really made my teeth chatter for a while." A metal fragment lodged in his neck (many years later it surfaced and was surgically removed).[22]

The regimental CP moved with the advance, often setting up directly behind the front lines. "It was sometimes more secure and safe than further back." Craig personally selected many of the command post sites, usually in a location that placed him in a position to control the movement of his Marines. On one occasion, the CP was set up in the thick jungle at the intersection of several trails and road junctions. "Shortly after I had picked the place ... a Japanese officer wandered into the middle of things and was shot as he started to pull his pistol. Later, a Japanese private was also shot ... at the important road junction." Shortly afterward, Craig went forward to check on the advance. "About 300 yards up the trail, I noted a well-worn path leading to a knoll. Steps had been carved in the steep slope." Craig stopped the jeep and got out to look it over. "I changed my mind and decided to get back in and continue to the front. Stopping a messenger, I told him to tell Major Lips [operation officer] to have a patrol investigate this area, and drove on to the front."[23]

Upon returning from the front, Craig was surprised to hear the sounds of a small battle. The patrol he had ordered to investigate the knoll was heavily engaged with a large Japanese force and had suffered several casualties. An Army battalion happened to be in the area. "I quickly explained the situation to the commanding officer and he immediately organized a full scale attack. Quite a battle ensued and the Army suffered many casualties before the place was overrun. It was found that the main position was a huge concrete underground bunker with steel doors. Inside was a complete headquarters with communications. It appeared that this was the secondary command post for the Japanese command on Guam. How thankful I was that I had changed my mind and decided not to investigate this interesting looking knoll."[24]

The knoll, officially known as Mount Mataguac, was attacked by infantrymen of the Army's 1st Battalion, 306th Regiment. After a spirited assault using flamethrowers, white phosphorous grenades, and massive charges of TNT, they overran the headquarters. The body of Lieutenant General Hideyoshi Obata, commander of the Thirty-first Army, was found inside the elaborate command post. Obata just happened to be on an inspection tour at the time of the invasion and was caught on the island. After writing a last message to the emperor he committed suicide, just before the Americans sealed the entrance.[25]

The 9th Marines advanced more than 6,000 yards and seized a critical road junction. Craig followed closely behind. As his jeep headed down a small valley, "We heard the sound of motors starting. Before we could locate the position of the noise, two enemy tanks rolled out of cleverly camouflaged positions on the side of the hill to our right and headed toward us firing machine guns and small caliber cannon. They were not over 100 feet away and I had visions of losing all my men who were in the immediate vicinity. A bazooka man ... and his assistant went into action immediately. With a calmness that was uncanny, they proceeded to knock out the two tanks in quick succession!" Two gutsy Marines jumped on the tanks, forced open a hatch, and dropped hand grenades inside, finishing off the crews. "We later found two well-camouflaged, unmanned tanks dug into the side of a hill, just a short distance away."[26]

During the advance toward the northern end of the island, Craig went forward to Tiyan Airfield, which had just been captured. "As I reached the southern end of the airfield, a Japanese tank suddenly appeared and cut right across in front of me. It turned and started down the road towards the 2nd Battalion assembly area. I had my driver follow it, and was not over 150 feet behind it. As it reached the battalion position, the top of the turret flew open and a Japanese officer started wildly firing his automatic pistol. The Marines were so surprised that the tank drove right through them and they did not fire a shot. The Jap tank continued on towards a jungle area and stopped. Three Japs jumped out and fled. It was one of those incredible Japanese actions for which there is never an explanation."[27]

"In another instance, we were in a small valley and heard tanks revving up their motors, and suddenly two of these tanks appeared and headed directly for us firing wildly. Two of my bazooka men knocked them out. We found four more tanks, supplies, and trucks that were camouflaged and abandoned in an area that had been the headquarters of a Japanese tank battalion. We used the trucks and two half-tracks for the rest of the campaign."[28]

As the 3rd Division's right flank unit, the 9th Marines was tasked to make contact with the 1st Marine Brigade, led by Craig's old friend Brigadier General Lemuel C. Shepherd. The brigade was working its way north on the Orote Peninsula. Craig was anticipating making contact on July 26. "I was in great hopes of pushing ahead and making contact with the brigade by nightfall." Instead, he received an order to fall back by the assistant division commander. "I tried to argue against such a move ... however, I didn't get very far." Instead, he sent a patrol to make contact. "I was most happy when at 2000 that night the patrol returned with a personal message from General Shepherd." The two finally made contact a few days later. "It was evening when General Shepherd ... came to visit me. He had just arrived when a number of artillery shells started to land in the very near vicinity of my CP. We both ducked behind a cement wall and continued our conversation while sitting on the ground." Just two old friends quietly reminiscing in the midst of a shelling![29]

By August 10, the end was in sight—one more push. Craig ordered a company to clear Peti Point and went along with them. "Nearing the point, we ran into a small group of the enemy, and in the short skirmish, one of my men was killed and one wounded. It was a sad sight because the buddy of the man shot through the head went temporarily insane. He had just had too much, and it was more than he could take. He ran screaming hysterical into the jungle and it was some days before he was eventually found."[30]

Guam was declared secure on August 11, although Japanese stragglers hid out for months in the thick jungles and caves of the island. In 1949, when Craig commanded the 1st Provisional Marine Brigade on Guam, his men captured two Japanese soldiers. They surrendered after seeing a photograph of Emperor Hirohito with two American MPs standing near him. The holdouts had clear, well-patched uniforms and lived in a well-stocked cave near the Marine officers' mess.

Craig's spot award of the Navy Cross was officially approved on September 18, 1947:

> The President of the United States of America takes pleasure in presenting the Navy Cross to Colonel Edward A. Craig (MCSN: 0-196), United States Marine Corps, for extraordinary heroism as Commanding Officer of the Ninth Marines, THIRD Marine Division, during action against enemy Japanese forces on Guam, Marianas Islands, from 21 July to 10 August 1945. An aggressive and inspiring leader, Colonel Craig constantly directed his men in combat in the face of intense enemy fire from the time of landing with the assault elements of his regiment until organized resistance ceased. On 30 July, charged with capturing a portion of high ground on the force beachhead line and making contact with the Army on Mount Tenjo, Colonel Craig remained with his leading assault elements during the entire advance and, by his coolness under fire, provided inspiration for his officers and men. Personally directing the final assault on Mount Chachao, he kept casualties at a minimum by his expert judgment. When one of his battalions encountered heavy enemy resistance near an important road junction during the advance to the northern end of Guam on 3 August, he took a position beside a tank advancing with the assault troops and, despite a constant stream of rifle and machine-gun fire, fearlessly remained there throughout the entire action of several hours to direct the attack which annihilated several hundred of the enemy. His outstanding ability, courageous leadership and devotion to duty were important factors in the success of the campaign and reflect the highest credit upon Colonel Craig and the United States Naval Service.[31]

CHAPTER 14

Operation *Detachment* (Iwo Jima)

"Shortly after the end of the campaign, Craig relinquished his command of the 9th Marines and reported to the Fifth Amphibious Corps as the G-3 (operations officer), a position of great responsibility. "I was given a one-page directive from Fleet Marine Force Headquarters to prepare operational orders for a landing on Iwo Jima [Operation *Detachment*]."[1] To facilitate planning, the Corps Commander, Major General Harry Schmidt, and his key staff officers, flew to Hawaii where the bulk of his force was in training. "I took this letter to Hawaii with me and began planning the operation. The 4th and 5th Divisions were the assault forces for the landing and the 3rd Division, which was still on Guam, was brought in as reserve or as needed."

"The orders for this operation included almost a hundred small units from the Army, Navy, Marine Corps and such organizations. My main difficulty in preparing the orders in Hawaii was getting in contact with these many units which were scattered all over the Hawaiian islands and in Guam. No orders seemed obtainable from the Army for the transfer of Army units which would take place in this operation. Accordingly, the Corps went ahead and issued their own orders to these units citing the overall order, which designated the unit as part of the Corps. The Army themselves would not issue orders for their transfer."

"We prepared for the initial landing with one alternate plan. The alternate plan was never carried out, and the original landing order was never changed. The orders were quickly promulgated to the divisions. Most of my time was spent on writing up various orders for attached units and making trips to the various divisions to coordinate our activities. Prior to leaving Hawaii, we carried one big landing exercise on the island of Maui. This was mostly a command post exercise [CPX], although the troops did get ashore before quickly returning to their ships."[2]

Sulfur Island

In October 1944, the Joint Chiefs of Staff directed Fleet Admiral Chester W. Nimitz, commander in chief Pacific Fleet, to seize the strategic Japanese-held island of Iwo Jima, 660 nautical miles southeast of Tokyo. The tiny volcanic island, barely eight square miles in area, was one of the most heavily fortified islands in the Pacific—and by far the toughest "nut" the Marines would have to crack. Intelligence reports indicated the island was honeycombed with multistoried blockhouses, camouflaged pillboxes, and thousands of yards of concrete-lined interconnecting caves and tunnels. Hundreds of artillery pieces, mortars, antitank and machine guns were sited to cover every square inch of ground. The formidable Lieutenant General Tadamichi Kuribayashi, onetime leader of the emperor's elite Imperial Guard, commanded more than twenty thousand combat veterans.

Kuribayashi, in a break with traditional Japanese all-out counterattack against the beachhead, adopted a policy of attrition. There would be no massive banzai attack to stop the invaders at the water's edge. Instead, he divided the island into five defense sectors and ordered his men to defend these positions to the death. He planned to slow the invaders with small infantry units supported by automatic weapons, while relying on artillery, mortars, and rockets emplaced to the north and south to enfilade the beaches and make them untenable.

Mount Suribachi, the major terrain feature in the south, was a 550-foot extinct volcano, which loomed over the landing beaches. It bristled with weapons of all types, ranging from casemated coast-defense guns and artillery to automatic weapons emplaced in mutually supporting pillboxes. Many of these emplacements were constructed of reinforced concrete with walls four feet thick and cleverly camouflaged to blend in with the terrain. The entire island was honeycombed with these defensive fortifications. Many had several levels that were constructed by tunnels and had multiple entrances, which allowed the defender to move throughout the system without being exposed to direct fire. Kuribayashi issued a last message two days before the landing: "I pray for a heroic fight."[3]

Major General Harry Schmidt commanded the veteran V Amphibious Corps (VAC). The 58-year old was a veteran of two Pacific campaigns— Roi-Namur and Saipan. VAC comprised three Marine divisions: the battle-hardened 3rd and 4th Divisions and the 5th Division, which was organized around a considerable number of combat-experienced troops. VAC was the largest force of U.S. Marines ever committed to a single operation—eighty thousand men, more than half of whom were combat veterans. In the opinion of historian Colonel Joseph H. Alexander, "The troops assaulting Iwo Jima were arguably the most proficient amphibious forces the world had seen."[4]

A Tough Proposition

Craig found that terrain dictated the landing plan and subsequent scheme of maneuver. "Selection of the landing beaches was a simple matter, there being only two available beach areas large enough to support a landing. Both were good beaches equally well defended, with the southeastern one perhaps better from the standpoint of fewer natural obstacles immediately inland. Because the prevailing wind was indicated being from the north and west in February, the southeastern or lee beaches were selected." However, Mt. Suribachi loomed over the entire southern end of the island, completely dominating either landing beach. In addition, the steep cliffs of the Rock Quarry overshadowed the right flank, sandwiching the landing beach between the two high grounds. The terrain north of the beaches compounded Craig's tactical dilemma. The land rose unevenly onto the Motoyama Plateau, falling off sharply along the coasts into steep cliffs and canyons. The broke, convoluted, cave-dotted landscape represented a defenders' dream and an attackers' nightmare.[5]

The final plan, issued on December 23, 1944, called for the simultaneous landing of four reinforced regiments, nine thousand men, in 45 minutes. The landing was to be preceded by three days of naval gunfire and aerial bombardment. Craig argued for a 10-day bombardment, but was overruled, much to the disgust of the naval gunfire expert Lieutenant

Colonel Donald M. Weller, USMC. "The issue was not the weight of shells, nor their caliber, but rather time. Destruction of heavily fortified enemy targets took deliberate, pinpoint firing from close ranges. Iwo Jima's 700 hard targets would require time to knock out, a lot of time." The Joint Expeditionary Force commander, Major General Holland M. Smith, gloomily predicted heavy casualties, possibly as many as 15,000. Secretary of the Navy James V. Forrestal, on board the flagship, said: "Iwo Jima, like Tarawa, leaves very little choice, except to take it by force of arms, by character and courage."[6]

In Harm's Way—Iwo Jima

The requirement for naval shipping to support MacArthur's campaign in the Philippines forced two postponements of Operation *Detachment*. Finally, in early December, VAC was notified that D-day was set for February 19, 1945. Loading started almost immediately. Corps troops and the 4th Division embarked from Maui, while the 5th Division loaded from Hawaii, "the big island." The landing force rendezvoused off Maalaea Bay, Maui, to conduct a week of rehearsal exercises. "This was mostly a CPX, although the troops did get ashore. They returned shortly thereafter to their ships." Craig emphasized their importance. "This rehearsal was conducted in every possible detail in accordance with the preferred (southeastern beach) plan of attack against Iwo Jima."[7]

The residents of the sleepy little Hawaiian island of Maui woke to find an armada of ships at their doorstep. Thousands of men swarmed ashore, tearing up the pristine beaches and quiet backcountry and completely shattering the pastoral setting. Distant explosions marked the detonation of naval gunfire and aircraft on Kahoolawe's live fire range. The seven-day exercise was closely monitored by the commanders and key staff of the landing force. They gathered aboard the command ship USS *Auburn* (ACC-10) for a critique of the exercise. Craig was generally satisfied with the results, although the absence of several assault organizations distracted from their overall value.[8]

The men were granted one last liberty on Oahu before sailing for the objective area. Historian Howard M. Conner explained that "One-quarter of the troops had regular liberty ashore each day and another fourth could go ashore in organized liberty parties to playing fields and beaches near Pearl Harbor and at Kaneohe Bay."[9] There was some concern that, with the number of men ashore, word would somehow leak out about their destination. Counterintelligence officers spread the rumor in Honolulu's bars and hotels that Formosa was the next target.[10]

With 23 days remaining before D-day, the immense convoy sailed for Saipan, the forward staging and final rehearsal area. Craig noted that the staff used the time to hone their skills. "While enroute to the forward area, an extensive CPX, coordinated with naval forces, was conducted on board the Auburn." Upon reaching Saipan, additional rehearsals were held. "Assault waves were boated and dispatched from the line of departure but were not landed. The sea was rough and several Marines were hurt as landing craft bounced up and raked them as they hung on the debarkation nets."[11]

Craig wrote two letters to his parents en route to the Iwo Jima operation:

> February 10, 1945, enroute to Iwo Jima:
> Dear Mother and Father:
> Am writing this on Saturday night as tomorrow will be a busy day as we will be at another big staging area [Saipan]. By this time next week, we should have entered combat again and you will be able to read in the papers ... how things are going ... this has been a long hard grind out here and it is not getting any better ... your loving son, Signed, Ned.

> February 16, 1945, enroute to Iwo Jima:
> Dear Mother and Father:
> This will probably be the last chance that I will have to write for some time ... Things are happening very fast, the raid by our carrier planes on Japan was [just] released ... and I hope they did plenty of damage there ... In a very short time now we will also be in combat and I pray that God will make it short and will bring us success with few casualties. It will be a very tough fight ... Your loving son, Ned.

Land the Landing Force

Dawn of D-day found the weather clear, with visibility virtually unlimited, the temperature about 68 degrees, wind eight to 12 knots from the north, surf conditions good. H-hour was set at 9am. At 8:30am,

68 armored, cannon-firing amphibious tractors (LVT(A)s) followed by more than 400 of their troop-carrying brethren, crossed the line of departure. Combat Correspondent Technical Sergeant Henry A. Weaver wrote: "There were the faintest grins on the faces of the Marines as they crouched in the landing craft that was bouncing toward the beach of Iwo Jima. It was D-day and this was one of the initial assault waves. On the inside of the ramp, the coxswain had painted with bold letters and heavy brush: 'TOO LATE TO WORRY.'" Naval gunfire thundered overhead, in a massive bombardment of the landing beaches. The assault waves hit the beach within two minutes of H-hour and advanced inland, against furious resistance. Jim Headley was in the assault wave. "Woody's company [Captain Elyn W. Woods, commanding Company I, who was wounded in action by a gunshot in his left side] was the first to hit the beach and I heard him report by radio that they had received no fire. Tom [Captain Thomas S. Witherspoon, commanding Company K, who was wounded in action by shrapnel in the neck], who was next to hit, reported that they were starting to receive mortar and small arms fire. L Company followed and then all hell broke loose. By the time four or five waves had hit, the entire beach and the Japs apparently waiting for the most opportune target, let go with everything they had." Hundreds of Marines hugged the black volcanic sand, pinned down by the relentless shelling. "Casualties were heavy ... officer casualties were so high that the men were without leadership."[12]

The beach resembled a junk yard. Disabled and broached landing craft, mired vehicles, abandoned equipment, and bodies littered the sandy terraces. Japanese artillery mercilessly pounded the wreckage into impenetrable rubble, jamming the beach approaches. Coast Guard Coxswain Marvin J. Perrett steered an LCVP (Boat number 21 from the USS *Bayfield*, APA-33) toward an opening. Wreckage prevented it from beaching properly. A motor mechanic dropped the ramp and the load of troops splashed ashore. One man fell beneath the ramp. Perrett applied full power to back away. Water poured over the stern and killed the engine. Plunging waves crashed over the sides. Number 21 joined dozens of other landing craft beneath the water.[13]

The Corps headquarters came ashore on D+5. A landing craft mechanized (LCM) came alongside the Auburn. Craig and his staff climbed into the boat for the run to the beach. As the small boat neared the island's northwestern beaches, he could plainly see the flag atop Mount Suribachi. The coxswain carefully maneuvered through the heavy boat traffic to bring the craft's bow against the beach. The ramp dropped and Craig stepped ashore. He immediately sank up to his ankles in the coarse volcanic ash. "I was immediately struck by how difficult it was to move through the black sand. There wasn't any traction, each step was an effort." A guide appeared and led him to the command post, "a little northwest of Mount Suribachi" at map coordinates TA 147R.[14]

"Our CP set up consisted of tents dug into the sand. It was crammed into the narrow southern end of the island, between artillery positions, first aid stations, supply dumps, and subordinate unit command posts, beneath Mt. Suribachi. It was a lucrative target for Japanese gunners. The Japs were shelling the area we were in with guns and spigot mortars. In addition, they had a form of rocket made from five-inch naval shells, which would periodically go over our CP. Most of these rockets dropped into the sea at the south end of the island, however."[15]

On February 25, 1945, at the base of Mt. Suribachi, he wrote to his parents:

> Dear Mother and Father,
> Am writing this in a blackout tent and, as I am very busy, it must be short. This is the toughest fight the Marines have had I believe. This place is a fortress defended by some 20,000 Japs with artillery covering every part of the island and hundreds of bunkers and caves defended to the death. We live in foxholes and dugouts at night because of the artillery fire and bombing. I hope we can finish this thing quickly ...
> Your loving son, Ned

Craig selected a site for his operation. "The small CP tent where I had my G-3 Section was placed in a slight defilade behind a small sand hill, but this, of course, did not protect against high-angle fire, and many shells fell around it." The Japanese had every inch of the area zeroed in and began a merciless shelling. "We were all congregated in this tent the first night ashore when suddenly the Japs opened up with everything they had. Shells were landing and exploding all around us. Rank was forgotten as well as dignity when all of the officers and men in the tent hit the deck in a pile three or four high. There we lay as the shells thumped and exploded around us. We fully expected that the entire G-3 Section would become casualties [in] one fell swoop. The shelling stopped as suddenly as it had begun, and we unscrambled from the pile and went back to work. This happened a number of times the first two or three days ashore."[16]

The heavy Japanese fire added impetus to the construction of shelters. Craig and his assistant, Lieutenant Colonel Joe Stewart, took time out to get underground. "The two of us decided to construct a double foxhole. We dug into the loose black sand and shored the sides up with whatever we could find but mostly sandbags ... [and] empty cardboard tubes the 105 shells came in filled with sand, and [with] some pieces of lumber, we covered the foxhole, leaving only a very small entrance at one side." Craig developed claustrophobia in the small space. "I will never forget the terror-filled moments in that hole when the Jap shells would be landing all around us. Joe and I would lie with our faces in the sand and pray that nothing landed on us as the explosions shook the sand down on us."[17]

Craig's G-3 Section prepared daily written orders for each division. "These orders usually got out to the units by about four o'clock in the afternoon, so the division naturally had to rush to get their order out to the various units down to the companies by the following morning. However, due to the short distance involved and the density of the troops on the island, this was not too difficult a situation as it might seem. The lines of communication were very short and could be handled by runners or verbally over the telephone in many cases."[18]

The Corps headquarters remained in the same location throughout the campaign, but Craig refused to wait for information. "I found that it was impossible for me to sit back at the Corps CP and have a clear conception of what was actually taking place at the front. My assistants were very capable, so I felt free at any time to go forward to check on the various units. This gave me the opportunity to talk with commanders and get their ideas on what could be done for the next day's operation." Craig also expected his subordinates to go to the front. "It was my policy as G-3 to require that at least one of my assistants go to the front each day and see for himself what the situation was and advise me on his return. I believe our Operations Section was always well informed as a result."[19]

On one occasion, Craig was by himself, on the way to a battalion headquarters. "I noticed a dead Marine with most of his lower body blown off lying nearby, and in an instant realized that he had stepped on a land mine. I stopped in my tracks, looked at the ground, and found that I was in the middle of a mined area ... so I carefully retraced my steps and got out without further incident." Craig worked his way forward to a company CP. While he was talking to the company commander, "a Marine crouching nearby yelled 'Look out, there's a Jap right there,' and pointed to a crevice in the rock almost beside me. Sure enough, there was a spider hole, as we called them, and tightly wedged in it, with a grenade in his hand, was a Jap soldier. A Marine covered him with an automatic rifle, and the company commander tried to induce him to come out by offering cigarettes and C-rations. The man was near enough to touch but would not let go of the grenade or move. Water was finally offered him and he still refused to move. A burst of fire finally settled the question and the war went on."[20]

By the second week of the campaign, Holland Smith's shocking prediction had come true. VAC had suffered 13,000 casualties, 3,000 of whom were killed in action. Assault elements of the three divisions were exhausted, and the end was not yet in sight. Craig personally observed the blooding. "I was watching a small advance of Marines over ground that was defiladed. A squad in rather close formation started to cross a knoll on which a number of dead Marines were lying. I heard someone shouting a warning to the squad to keep off the knoll. They had reached the dead Marines and some of them had bent over to examine one of them who was apparently only wounded. A sharp burst of fire from an unseen place mowed down seven of the squad. Others were wounded but managed to roll down out of the danger area. I had never seen so many Marines shot down at once before, and it made me feel very depressed."[21]

Iwo Jima was not a place to visit. "Looking toward the knoll on my right hand," continued Craig, "I noticed a huge figure of a man dressed in a new camouflage uniform lying on a litter where he had been abandoned by stretcher bearers. As none of our personnel were dressed in camouflage, I noticed him particularly and wondered who he was. He must have been over six feet four and built like a giant. The front of his jacket was red with blood. I never did find out who this casualty was, and surmised at the time that he must have been an observer sent ashore from some ship."[22]

Death Valley

By D+25, depleted regiments of the 5th Division had reached the Japanese commander's final command center, an 800-yard pocket of incredibly broken terrain, which the troops dubbed "Death Valley." Craig went forward to check on the situation. "This area had been held by some six or seven hundred Jap troops and was their last stronghold on the island. The Gorge was a jumble of rocks surrounding an area some 700 yards by 300 yards. It had steep sides and the Japs were concealed in the crevices and caves along these sides. It was almost impossible to locate where defensive fires came from due to excellent concealment, and the smokeless and flashless powder that the enemy was using." The Marines pressed forward in cave-by-cave assaults with flamethrowers and demolitions. Casualties were heavy.[23]

As Craig approached the Gorge, he "passed long lines of dead Marines laid out on the ground ... covered with ponchos, their booted feet sticking out." He found a young platoon commander, who commenced to brief him on the situation. "In the middle of the briefing, a barrage of phosphorus shells fell around us. I thought that the end had come, and we lay crouched down in the hole with our faces in the dirt for a long time, it seemed, before the barrage stopped. Phosphorus shells are most terrifying when they are landing almost on top of you." Inching forward, Craig watched a squad cautiously move among the rocks. "I saw a Marine fall, shot directly through the head at very close range. He never saw the enemy. Another was wounded and then a third shot through the head from the rear. Others were wounded while I still watched as though from a seat in the audience at a theatre." One Marine exclaimed: "How the hell can you fight something you can't see? The thing that made it so tough was the Japs were completely concealed in caves, pillboxes carved out of rock, or crevasses, and there were so many of them you could never tell where the next shot came from."[24]

The men that Craig watched were new replacements, brought up from the rear and hastily thrown into the attack. "It looked like murder to me. These men did not know war; they did not even know the squad leader in some cases." Craig made a strong recommendation to land the veteran 3rd Marine Regiment, the Corps reserve. His request fell on deaf ears, as Holland Smith refused to send them in, with the comment: "You got enough Marines on the island now; there are too damn many here." The problem was not with the number of Marines, but the fact that the replacements lacked experience. "The new men ... were not only new to combat, but they also were new to each other, an assortment of strangers lacking the life-saving bonds of unit integrity." Craig "returned to the Corps CP sick at heart, knowing that this slaughter would probably go on till the Gorge was secured."[25]

The 9th Marines were engaged in a bitter fight to take Motoyama No. 2, the center airfield. "I had not been back to my old regiment since leaving them for the Corps assignment, so I decided to visit them and see how they were getting along. As I approached the CP area, I heard someone yell from the distance, 'Hello Colonel Craig.' At that, it seemed that heads arose from foxholes in all directions and hands waved at me. In talking to the men, I found that casualties had been high, and many names were mentioned to me as having been killed. The same old spirit was still there though."[26]

On March 11, 1945, at the base of Mt. Suribachi, he wrote:

> Dearest Mother and Father,
> This thing is dragging on and is costing us plenty. However, I believe it will be over in two days more, as we have the remnants pinned down at the end of the island. The place where they have been fighting this past two weeks is a weird looking area of jumbled rocks and ravines with sulfur smoke, which causes a haze. It is literally honeycombed with pillboxes, blockhouses and caves. It is heavily mined and manned with enemy who will not retreat but die at their posts after exacting heavy casualties on our men. This was not unexpected, however, and

was the reason the Marines were assigned the job ... all our plans for landing worked out perfectly. Will be glad to get out of here, God willing.
As ever, your loving son, Ned.

Craig was asked to summarize the tactics that brought about victory: "By a determined main effort in the center of our line just north Airfield No. 1, the enemy forces were split ... This breakthrough enabled our forces to envelope enemy troops on the right and left flanks and to continue the attack down the rocky corridors and ridge lines on our flanks instead of assaulting frontally these ridges and cross compartments."[27]

Work Through the Pain

The pressures on Craig were tremendous—little sleep, poor and inadequate food, and the constant threat of death or injury took its toll. "Towards the end of the Iwo Jima campaign, I noticed an increasing symptom of stomach trouble. I could not eat much, and many times threw up what I had eaten. Pains in my stomach made it almost impossible to sleep at night for any length of time. I threw up and noticed some blood was in the residue." He refused to turn himself in to sickbay as long as the battle lasted. Finally, the Corps headquarters evacuated the island and returned to Hawaii.[28]

Butcher's Bill

The battle for Iwo Jima far exceeded even Holland Smith's grim prophecy. One-third of the assault force became a casualty—24,053 Marines and Navy personnel, of which 6,140 died. Japanese losses were more than 22,000 dead. Military historian Dr. Norman Cooper said: "Nearly 700 Americans gave their lives for every square mile. For every plot of ground the size of a football field, an average of more than one American and five Japanese were killed and five Americans wounded."

Craig related that "At the end of the Iwo Jima campaign, I was ordered to fly back to Hawaii, go to Maui, and find a place for the Corps headquarters to set up. This I did, and when the Corps arrived by ship, we had suitable accommodations set up for all Corps troops." Shortly afterward, Craig came down with an ulcer, which he had had for some time. He spent three weeks in the hospital, on a soft diet, before being released for duty as executive officer, Marine Training and Replacement Command, Camp Pendleton, California.[29]

CHAPTER 15

1st Provisional Brigade: Guam

In 1946, after a series of assignments in the United States—Training and Replacement Command/Redistribution Regiment (Camp Pendleton), Troop Training Unit (San Diego and Japan), Amphibious Review Board (San Diego)—Craig was promoted to brigadier general in 1947 and assumed duties as assistant division commander, 1st Marine Division, Tientsin, China. A year later, the division was withdrawn from China and the First Provisional Marine Brigade was activated on Guam, with Craig as its commander. "I arrived on May 19, 1947, and reported to the Naval Governor." The brigade's personnel arrived shortly thereafter by naval transport and were allotted an area that had been used by the 3rd Marine Division during the war. The unfinished camp, named Camp Witek, in honor of Private First Class Frank P. Witek of the 9th Marines, who was posthumously awarded the Medal of Honor in the recapture of the island, was located on the high ground in an overgrown jungle area above Ylig Bay on the east side of the island.[1]

The brigade comprised two Battalion Landing Teams, each with its own artillery battery, tank platoon, antitank platoon, and support units. The basic mission of the brigade was to train Marines for contingency operations in China during the communist takeover of the country. "I had top secret orders at the time to be prepared to move out with the brigade prepared for combat on a few hours' notice to Saudi Arabia. We also had orders to reinforce the garrison at Tsingtao. Eventually we did send men by air and ship there on an emergency in 1949."[2]

"This situation required that I keep up an intensive troops training program and at the same time build up the cantonment." Training was interesting. "Besides battalion and brigade field problems and landings, we conducted air-lift exercises, and were able to assemble enough transport aircraft to lift a battalion, with necessary supplies, to Saipan on three different occasions."[3]

"Camp Witek was a new Marine Corps installation," General Raymond G. Davis recalled. "Troops were housed in Quonset huts and tents. There were no quarters available for married officers and staff non-commissioned officers (SNCOs). As a result, the assignment was designated as an 'unaccompanied tour,' meaning families could not accompany their sponsors."[4]

Craig was determined to provide quarters for the members of his command. "My first priority was to finish barracks, mess halls and battalion clubs for the enlisted men. My second priority was to construct bachelor officers and SNCO quarters, and my last priority would of necessity be quarters for married officers and non-commissioned officers. I was informed that in the jungle were 900 new Quonset huts in crates, plus a large number of large jumbo Quonset huts that could be used for storage. This was all World War II surplus." He was able to secure $300,000 for construction materials, but it had to be shipped from the United States.[5]

With that start, he was able to get underway. "Fortunately, I had an engineer company and a shore party company with heavy engineering equipment as part of my brigade." He turned out the entire brigade "from early morning till four thirty in the afternoon, sometimes longer. The Marines worked tireless to finally complete a cantonment which any commander could be proud." To maintain morale, he pushed for the construction of a huge club, complete with pool tables, bowling alleys, restaurant, and bar. "I also pushed athletics and, despite the hard work being performed by the men, we put out champion football, baseball and basketball teams."[6]

Craig next completed his second priority and started on his third, the officers and SNCOs. "I told them that I realized the hardships of long separation from their families but that they were Marines and their duty came first to the Corps." He went on to tell them that "If they desired to put out extra work, they could bring their families to Guam by constructing modified Quonset style quarters. A board of officers would inspect it and if it passed specifications, the builder would be given permission to bring his family to Guam."[7]

This plan met with instant approval by the great majority. "I also told them that if there were any who felt they could [not accept] the plan and felt they did not want to continue duty with the brigade, they should tender their resignations." Some six or eight officers put in their "papers" and were sent back to the States for discharge. "I was glad to get rid of them," Craig said.[8]

"We had to build our own quarters," Ray Davis emphasized. "I was issued a vacant lot and a knocked-down Quonset hut. The hut consisted of a half- moon structure build with semi-circular metal frames: three feet by six feet pieces of tin roof; and four feet by six feet plywood slabs for the floor. Pieces of tarpaulin were attached to the outside walls to serve as screen-covered 'windows' during the heavy intermittent rains the swept Guam almost daily. No glass was allowed, since strong gusts of wind would have broken them out. We also had to personally order other essentials, such as commodes, stoves, and refrigerators from the States."[9]

"Because there were a number of officers awaiting families, the whole thing was kind of a do-it-yourself community. I was a pretty good plumber, as I put plumbing in four or five houses. Somebody else was an electrician, another was a carpenter—so it was a trade-off effort. I do not know of any other time in the Corps when officers had to get out and build their own quarters. Many of them would work late at night under floodlights, after a long hard day of training. It should be noted, that after building these Quonsets, along with sending of substantial amounts of personal funds, the Marines had to give up their full quarters allowances in order to live in them!"[10]

"It worked out well in the end. By the time I left Guam," Craig asserted, "there were some 350 good sets of quarters completed and occupied."[11]

Craig took a Sunday off from the pressures of the assignment, haunted by the wartime memories. "I drove my jeep to the northern end of the island to look again at the small crossroads hamlet of Finegayan, where one of my battalions had such a tough time and suffered heavy casualties. It was near here that my runner and I had been pinned down by machine gun fire and barely escaped with our lives. As I left the crossroad and headed north, I found instead of the familiar jungles, unrecognizable housing areas. I looked and looked for familiar landmarks ... but the place no longer existed. Civilization had caught up with it and bulldozed it under. I turned back, disappointed that I had been unable to see once again the place where my Marines had put up such a gallant fight. In my mind's eye I could see every detail of the action. As I drove back, I thought to myself that even though the place had changed, it will always exist for those who fought there ... the place where the Japanese made their last fanatical stand ... it was tough."[12]

Even though the war had been over for several years, Japanese holdouts would occasionally surrender. On May 12, 1948 two Japanese soldiers surrendered to civilian police. "They were picked up and hauled off to be repatriated," Davis recalled. "There were also several war criminals incarcerated on the island and, after the war crimes trials, some were executed." In 1947 and 1949, 13 Japanese Army or Navy officers were found guilty of torturing and murdering American servicemen, including nine Marine Raiders captured on Makin Island. The men were hanged inside a Quonset hut and buried in unmarked graves on U.S. military land on Guam.[13]

In 1949, Craig completed a two-year tour and resumed duties as assistant division commander, 1st Marine Division, Camp Pendleton, California. "When I finally left Guam, I felt that I had accomplished my mission." In the summer of 1950, Major General Graves B. Erskine, the division commander, received classified orders to go to South Vietnam, making Craig the acting division commander.[14]

USMC World War I recruiting poster that Craig became so enamored with. (Library of Congress Prints and Photographs Division)

Second Lieutenant Edward A. Craig. (USMC)

Colonel Charles F. Craig (1872–1950), a pioneer in tropical medicine, pathology, and bacteriology, served in the U.S. Army Medical Corps; after retiring from the military in 1931, he joined Tulane University. (Smithsonian Institution Archives, Accession 90-105)

"Banana Wars" Marines in field uniforms armed with heavy weapons: "Tommy guns," Browning Automatic Rifles and .45 caliber service automatics. (USMC)

A tough-looking squad of Marines in the "bush." (USMC)

U.S. Marines with the captured flag of Augusto César Sandino in Nicaragua in 1932. (USMC)

Augusto Cesar Sandino, one of the main guerrilla leaders during the 1920s in Nicaragua. (Marine Corps Archives & Special Collections)

Landing craft circle while awaiting orders during the Cape Torokina landings, Bougainville, November 1943. (USMC 67319)

Beach landing on Bougainville. (USMC)

Brigade Commander and Staff, 2nd Marine Brigade, 1936. Emile Phillips Moses (May 27, 1880–December 22, 1965) was a distinguished officer in the United States Marine Corps with the rank of major general. A veteran of 40 years of service and several expeditionary campaigns, Moses is most noted for his service as Commanding General, Marine Corps Recruit Depot Parris Island, during World War II and for his efforts in the development of Marine Corps amphibious warfare doctrine, especially the development of the Landing Vehicle Tracked. Craig is sat in the front row on left. (USMC History Division)

Marines advancing toward Japanese positions on Bougainville. The Marine in the foreground has just tossed a hand grenade. (USMC)

U.S. Marine Raiders gathered in front of a Japanese dugout on Cape Torokina on Bougainville, Solomon Islands, which they helped to take, in January 1944. These men earned the bloody reputation of being skillful jungle fighters. (USMC)

A bloody encounter on November 14, 1943, at the junction of the Numa Numa and Piva Trails. Marine infantrymen had been stopped by well dug-in and camouflaged enemy troops. Five Marine tanks rushed up and attacked on a 250-yard front through the jungle. (USMC 65162)

In a field hospital on Bougainville wounded Marines are given first aid by doctors and Corpsmen on November 29, 1943. (USN)

D-day: climbing down cargo nets into landing craft for the ride to the beach, Guam. (US Coast Guard)

Enemy anti-tank guns accounted for these two tanks burning near Yigo, Guam, during the Marine and army invasion of the island. The crews escaped safely from the burning machines, as the Marine infantry continued their advance. (USMC)

Marines from the First Marine Division at Camp Pendleton loading up on July 11, 1950, prior to departing for the Korean War. (USMC)

Men of the First Provisional Brigade arriving in Pusan, Korea. (USMC)

A South Korean army band greeting Marines on the dock at Pusan. (COLL/3948, Marine Corps Archives & Special Collections)

Brigadier General Edward A. Craig in Korea commanding the First Provisional Marine Brigade. (USMC)

Craig as the Commanding General, 1st Provisional Marine Brigade, Korea 1950. (Author's collection)

At the CP of 1st Marines, September 25, 1950. Left to right: Colonel Lewis B. Puller, CO 1st Marines, and Brigadier General Edward A. Craig, Assistant Division Commander, 1st Marines. (From the Oliver P. Smith Collection (COLL/213), Marine Corps Archives & Special Collections)

Cake cutting at Division Headquarters at Hungnam, November 10, 1950. Left to right: Major General Oliver P. Smith and Brigadier General Edward A. Craig. (From the Oliver P. Smith Collection (COLL/213), Marine Corps Archives & Special Collections, Official USMC Photograph)

Brigadier General E. A. Craig and Colonel "Chesty" Puller studying map in Korea "on the way to the liberation of Seoul." (USMC)

Brigadier General Craig aboard ship, Korea 1950. (USMC)

Marine amtracs crossing the Han River and onward for the liberation of Seoul, capital of South Korea. (USMC)

From left to right: Major General Oliver P. Smith, 1st Marine Division Commander; Major General Frank E. Lowe; Brigadier General Edward A. Craig, Assistant Division Commander at 1st Marine Division CP, Inchon, Korea. September 1950. (Harry S. Truman Library & Museum)

Secretary of the U.S. Navy Francis P. Matthews (right) is shown shaking hands with Brigadier General Edward Craig, Assistant Division Commander, 1st Marine Division, while visiting the Korean War front in November 1950. (Harry S. Truman Library & Museum)

The forces retreating from Chosin in late 1950 were almost lost when they reached a damaged bridge over an impassable chasm at Funchilin Pass. Working with army riggers, eight USAF C-119 crews airdropped 16 tons of portable bridge spans. This operation, never done before, enabled U.S. units to escape over the gorge. (USAF)

Photograph of Craig from his officer's file. (USMC)

Author with Lieutenant General Craig at the Marine Corps Recruit Depot, 1986. (Author's collection)

Lieutenant General and Mrs. Craig at their home in San Diego, California, 1986. (Author's collection)

PART IV

Korea

CHAPTER 16

Police Action

The predawn darkness was broken by the sharp flash and crump of exploding mortar and artillery fire. The detonations spewed jagged metal in a lethal arc of death and destruction. This deadly orchestration began in the early morning hours of Sunday, June 25, 1950 (5pm, June 24 in Washington, D.C.). The telephone rang in the room of the commanding officer of South Korea's 1st Division, Colonel Paik Sun Yup, at 7am: "Sir," his G-3 announced breathlessly, "the North Koreans have invaded. They're attacking all along the border."* Paik hurriedly

---

* Captured North Korean documents offered proof that the invaders had already set the machinery of aggression in motion while making their pleas for peace. This evidence included the written report of instructions given by one Lieutenant Han to a group of picked men on an intelligence mission. On June 1, 1950, they were to proceed by power boat to an island off of the mainland. "Our mission," explained Han, "is to gather intelligence information concerning South Korean forces and routes of advance ahead of our troops. We will perform this task by contacting our comrades who are scattered throughout the length and breadth of South Korea." The lieutenant explained that the forthcoming attack on South Korea was to be the first step toward the "liberation" of the people of Asia. And his concluding remarks leave no doubt as to the complete confidence with which the Korean communists began the venture: "Within two months from the date of attack, Pusan should have fallen, and South Korea will again be united with the North. The timetable for this operation of two month's duration was determined by the possibility of United States forces intervening in the conflict. If this were not so, it would take our forces only ten days to overrun South Korea." Source: Lejeune Leadership Institute, Marine Corps University, *A Case Study: Brigadier General Edward A. Craig, USMC and the Fire Brigade at the Pusan Perimeter, August 1950* (Marine Corps University, 2019).

dressed, flagged down a passing military jeep, and hitched a ride to ROK Army Headquarters, which he found "in a state of bedlam." The situation only got worse as Paik learned of the extent of the North Korean invasion.[1]

Seven Russian-trained infantry divisions and an armored brigade of 35-ton Russian-made T-34 medium tanks of the North Korean People's Army (NKPA) stormed across the 38th Parallel. The main attack, two divisions and most of the tank brigade, struck south, through the Uijongbu, the historic invasion route that led straight to the South Korean capital of Seoul. Soviet records[2] indicate that in January 1951Kim Il Sung visited Moscow to argue his case for invading South Korea. Immediately after the visit, the Soviet Union provided military advisers and huge amounts of weapons and supplies.

In a coast-to-coast coordinated attack, the In Min Gun (NKPA) brushed aside the ineffective resistance of the Republic of Korea (ROK) frontier force. Within three days the invaders seized Seoul, the capital, 35 miles south of the 38th Parallel, forcing the South Korean government to flee and turning its citizens into fugitives desperate to escape the fighting. The NKPAArmy was executing its operational plan, which called for advances of 9–12 miles a day with main military operations completed within 22 to 27 days.

In that summer of 1950, North Korea fielded an Army of more than 100,000 men. Almost one-third were seasoned veterans who had served in the Chinese communist Eighth Route Army in World War II and in the civil war against Chiang Kai-Shek's nationalists. Three of its front-line divisions were almost entirely composed of veterans. The technical branches were largely staffed by Koreans who had served in the Soviet armies or had received a military education in the Soviet Union. All political officers and lower-level cadres were Soviet-trained. The senior commanders were graduates of the Whampoa Military Academy, China's West Point, and many held commissions in the Soviet Army during World War II.

Facing them were four poorly trained ROK divisions, armed primarily with light infantry weapons. They did not have any tanks, medium artillery, or effective antitank weapons. Most of their equipment was cast-off American World War II material. Their senior leadership was not professionally qualified. Many were political appointees, with little military experience. Junior officer and NCO leadership left a great deal to be desired, although many were tough and courageous, as would be seen in the first weeks of the war. Unfortunately, bravery alone could not stand up against the well-trained, ruthless In Min Gun.[3]

Call for Help

U.S. Army Captain Joseph Darrigo of the Korean Military Aid Group (KMAG), and the only American near the onslaught, barely managed to escape the advancing North Koreans. Awakened by the massive shelling, he struggled into shirt and trousers and raced for his jeep. Small-arms fire chipped stone from the outside walls of his house. After a harrowing night-time drive through darkened streets filled with In Min Gun troops, Darrigo reached the ROK 1st Division headquarters at Munsan just minutes before it was overrun.[4]

The alarm spread up the chain of command. The U.S. Ambassador, John J. Muccio, received Darrigo's sketchy report and cabled the State Department with a priority night dispatch: "According to [South] Korean Army reports, which are partly confirmed by [a] KMAG field adviser report, North Korean Forces invaded ROK territory at several points this morning. It would appear from the nature of the attack and the manner in which it was launched that it constitutes an all-out offensive against the ROK."[5]

A United Press correspondent, Jack James, sniffed out the story and beat Muccio by sending it to New York as an urgent news flash. "Fragmentary reports indicate North Koreans launched Sunday morning attacks generally along entire border. Headquarters ROK's 1st Division fell 9am. Tanks supposed [to have been] brought into use at Chunchon, 50 miles northeast of Seoul." James scooped his buddies; they were still sleeping off a late-night drinking binge.[6]

Muccio's encrypted cable arrived at the State Department's communication room at 9:26pm, where it was decoded. Secretary of State Dean Acheson held up the communiqué for several hours trying to verify its contents before calling President Truman at his vacation home in Independence, Missouri. Truman had just finished dinner and settled down in the living room to read when the security phone rang. It was Acheson: "Mr. President, I have serious news, the North Koreans are attacking across the 38th Parallel."[7]

As the North Koreans approached the capital, harried embassy staffers threw boxes of classified papers and documents onto a bonfire in the parking lot. They piled suitcases, boxes of clothing, and personal effects in the building's hallways. Muccio was eating lunch with Colonel Sterling Wright, Chief of the KMAG, when two North Korean Yaks strafed the building. The two jumped into a vehicle and took off, starting a mass exodus of employees.

The ambassador, his staff, and the Marine Embassy Guard crossed the Han River Bridge, just hours before it was blown up by panic-stricken ROK engineers. Thousands of Korean troops were trapped on the outskirts of Seoul, along with all their heavy equipment and rolling stock. Hundreds more were killed when the span tumbled into the river. The engineer commander was summarily executed for cowardice.[8]

Trygve Lie, Secretary General of the United Nations, called the Security Council into emergency session and declared the North Korean aggression a breach of the peace and demanded their immediate cease-fire and withdrawal. Two days later, after hearing nothing from the North Koreans, the Security Council passed another resolution, calling upon UN members to provide economic and military assistance to embattled South Korea. The United Nations was in the fight. Fortuitously, the Soviet delegation was absent when the vote was taken, or certainly they would have vetoed the resolutions. Documents from the Soviet archives[9] suggest that Stalin supported the North Korean invasion because he didn't think the United States would get involved. U.S. Secretary of State Dean Acheson may have inadvertently given the Soviet leader that idea at a press conference in mid-January 1950, in which he described the American sphere of interest in the Pacific and did not explicitly mention Korea.

Acting quickly, President Truman ordered American naval, air, and ground forces into action. The first contingents to arrive were hastily assembled occupation troops from Japan. They were understrength, soft from occupation duty, and short on heavy weapons and equipment. Marine General Lemuel C. Shepherd considered: "In retrospect, the

Army had a couple of 'makee-learnee' divisions in Japan. It was during the Occupation period. The men were living in the lap of luxury in Japan. They weren't worrying about any war. A lot of them had come in after World War II and had no combat experience—and there were very few veterans there."[10]

The American formations were immediately thrown in to battle the North Korean advance. They were chewed up by the tougher, Soviet-trained and equipped NKPA, who totally outfought the unprepared and ill-equipped Americans. They retreated in the face of the North Korean onslaught, trading space for time in an effort to regroup and establish a sustainable defensive perimeter. Even with the arrival of additional reinforcements, American forces were pushed further and further south, toward the vital seaport of Pusan. Shepherd felt there was a definite quality difference in the opposing forces. "They [U.S. forces] were not trained soldiers. All of a sudden they were thrown into battle against a strong enemy. These North Koreans were fighters and had successfully overrun South Korea. I can't blame or criticize the Army too much—they just were not prepared for combat against a determined enemy."[11]

Send in the Marines

The plight of the American forces reached Hawaii where Admiral Radford, Commander of the U.S. Pacific Fleet, suggested to Shepherd that he "better go out to see General MacArthur and find out what the situation is out there [Korea]. We're getting a lot of dispatches here which are rather confused. I want somebody to tell me what the situation is out there." Shepherd knew MacArthur from World War II. He had been the assistant division commander in the 1st Marine Division under MacArthur in the Cape Gloucester campaign. In addition, MacArthur's chief of staff, Major General Edward M. "Ned" Almond, and several others in the Far East Headquarters were fellow "ring-knockers" from Virginia Military Institute. "I did have a number of Army friends in the Far East Headquarters. During my two years' experience overseas with the Army in World War II, I met a lot of Army people, and I didn't have the antagonism towards them that a lot of Marines did." Shepherd respected the Army general. "[MacArthur] had a keen mind ... [he was] a great leader ... a fearless, courageous man. I believed, as all of us did during World War II, that MacArthur was a political general—everybody was calling him 'Dugout Doug.' I don't want to hear that about General MacArthur again—I'm telling you, he had the guts!"[12]

MacArthur, always the gracious host, welcomed Shepherd as an old comrade-in-arms. "We had a lengthy conversation in his office. You know he always wanted to talk. My God, talk, talk, talk, 40 minutes, telling me all his experiences. We talked about Korea, we talked about this and that, and as we got up and went to the door of his office." A large map of Korea hung next to the door. MacArthur put his hand on Shepherd's shoulder and pointed, with his ever-present pipe stem, to a spot on the map adjacent to Seoul on the west coast of the peninsula. "Lem, if I had that 1st Marine Division as I had at Cape Gloucester, I'd land here at Inchon and cut the North Korean lines of communication." Shepherd was not taken aback; he had been thinking about the commitment of Marines a great deal. "[If] We have only a Marine brigade in Korea, its identity will be lost among all those Army divisions. On the other hand, if we could get a Marine division ordered to Korea, it would be a unit of sufficient size to take care of itself independently. With a major general in command, he would not permit his division to be pushed around."[13]

Shepherd had made up his mind to push for the commitment of the 1st Marine Division if the opportunity presented itself—and here was the opening he needed. "General, why don't you ask for them? They're under my command, as part of FMFPAC [Fleet Marine Force, Pacific], but I can't order them from the west coast to the Far East without the Joint Chiefs of Staff approval." Shepherd had received a report from an aide that President Truman was going to call up the reserves. "It was on this promise that I based my decision, because I knew that we had expended everybody on the west coast to get the brigade going, but with the reserves being called up, we would be able to mount out a full division."[14]

MacArthur, not batting an eye, said: "That's the kind of talk I like to hear," and immediately asked Shepherd to write a message for him. "Sit down at my desk and write a dispatch to the Joint Chiefs of Staff [JCS], requesting that the 1st Marine Division be sent out to my theatre of command." Shepherd took one look at MacArthur's huge desk, four times the size of his own, and knowing that MacArthur would scrutinize every word, he was terribly disconcerted. After all, the far east commander had five stars and Shepherd was a junior three star. MacArthur had an aura, a presence that was almost larger than life. "It really shook me, so I said, 'Well, General, I will go out to the office of your chief of staff [Almond] to draft this message and bring it in to you for approval.'" Shepherd scrounged a message pad and jotted down his thoughts. It took him three drafts before he got the delicately worded message in a form that he thought was acceptable. "I finally came up with a draft that I believed suitable. It was a delicate dispatch to compose. Here I was, recommending that a Marine division be sent to Korea, and the Commandant [of the Marine Corps, General Clifton B. Cates] didn't know anything about what I was doing. It was a hell of a spot to be in, but the ball had been dropped in my hands and I felt I must run with it." MacArthur approved the request without change, but the joint chiefs turned it down—and three more times—before finally approving the fifth message.[15]

Shepherd's next task was to convince the commandant that it was the right thing to do. Cates had recently committed the 2nd Marine Division to a NATO mission, which did not leave enough men to form the 1st Marine Division. The two senior officers met in San Diego to wish the brigade good bye as it shipped out. Cates was somewhat put out with Shepherd for committing his Marines without consulting him. Fortunately, the two men were friends of long standing, or it could have turned out badly. Shepherd pleaded his case: "Clifton, you can't let me down. I have recommended the commitment of a Marine division to MacArthur for Korea. Please back me up." Cates responded, "We haven't got the men, we haven't got the men." But Shepherd won the day with: "Clifton, we're fighting a hot war over there in Korea. NATO is something they're forming on paper. We belong in the Pacific. The Western Pacific is our theatre." Cates finally gave the commitment his full backing. Victor Krulak, Shepherd's G-3, described the meeting: "I remember there was a pretty spirited dialogue at Camp Pendleton between General Cates and General Shepherd ... about what we could or couldn't do. Neither General Shepherd nor I was very popular at that time because we had obviously overextended. We did exactly the right thing. We marched to the sound of the guns...."[16]

General MacArthur, with his back to the wall in Korea, fired off a message to the JCS: "Request immediate dispatch of a Marine Regimental Combat Team and supporting Air Group for duty this command—MacArthur." In the meantime, General Cates sent the 1st Marine Division at Camp Pendleton, California, a "be prepared to deploy" warning order. He continued the pressure on the joint chiefs by showing up uninvited when they met to discuss and finally approve MacArthur's request. Cates diary entry for July 3, 1950 noted: "Orders for employment of FMF [Fleet Marine Force] approved."[17]

In a June 27, 1950 letter to his parents, Craig told them,

> I am really busy here right now as General Erskine [division commander] leaves tomorrow and I have already taken over [1st Marine Division] ... Things look bad in the world today and we are wondering what next ... it looks like they might decide to use the 1st [Marine] Division here for something....

General Cates' warning order reached Camp Pendleton, California, and was delivered to Craig in the early morning hours of July 3. "My wife and I [Craig had remarried, to Marion Honor Mackle after returning from Guam] had spent a very pleasant weekend at Pine Valley [in the eastern San Diego County mountains] and were returning to Camp Pendleton when we heard on our car radio the news that the North Koreans had invaded South Korea. I remarked to my wife, 'Well, this is it again, and it looks like another war for the Marines." Shortly afterward, he received a phone call from the assistant commandant, Major General Oliver P. Smith, ordering him to take command of the 1st Provisional Marine Brigade and "have it ready to move out at the earliest possible date."[18]

Craig wrote in his Field Notebook on July 2, 1950:

> Received telephonic orders from Headquarters Marine Corps, Maj. Gen. O. P. Smith, to prepare plans for organizing and mounting out a brigade consisting of one reinforced infantry regiment and one air group. The orders for execution would come from Fleet Marine Force, Pacific.

Shepherd's ciphered "activation order dated July 7, 1950, as a combined air-ground team for combat duty in the Far East, with Brigadier General

E.A. Craig in command," reached the division communication section four days later. "Take whatever is required and available in troops and equipment from the 1st Marine Division and 1st Marine Aircraft Wing, plus what Marine Corps Headquarters provides from other sources, make a provisional brigade consisting of the 5th Marine Regiment Reinforced and Marine Aircraft Group 33, both at reduced strength, embark them in ships the Navy will provide, and set sail for the Far East."[19]

"We had an annual carnival and rodeo at Camp Pendleton which was quite a big affair. We built a big rodeo area, and the carnival was brought in from various companies that furnished that type of equipment and by rodeo companies that furnished the mounts and the cattle." Craig was the senior member of the committee that had made all the arrangements and everything was set up ready to go when he received the call from General Smith to organize the brigade and be ready to mount out. Needless to say, the carnival had to be cancelled. "We ran one night of the carnival and cancelled the rodeo."[20]

The next day, the division was scheduled to have a full-scale combat review. "I decided to go ahead with this review because we had all the equipment on the field already—rolling stock, artillery, etc.—and the troops were all set to go, with everything the men would actually carry."[21]

The review was held and then the 1st Marine Brigade was organized. Craig had his work cut out for him. The division was seriously undermanned because of cuts imposed upon the Corps by Secretary of Defense Louis Johnson after World War II. Lem Shepherd noted that "Louis Johnson hadn't helped us along, and the Marine Corps was just about to go out of existence. We had only about sixty thousand to seventy thousand Marines at the time. To form the brigade took a great deal of effort just to get out the initial orders."[22]

O. P. Smith in his oral history said: "Johnson was not a friend of the Marine Corps ... he kept cutting us down on strength until we were down to nine battalions and very few [air] groups ... he was trying to destroy the Marine Corps."[23]

Craig was able to field one understrength infantry regiment, the 5th Marines, commanded by Lieutenant Colonel Raymond L. Murray. "I received quite a bit of pressure to take a full colonel, but considered that he [Murray] was the best man available to command the regiment, and he was one of the outstanding regimental commanders of any regiment in Korea."[24] "The 5th Marine Regiment was a well-trained, peace-strength organization and participated in many field problems in the Pendleton area; moreover, many of the men had received additional training in other places. The regiment was entirely inadequate for combat."[25]

"To bring the brigade up to strength I had to strip the division, and being in command of the base and the division at the same time, [Major General Erskine, the division/base commander was absent, leaving Craig in command] I had the choice of taking anybody I wanted," Craig said. "Naturally, I took the best I could find."[26] "I think when we left Pendleton there were some 2,000 men remaining that we had to use as a nucleus to form the 1st Division on."[27] Lieutenant Colonel Murray admitted that "We pretty well cleaned out Camp Pendleton."[28]

Even with these efforts, the brigade had serious shortages of personnel. "We were on a peacetime strength basis, and the 5th Marines consisted of three infantry battalions with only two rifle companies; and those two companies had only two platoons each. I immediately sent dispatches requesting that the third platoon be added to each infantry company and that the third company be added to each battalion and that various other units be augmented, such as the artillery with six guns instead of four." A third platoon was added to each company just prior to shipping out. However, the brigade did not get a third company for each battalion until the Inchon landing. Craig felt that with two-company infantry battalions, commanders were at a tactical disadvantage in every engagement. Without a third maneuver element they lacked flexibility in the attack. When defending, they had to scrape up whatever they could to have a reserve. "I was convinced it would cost us lives in the end if we did not. This turned out to be correct during the first battle of the Naktong."[29]

An extract from Craig's field notebook, July 3, 1950:

> Absence of third rifle company in each battalion will be critical but people who made decision to deny me this will be in safe place, and the cost will be in lives—not theirs.

A few miles up the road at Marine Corps Air Station, El Toro, the 1st Marine Aircraft Wing was doing the same thing. Brigadier General

Thomas J. Cushman formed Marine Aircraft Group (MAG) 33, consisting of four squadrons: Marine Fighter Squadrons (VMF) 214 and VMF-323, VMF (Night-fighter)-513, and VMO-6, an observation squadron, which included four HO3S1 helicopters and four OH light observation aircraft. A naval aviator for more than thirty years, Cushman, like Craig, served in the "Banana Wars" and saw action as a Commanding General during World War II. Designated as deputy brigade commander, Cushman brought a wealth of aviation experience, which complimented Craig's ground expertise. Together, they formed an extremely effective air-ground command team.[30]

The Marine Corps Supply Center at Barstow, in the California desert, was ordered to equip the brigade with rolling stock—tanks, trucks, jeeps, and amphibious vehicles. At the end of World War II, the Marine Corps established a stockpile of war reserves. Code-named "Operation *Roll-up*," everything that could be shipped back from the Pacific was repaired and squirreled away in the desert center, including "abandoned" Army equipment that could be rehabilitated. Nobody looked closely at unit designations, and after a new "Marine Green" paint job, a stenciled "USMC", and new serial numbers, the equipment certainly looked Marine! The center went into high gear. Reconditioned tolling stock jammed the highways between the two bases. According to Andrew Geer in *The New Breed: The Story of the U.S. Marines in Korea*, "There were more veterans of Iwo [Jima] and Okinawa among the vehicles than there was among the men who would drive them."[31]

To make up some of this personnel shortfall, Marines from all over the United States were ordered to "get to Camp Pendleton NOW!" By train, plane, and bus, dozens of former recruiters and guard company troops poured into the base. Lieutenant Colonel Raymond G. "Ray" Davis, the Inspector-Instructor of Chicago's 9th Marine Corps Reserve Infantry Battalion, received the mobilization orders for his unit to hop on a train for Camp Pendleton. Within days the battalion was on the way west, including youngsters just out of high school.

Captain "Ike" Fenton remembered:

> These men were shipped from the posts and stations by air, most of them arriving with just a handbag. Their seabags were to be forwarded at a later date. They

didn't have dog tags and had no health records to tell us how many shots they needed. Their clothing consisted of khaki only, although a few had greens. They had no weapons and their 782 gear [web equipment] was incomplete. We had a problem of trying to organize these men into a platoon and getting them squared away before our departure date.

Fortunately, most were veterans and needed only a short "snapping in" period to bring them up to speed, much of which was done on the transports at sea.[32]

Among the newcomers was the brigade chief of staff, Colonel Edward W. Snedeker, who was returning to the States from overseas when the war broke out: "Upon arrival in San Francisco with my family, on July 5, I had orders waiting to report immediately to Camp Pendleton. I called General Craig, who gave me enough time to get the car off the ship and to drive down to the base." Snedeker hurriedly loaded a surprised wife and kids into the car and sped off, arriving early on the 7th. He immediately immersed himself in work, leaving his wife to settle the family. Seven hectic days later, he sailed with the brigade, 6,534 Marines, of whom 90 percent of the officers and 65 percent of the SNCOs were combat veterans. However, only 10 percent of the junior enlisted men had seen action. Craig recalled that "All the units of the division were so far understrength, so inadequate for the mission as a division unit that they hardly could fill the duties of a brigade unit; however, such personnel, as we had, were well trained and were in high spirits."[33]

The brigade's final destination remained something of a mystery, although "indications were that the brigade would be used in an amphibious assault against the enemy." Craig was told that it would probably not go directly into combat, but rather stage in Japan and wait for the rest of the division before being committed to Korea. However, Craig believed otherwise: "It was my opinion that being a Marine unit we should be prepared for any eventually. The chips were down; the Marine Corps was on the spot; it was up to us to put up or shut up. It was a real test of the Marine Corps."[34]

Craig made sure that most of the ships were combat loaded, just in case they had to make an assault landing in Korea, however; therefore, many ships had cargo piled on deck. He was well aware of the 1st Marine Division's fiasco on the New Zealand docks before Guadalcanal. The ships had not been combat-loaded in the United States and had to be reconfigured prior to sailing. Contemporary World War II accounts tell of docks awash in soggy pasteboard, mounds of unmarked boxes, and containers and harassed working parties. "I was not allowed to take my full allowance of combat transportation. Some 150 to 200 vehicles were left behind."[35]

As Craig's staff struggled to complete the brigade's movement orders, the Navy was trying to find enough amphibious shipping. O. P. Smith recalled: "The Navy did the best they could. They grabbed ships from all up and down the coast; merchant ships, anything they could find. All the amphibious shipping was in the far east."[36]

At the end of World War II, most of the amphibious ships had been sold off, mothballed, or broken up for scrap. A nation that leapfrogged across the Pacific—island by island—from thousands of ships was forced to lease those same vessels from its former enemy. For the Inchon landing, American-built Landing Ship Tanks (LSTs) were chartered from and manned by Japanese merchantmen. Because of this shortage, Craig was forced to depend on the Army's largesse for transport.

Hot Water

On the morning of the 12th, General Shepherd, Craig's boss, arrived by plane from Hawaii. "It was a complete surprise to me when he greeted me rather coldly and wanted an immediate conference with me at headquarters. On arrival, he took off in a temper telling me that I had put him in a difficult position by requesting additional shipping after he had already given the Navy our requirements."* Shepherd also

---

* Designated Task Force 53.7, the convoy included 10 ships: five Attack Transports (*Anderson* APA-8, *Achernar* AKA-53, *Pickaway* APA-222, *George Clymer* APA-27, and *Henrico* APA-45), two Dock Landing Ships (*Fort Marion* LSD-22 and *Gunston Hall* LSD-44), two Attack Cargo Ships (*Alshain* AKA-55 and *Whitside* AKA-90) and the escort carrier *Badoeng Strait* (CVE-116).

"chewed" him out for taking too many vehicles.* "He said I would not need them ... the brigade was only going to Japan to wait for the rest of the [1st Marine] division ... and then be absorbed by it. He complained that I was taking too many key members of the division to staff the brigade and finally, he was critical of my request for an additional rifle company to fill up the 5th Marines."[37]

Craig tried to justify his requirements. "I reminded him that the brigade was going to a war zone and might be called on for combat immediately on arrival and that the reputation of the Marine Corps was at stake. Before the conference was over, we were both talking a little loud and I took the occasion to have the doors of my office closed." However, "the outcome was that I did not get the additional ship, nor the missing rifle companies." Craig was soon justified in all his requests: "One month later, when we had to borrow and steal trucks and jeeps from the Army to give us mobility ... and at the first battle of the Naktong when the additional infantry companies would have meant the saving of Marine lives and a quicker decision over the enemy."[38]

Shepherd pulled Lieutenant Colonel Joe Stewart off Craig's list. He was slated to be the brigade's operations officer (G–3), a key position, and one that Craig was willing to go to "war" over. Craig interceded with the commandant, who agreed and directed Shepherd not to "touch" Stewart. "I disliked doing things in this rather underhanded way, but felt the Marine Corps needed Stewart in the brigade as much as I did ... he certainly proved his worth. Despite the rather heated conference, Lem Shepherd remained a good friend."[39]

Shipping Out

The brigade had just seven days to get organized. No one slept during that final hectic week, working around the clock under the watchful eye of the brigade commander. Craig recounted: "During this time I was

---

* It was necessary for Craig to go to the Army for transportation. "The Army was very good about this, and they not only furnished the trucks, but many jeeps for our reconnaissance company. They were completely equipped, even with .50-caliber machine guns." Craig, Incidents.

busy with a thousand details of the organization and move." Craig was everywhere, encouraging, cajoling, and sometimes just plain "kicking ass," when and where it was needed, in his own quiet but forceful manner. "Before the brigade left for Korea, we worked from 7am until 2 or 3am in the morning every day." One day, First Sergeant John Farritor was working in the [artillery] storeroom at 2am and General Craig walked in. Farritor recounted: "I was a little surprised. He said he just wanted to know how things were going. He was a hands-on general." Having shipped out more times than he could count—Haiti, Nicaragua, China, Guadalcanal, Bougainville, Guam, Iwo Jima—Craig knew what had to be done, and how to do it. Craig, however, was not a micro-manager. He provided guidance to his staff and commanders and then stood back to let them carry it out. "I learned early in my career to rely on my non-commissioned officers, and they never let me down. When I became commander of a unit and had staff officers, I gave them full rein and trusted them, and they, too, never fell down on me. I believe that what success I had in the Marine Corps was the result of the work of those officers and men."[40]

As the deadline for embarkation approached, the pressure became even more intense, but Craig's steady hand brought a sense of organized urgency out of mad confusion. As usual, most of the grunt work fell on the shoulders of the small unit leaders—the junior officers, staff and non-commissioned officers—who had to organize hundreds of newcomers into fire teams, squads, platoons, companies, and battalions. Conflicting priorities—working parties, administrative processing, weapons and equipment issue, inspections, and a hundred and one other details—were enough to make a grown man cry. In fact, one detail brought even the strongest to their knees; according to Lieutenant Jack Buck, "inoculations had to be given. I recall receiving seven shots at the same time. It was still the era of 'heavy needles.' After a number of penetrations of muscular biceps, it came close to feeling like a heavy punch." Yet somehow, the brigade shaped up, as the old salts knew it would. However, it was still a great sense of relief that embarkation day finally arrived. The brigade surgeon, Captain "Doc" Herring, USN, recalled "Went on board USS *Clymer* to count noses. Drunk or sober, they're all here and that's phenomenal."[41]

Craig told them where they were going just before embarking. David Douglas Duncan, the famed war photographer, was there to record their reaction. "The men were dead-panned, for they had seen pictures and read reports of soldiers who had been caught wounded by the communists on the field of battle. Craig reminded them of the Marines' historic role in meeting their country's emergencies. They were still expressionless. Craig, with the brigade surgeon standing by his side, told his men that "As long as there were any Marines alive in Korea who could still fire a rifle, or toss a grenade, no other Marine would be left behind on the battlefield, either wounded or dead." Over 4,000 men cheered in unison as his Leathernecks gleefully slugged each other in the ribs, grinned happily, and wanted to know when the hell they were going aboard ship.[42]

The decks were crowded with family and friends, as well as the curious and a host of well wishers. A large contingent of press was also on hand to record the occasion for posterity. "There is nothing like the atmosphere of a Marine unit sailing to war. It is ribald, loud, and raucous. Even the families on the dock, for the most part, hide their faces and grief and respond to the carnival spirit." The division band livened things up with John Philip Sousa marches. The bandsmen, caught up in the spirit of the occasion, played their collective hearts out, knowing that their turn would come soon enough. Suddenly they sounded "ruffles and flourishes," the general officer's call, and General Cates came forward to address the formation. "I didn't come here to wave the flag. I came to say good-bye. You boys clean this up in a couple of months, or I'll be over to see you." With the formalities over, the formation broke up and the men filed aboard ship. "The band struck up the 'Marines' Hymn': lines were slipped, and as the ships slid away, there was a great, gusty roar that drowned out the band."[43]

As the ships of Task Group 53.7 sailed past the breakwater of San Diego harbor on July 15, Generals Craig and Cushman, together with a small staff, flew to Pearl Harbor on the 16th to confer with Lem

Shepherd. The two old friends took a few minutes to reminisce and then got down to the serious business of war planning. The brigade needed more men, motor transport, and artillery. Craig stated his case forcefully, and Shepherd promised to work on it. The meeting took on a more somber tone when Craig asked for an 800-man draft to replace losses. Both officers were well aware of the cost of war, but Craig was particularly affected by casualties. Shepherd knew of his friend's kindly, avuncular attitude toward his men. "I've known Eddie Craig for over 30 years. If he has a weakness, it's the inner torment he suffers when his unit takes casualties." The meeting broke up with Shepherd promising to do all that he could.[44]

Conference with the Great Man

The entourage continued to Japan on the 19th, to confer with senior Army and Navy commanders—Vice Admiral Turner Joy, Commander Naval Forces, Far East; Lieutenant General George Stratemeyer, Far East Air Forces; and a 45-minute audience with General Douglas MacArthur. Craig was welcomed graciously by the legendary commander. "He lit his pipe and talked at length on the situation in Korea. He expressed his pleasure at having Marines under his command again and said that he had the greatest admiration for the Corps after having had the 1st Marine Division and an air wing under him in World War II."[45]

"MacArthur told me that at present there was no indication of committing the Marine brigade, that we would stay in Japan but if it were necessary, i.e., if the military situation dictated it, that he would send the brigade to Korea. MacArthur then went into a long discussion as to how he was going to employ the Marines after the remainder of the 1st Marine Division arrived in Japan. He said that he specifically requested Marines because he needed them for the amphibious landing at Inchon and he was going to land there and cut the North Korean forces off by advancing on Seoul and [go] north. That he would cut their lines of communication and cause the Pusan Perimeter to collapse thus allowing the Eighth Army to advance and complete the defeat of the enemy ... [The Marines are] going to turn the tide of the war."* The landing, when it did take place, was more or less similar in all respects to the way he visualized it at the time.[46]

Craig briefed MacArthur on the peculiarities of the brigade, specifically the close bond between Marine air and infantry. "I told General MacArthur that this brigade, if used as a unit with its air force and with its ground unit intact, was a potent unit with great capabilities. He [MacArthur] agreed that any time the Marine brigade was committed, that our Marine air force would support us. These instructions were always carried out, and we were never without our Marine air support, which paid dividends in the end by keeping the brigade intact."[47]

Craig wrote in his field notebook on July 19, 1950:

> After the conference with General MacArthur on July 18, which lasted some 45 minutes, he directed his G-3, Brigadier General Wright, to draft a dispatch to JCS and War Department asking that the Marine 1st Brigade and the remainder of the 1st Marine Division as well as the air wing, be brought up to full war strength. Dispatch was sent on July 20.

Craig was told to go to Kyoto, where he would find abandoned Army billets that had been vacated by troops then in Korea. The brigade would not be committed to Korea unless the military situation deteriorated further. "I left the office feeling that General MacArthur was behind us in every way. I also had the feeling that I had talked to a great man and a real general. I have always had the highest respect and liking for General MacArthur."[48]

Craig had been in the air about thirty minutes when he was ordered to return to Tokyo. On arrival, he was informed by MacArthur's chief of staff that the brigade was to be immediately committed to the defense of the Pusan Perimeter. The situation had dramatically worsened. The NKPA had broken through the U.S. and South Korean lines, forcing them to

---

* In a personal interview with the author 30 years later, Craig enthusiastically recalled the meeting, becoming quite animated in describing MacArthur's "I like Marines" proclamation. On a trip through Tokyo, Commandant Cates asked MacArthur "why he was so down on Marines," and MacArthur replied: "I'm not down on the Marines. The Marines are (were?) the best outfit I had in World War II. When I want anything done, I know I can get it done by the Marines."

retreat toward the vital seaport of Pusan, the last foothold in Korea. Three badly shot-up U.S. and four ROK divisions dug in, forming a ragged, horseshoe-shaped defense line 120 miles long and 60 miles wide, for a last stand. Arrayed against them were 11 well-trained and well-armed NKPA divisions, including an armored division of 40 tanks. If the allied force failed to hold, Pusan would fall and, with it, all of Korea.

On July 28, Craig wrote in his field notebook:

> Situation in north and southwest is critical. Lines will probably be drawn back in order to shorten them and provide more depth in defense. Chief of Staff Eighth Army in conversation with me today indicated that the brigade would probably be committed on left flank of the Allied lines and would be landed at Pusan.

The Pusan Perimeter was a defensive line in name only. Its American and South Korean defenders were stretched to the breaking point, unable to man the entire line. There were large gaps between units that were exploited by the NKPA to infiltrate small units into the rear areas, sowing confusion and fear. Larger NKPA formations massed to attack, threatening a breakthrough, and there were precious few reserves to stop them. The Marine brigade was desperately needed to help plug holes and shore up the perimeter.

Fire Brigade

On the 26th, Craig flew to Taegu, South Korea, to report to Lieutenant General Walton Walker, Commanding General Eighth Army. "He was very cordial but told me that he did not know exactly where the Marines would be used at that time; that the situation was changing so rapidly that they might be used anywhere on the perimeter; but that probably I would be used on the left flank." Walker's Eighth Army was having a rough time of it. The men were exhausted and demoralized, units were scattered and riddled with casualties, and panic was not too far below the surface.[49]

While in Taegu, Craig was given General Walker's plane to use. "I flew all over the battle area; all over the Pusan Perimeter and observed the various locations and positions of the troops. This was very helpful to me and gave me a very good idea of the extent of the perimeter and the scarcity of men. I was impressed with the way the troops were thinly spread out, sometimes without contact on their flanks."[50] Extracts from Craig's field notebook, July 29–August 1, 1950:

> At Eighth Army Headquarters at Taegu. Attended briefing on situation which continues serious. Left flank [Pusan Perimeter] is being enveloped and there is a general air of uneasiness around the headquarters. Brigade will be committed on left flank unless situation changes. Brigade is due to arrive on August 1st, and will be committed on August 2nd or 3rd. Requested that Marine air group be made available to support the brigade on August 2nd. As of July 31, the situation on the left flank was extremely critical with our forces driven out of Chinju and air field there in enemy hands. 1st Brigade still at sea but expected tomorrow [August 2nd]. The situation in area very critical. Build up of enemy forces continues.

Craig's potent fighting force was desperately needed to stop the North Korean advance. Craig, realizing that his men would be immediately thrown into the fight, recalled: "I wrote out a preliminary order telling the various units of the brigade what they should do upon landing. I sent this dispatch through the 8th Army communication system."[51]

Crisis at Sea

There was great concern among the embarked Marine leadership that the brigade might not even reach Korea. Snedeker, the senior officer afloat, saw one disaster after another strike the small fleet. "One of the transports (USS *Henrico*, APA-45) developed a vibration in its drive shaft and propeller and was declared temporarily unseaworthy. It had to leave the formation and go to San Francisco to get repair work done." A third of the brigade's infantry was aboard, and no one knew how long the repairs would take. The *Henrico* would not rejoin the convoy until the day before the landing at Pusan. The USS *Fort Marion* (LSD-22) accidentally flooded its well deck, immersing all the brigade's M26 tanks, 300 90mm projectiles (then in critical supply), and 5,000 rounds of .30-caliber ammunition in six feet of water. Snedeker recounted that "These were our new type tanks, which had just been received only through a great deal of effort. Their loss was critical." The M26 with a 90mm gun was essential to defeat the NKPA's Russian T-34 tanks, whose 75mm guns were terrorizing ROK and U.S. forces. Crewmembers turned to and were able to fix the tanks, much to Snedeker's relief.[52]

The *Henrico* limped into Oakland Naval Supply Depot on the 16th, where workmen immediately began repairs. The ship attempted to sail twice but had to turn back each time. Meanwhile, hundreds of embarked Marines could only stare longingly at the beckoning lights of the Bay City, much to the chagrin of the cloistered liberty hounds. They were forbidden to leave the ship because of security concerns. Finally, the third time was the charm, and *Henrico*, now sarcastically nicknamed "Happy Hank," steamed under the Golden Gate Bridge in time to rejoin the convoy on the morning of its arrival at Pusan.[53]

Lieutenant Colonel Murray explained that "The ships were crowded and uncomfortable, with every nook and cranny jammed with Marines or their supplies and equipment." Despite the conditions, unit leaders found space to conduct classes on the squad and platoon level and used the two-week voyage as a time for training and indoctrination. First Lieutenant Francis I. "Ike" Fenton, executive officer Company B, 1st Battalion explained: "It was impossible to get the whole company together. Consequently, we used passageways, boat decks, holds—any space we could find to lecture to the men and give them what little information we had on what was happening in Korea. A lot of time was spent on blackboard tactics for the fire teams, platoons, and company. We also emphasized first aid, hygiene, water discipline...." Weapons training and familiarization firing was done off the deck against floating targets. The only thing the leaders couldn't do was give them an indoctrination on the North Koreans ... intelligence was just not available.[54]

Late in the afternoon of August 2, USS *George Clymer* (APA-27), nicknamed "Greasy George" by the embarked Marines, edged alongside the pier. Craig stood impatiently on the dock, looking in vain for signs that his men were ready to fight. Hundreds of rubbernecking Marines lined the rails, as if they didn't have a care in the world. A South Korean band serenaded them with a tinny and slightly off-key rendition of the "Marines' Hymn." Craig spotted his chief of staff, and shouted "What battalion is the advance guard?" Sensing the look of surprise on Snedeker's face, he asked again, "Did you receive my orders?" They had not;

something had gone amiss. "Through some snafu in the Eighth Army channels, my dispatch was never received by the convoy. Consequently, when the brigade arrived, it had no intimation that it would be landed immediately."[55]

While the ships unloaded, Craig convened a hasty conference on the ship at 2100 to bring his key officers up to speed on the tactical situation and issue Brigade Operation Plan 3-50. The intelligence officer (G-2), Lieutenant Colonel Ellsworth B. Van Orman, led off the briefing with a grim narrative of the situation, followed by Lieutenant Colonel Joseph L. Steward, the operations officer (G-3), who sketched in the operations plan. Finally, Craig summed up the meeting: "The situation is serious. We're going into battle against a vicious, well-trained enemy. The Pusan Perimeter is like a weakened dike, and we will be used to plug holes in it as they open. We're a brigade, a fire brigade."[56]

CHAPTER 17

Pusan Perimeter

The Pusan Perimeter positions taken up by the American and ROK forces on August 4 enclosed a rectangular area about 100 miles from north to south and about 50 miles from east to west. The Naktong River formed the western boundary of the Perimeter except for the southernmost 15 miles below the point where it turned eastward after its confluence with the Nam River. The Sea of Japan formed the eastern boundary, and the Korea Strait the southern boundary. An irregular curved line through the mountains from above Waegwan to Yongdok formed the northern boundary. Yongdok on the east coast stood at the northeast corner of the Perimeter, Pusan was at the southeast corner, Masan at the southwest corner, and Taegu near the middle from north to south but only about 10 miles from the western and threatened side of the Perimeter. From Pusan, Masan is 30 air miles west, Taegu 55 miles northwest, P'ohang-dong 60 miles northeast, and Yongdok 90 miles northeast. With the exception of the delta of the Naktong and the east-west valley between Taegu and P'ohang-dong, the ground is rough and mountainous. The mountains are particularly forbidding in the northeast.[1]

That night the Pusan docks were a bedlam of noise and organized confusion, as the supplies and equipment for thousands of men were taken from the holds of ships and organized into supply points and vehicle parks. Working parties struggled to unload pallets and break open crates for long lines of Marines forming up to draw ammunition, hand grenades, C-rations, and medical supplies. The men worked through the night, and by 6:30am the first elements were ready. "I had to direct that practically all our stores be left behind on the docks," Craig explained.

"The men carried only their combat loads. The Army would establish dumps for us to draw on. We moved out from Pusan by truck and train. The tanks were put on flatcars, and the troops—most of them—moved by truck."[2]

As the troops clambered aboard the trucks, rumors were rife, Lieutenant Robert D. Bohn, recalled: "The thing I remember most about arriving in Korea is being briefed by some Army people who, in retrospect, had obviously never been out of Pusan. These fat lieutenants told us all those horror stories. Although they didn't know what the hell they were talking about, they were very successful in scaring us. We all began to think the North Koreans were about 10 feet tall."[3]

"The brigade moved out with the leading battalion carrying out all security measures," Craig said. "I had previously picked by helicopter the area where the battalions would bivouac. Scouting parties from the various units preceded the movement as security to locate the designated bivouac areas. The brigade arrived in Chindong-ni late in the afternoon of August 3. My idea was to cover the road where the fighting was then going on, and where the communists were trying to break through. This was the first time the brigade was able to operate as a unit in the field in a combat formation. I established my command post there close to the front line."[4]

"Our advance post set-up was very simple. It consisted of what the various staff officers with their jeeps and trailers could carry, sometimes just myself and two or three key members of the staff with what we could transport by helicopter. It normally was set up with two or three CP tents—sometimes just a tarp.

"My method of controlling the brigade was more or less unorthodox. Initially, I went forward to the leading elements by jeep and helicopter with my S-3 and directed movements by contact with both battalion commanders and the regimental commander as necessary. In many cases, the brigade was spread out over miles of road and it was necessary to make five or six landings in helicopters each trip to make contact with various elements to give information or instructions on the spot. This worked out very well. I was able to get around much faster than if I had tried to use a jeep.

"I found out throughout my operation in Korea that the closer I could get to the front, the better control I had. I also found that the matter

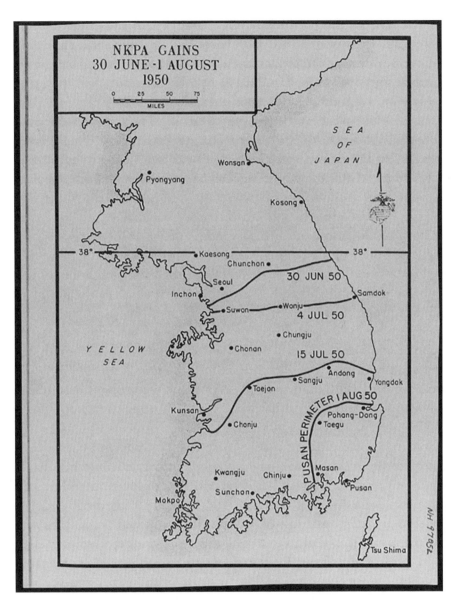

The Pusan Perimeter: the North Koreans had pushed UN forces and were on the verge of sweeping them out of Korea

of security was generally solved by being close to the front lines where the combat units were. Consequently, in most of our moves in Korea, we kept well closed up with both our support elements well up toward the front and our artillery the same way."[5]

"The artillery had been trained in [Camp] Pendleton in the methods of security. They were armed with bazookas, .50 caliber machine guns, and everything that the infantrymen would need to defend a position; and they were well trained in defense of their positions. And they, from that day on, took up defensive positions whenever they moved."[6]

"As a result, we never had a gun overrun. There were attempts at sniping and so forth, but we never had a gun taken or overrun; whereas I noted that the Army, on a number of occasions, lost whole batteries. It was simply, I think, because the artillerymen were not trained along the same lines as the Marines."[7]

Craig decided that "going into bivouac would leave us wide open for surprise. To ensure our security and be prepared for any eventuality, I deployed the brigade tactically and immediately started digging in on the high ground along the road, preparing for its first night in combat. With the gathering darkness, a phantom Army invaded the perimeter and was taken under fire by the inexperienced troops. A single shot was followed by a deadly barrage of automatic weapons fire, as the apprehensive Marines blasted bushes and shrubs that, in their minds, had mysteriously turned into North Korean infiltrators. Veteran CBS radio correspondent Bill Dunn recalled: "Anything that moved they took a shot at. I was disgusted ... [but] Do you know, they went into combat in a few days ... they became terrific...."[8]

Sometime before dawn, order was restored by veteran NCOs. Craig reinforced the message, making it known, in no uncertain terms, that he would not tolerate a repeat performance. In a personal interview with the author John A. "Jack" Buck, Craig's aide and longtime friend, Jack related that Craig came out of his tent that night and ordered Buck to stop the firing. Jack walked to a small hill and had a jeep turn on its light on him. He shouted out for the troops to "knock it off!" Fortunately, they did, without ventilating him in the process. "That was the only time it ever took place in the brigade," he said.[9]

Despite being a "little trigger happy," Craig said tongue in cheek: "There was some wild firing but not to any great extent. That was the only time it ever took place in the brigade. We were ready for combat, even though situated behind the so-called front lines. During the few days we were there, we knew we were observed by the enemy observation posts and patrols off on the flank. They did not bother us. A major penetration of the U.S. Army at Chindong-ni could have been caught in bivouac."[10]

Despite the evening disruptions, Craig took off early on August 3 in one of the Marine helicopters and put in a remarkable day that demonstrated the amazing versatility and usefulness of the new aircraft. He stopped to give instructions to the lead battalion on the march; he then selected a site for his forward CP; and he then flew to Masan to confer with Walker and Major General William B. Kean, commander of the U.S. Army's 25th Infantry Division, to which the brigade would be attached. Finally, on his return trip, Craig landed three more times to meet with his unit commanders.[11]

Craig thought that the helicopter was "one of the greatest things that is being developed for liaison and transportation of key and staff personnel today and for the evacuation of wounded and furnishing the men with supplies. Time was always pressing. Fortunately ... helicopters ... were always available for observation, communications, and control ... Without them I do not believe we would have had the success we had. Our only complaint was that we didn't have enough, and they couldn't carry enough." Craig made two requests for troop-carrying helicopters then based at Quantico but his request was turned down.[12]

On August 5, 1950, "Routine security patrols continued. No enemy contact. A warning order was received from brigade at 2130 directing 5th Marines to be prepared to move by motor to vicinity Chindong-ni and be prepared for offensive operations against the enemy."[13]

Task Force Kean—The First American Counterattack

At 1400 on the 5th, Craig received orders from Walker attaching the brigade to the 25th Infantry Division. Craig met Walker and Kean at their headquarters near Masan. "General Walker told me that he was going to carry out an offensive from Chindong-ni against the communists." Up to that time, the American troops had been retreating or holding the line and had not carried out an offensive. General Walker wrapped up the briefing by stating: "No one is to fall back again to the rear. We are going to stop the enemy where he is and, if necessary, we will fight to the death." It was a rather chilling send-off for commanders who were about to launch the first ground offensive of the war. Craig noted, rather tongue in cheek, that "General Walker made these points rather strongly." In fact, Walker's "no retreat" message was akin to Craig's orders to the brigade prior to leaving the States: "You will never receive an order to retreat from me."[14]

Hurrying from the conference, Craig climbed aboard a Sikorsky HO3S-1 three-seat helicopter for a quick flight to brief Lieutenant Colonel Murray on the operation. The pilot, Lieutenant Gus Lueddeke, radioed 5th Marines that "Warrior Six"—Craig's radio call sign—was inbound. This simple flight represented a tactical innovation—a revolution in the manner in which commanders controlled widely dispersed units—foreshadowing the development of heliborne tactics in the 1960s.

Crisis at the Crossroads

The brigade was ordered to start the first genuine offensive of the war, an attack to the southwest toward Masan. The situation was critical, because the NKPA seemed invincible. "In late July and early August 1950, the North Koreans had rapidly advanced along the coast to a point less than 35 miles from Pusan, a vital United Nations (UN) communications and supply complex centered in the Masan-Pusan area. A break-through at this point would have caused the collapse of the entire UN perimeter."[15]

The scheme of maneuver for the attack called for the 5th Regimental Combat Team (RCT) [Army] to pass through the 27th Infantry and clear the Tosan Road junction west of Chindong-ni. The Marine brigade would then jump off from the junction and attack along the road to Sachon and Chinju, some 30 miles to the west. "The nature of this operation ... was never divulged to me," Craig said. "We were told to attack and take Sachon ... and this we were prepared to do...." The attack was scheduled to commence on August 7, the eighth anniversary of the Marine landing on Guadalcanal and only one month since the brigade's activation.[16]

Corsairs from VMF-323 and VMF-212 aboard the USS *Badoeng Strait* and USS *Sicily* prepared to support the brigade. The two squadrons kept approximately six aircraft overhead during daylight hours. Their average load consisted of either a 500-pound bomb or a napalm tank, eight rockets, and a full load of machine gun ammunition. "The personnel in the Marine ground tactical air control parties were the same people with whom the Marine fliers had been rehearsing close air support at Camp Pendleton a few weeks earlier."[17]

"At Chindong-ni I found the most confused situation that I've encountered in the Marine Corps. It seemed to me that everything was combining to make this first attack a failure. That it succeeded was due solely to the fine Marines that I had under my command—who despite the many difficulties, pushed the enemy back over 28 miles in four days and inflicted over 1,900 casualties on the North Korean Army.

"The brigade was told to start an offensive as soon as the 5th Marines had cleared the Tosan Road junction, which was just ahead of our line. The 27th RCT was in position holding the line. The 25th Division was on our right. The 24th Regiment, another RCT of the Army, was due to come into Chindong-ni area and was to be attached to the brigade. Finally, due to the inability of the Army to clear the road junction, our offensive was held up one day."[18]

Extracts from Craig's field notebook, August 7:

> General attack stalled as the 5th RCT [U.S. Army] had one battalion held up by enemy necessitating commitment of 2/5 Marines to extricate them. Casualties for brigade about 25, plus one 105mm howitzer knocked out be direct hit.

At first light on the 8th, after a short air-artillery preparation, the 5th RCT Army jumped off in the attack, only to be stopped dead in its tracks by heavy NKPA automatic weapons and mortar fire from Hill 342, overlooking the road junction. With casualties mounting and the attack stalled, Major General Kean ordered Craig to assume command of all Army as well as Marine forces in the Chindong-ni area—making him, in essence, a division commander. "The orders were that the force commander with the most troops in the area would assume command during the turnover. Accordingly, as I had the preponderance of troops, I took over command from the commanding officer of the 27th Infantry."[19]

Craig went forward on a personal reconnaissance of the road junction. He arrived at the front in his helicopter and found it jammed with vehicles and equipment, creating an irresistible target for the NKPA gunners. "Suddenly, the NKPA artillery and mortars dropped a concentration all around us. My G-3 [Joe Stewart] and I took off at a run and gained cover behind a low stone wall running out from the village but found that we were in the middle of an odorous pile of Korean fertilizer ['night soil'/human excreta]. We finally gained the road and with artillery still falling, climbed the steep hill to confer with Lieutenant Colonel Bob Taplett, Commanding Officer, 3rd Battalion."[20]

David Douglas Duncan, the famed photographer for Time and Life magazines and a former World War II Marine, happened to spot Craig as he observed the action: "A helicopter came churning over the valley from our rear, then landed out in the nearby dry riverbed below. We both spotted the snow-white head of Marine Brigadier General Edward Craig as he stepped from the aircraft. With his men scheduled to attack, Craig had moved up, taking personal command of the assault. Watching a slow smile start across his lean, deeply tanned face, while a pair of cool blue eyes swept the nearby hills where his Marines were deepening their foxholes, I knew this veteran of Iwo Jima and Bougainville could take anything Korea could hand out."[21]

Lieutenant Colonel Harold S. Roise's 2nd Battalion, 5th Marines, was ordered forward to seize Hill 342 and relieve an Army battalion and a Marine platoon that were desperately clinging to the crest under heavy pressure. The battalion ran into the same suborn resistance that stopped the initial advance and was forced to dig in for the night. Company D had a particularly tough time, losing eight killed and 28 wounded, including the company commander and three lieutenants. Master Sergeant Harold Reeves, the company gunnery sergeant, was awarded the Silver Star for taking command of the leaderless men and holding the position until relieved the next day. Private First Class Doug Kock remembered Reeves had "somewhat over 21 years in the Corps. When he chewed you out, he had the blackest eyes. You could see the sparks flying from them when he really got worked up."[22]

By the next day, the communist troops were gradually falling back. They were unprepared for a quick thrust by the brigade. However, Craig was quick to point out that they had the capability of being quickly reinforced. "In view of this I ordered a night attack in order to gain ground, surprise the enemy, and keep him off balance." He did not make the decision lightly but "only after mature deliberation...." However, "I believed the decision was justified if the brigade could advance rapidly and gain its objective before the enemy could move in his reserve and oppose us in force."[23]

"It was shortly after midnight that I received a message from Lieutenant Colonel Ray Murray that a tank had broken through a bridge and that the night attack would be delayed." Craig hurried forward and met Murray, who was "trying to figure out how to get the tank back on the road. General Craig informed me in no uncertain words that others could figure it out and it was my job to get on down the road. He had a way of telling you to do things that weren't nasty, but you knew you had to get them done. I admired him very much." A bypass was constructed, and the night attack was launched. "It succeeded by the fact that only small delaying forces were encountered, and these were quickly brushed aside," Craig reported.[24]

Extracts from Craig's field notebook August 10, 1950:

> Report from CO 5th Marines that a tank had broken through a bridge in the dark ... went by jeep to investigate and initiated immediate measures to make a bypass. One and a half hours later jeeps could cross, and by 1200 trucks and tanks.

After 54 hours of intense infantry action, including hand-to-hand combat, the enemy started withdrawing southwest toward Kosong. They suffered an estimated 600 casualties. Captured documents revealed that U.S. forces had been opposed by elements of the 13th and 15th Regiments of the NKPA's 6th Division. The division was formed by Korean veterans of the Chinese People's Liberation Army (PLA). Early in the war, it was awarded the title of "Guard" because of its fighting spirit.[25]

Historian Lynn Montross described the battle skills of the NKPA: "The Marines learned to respect a hardy enemy for his skill at camouflage, ambush, infiltration, and use of cover. They learned that supporting air and artillery fires often had limited effect on a foe making clever use of reverse slope defenses to offset Marine concentrations. A ridge might protect and conceal an enemy strong point until attackers were too close for supporting fires. When this situation developed, with the heavy firepower of the Marines neutralized, their attack was reduced to the familiar basic essential of small arms fire fights. In these circumstances, the NKPA was able to meet them on even terms, man-to-man."[26]

Kosong Turkey Shoot

On August 11, 1950, "The night passed quietly with only sporadic rifle fire in defense position. At 0700, 3rd Battalion was directed to insure that battalion area was clear of enemy troops. No enemy found and at 0808, G Company led the attack toward Kosong."[27]

The brigade continued to rapidly advance to Kosong and was within three miles of Sachon on the 11th, when its supporting artillery (1st Battalion, 11th Marines) fired a barrage on a crossroads west of Kosong. Thinking its position had been discovered, a major part of the North Korean 83rd Motorized Regiment took flight. "This is the only organization of this kind that I have seen in Korea. It was equipped with Russian jeeps, trucks, anti-tank guns, and motorcycles with side cars, equipped with machine guns. A long column of approximately 200 vehicles loaded with troops, ammunition and supplies got on the road. A flight of four F4U4B Corsairs led by their commanding officer, Major Arnold Lund, from the Badoeng Strait circled overhead."[28]

The Corsairs made an immediate low-level strafing run in an effort to bring the column to a halt. The aircraft spewed rockets and machine gun bullets into the column. Vehicles crashed into one another or piled up in the ditch while enemy troops scrambled for cover. Soviet-made jeeps and motorcycles were stopped or abandoned. The North Koreans fought back with small arms and automatic weapons and seriously damaged two of the low-flying planes; Lieutenant Doyle Cole ditched in a nearby bay to be rescued by Craig, who pulled the downed pilot into his helicopter using a winch. "Grinning and happy at his quick rescue, Cole slapped the general on the shoulder and said, 'Thanks for the lift, buddy.' His grin faded as he saw the stars on the dungaree jacket. 'Thank you, sir,' he said, trying to recover. 'Glad to be of service, Lieutenant,' Craig responded, smiling. Later, Captain Vivian Moses crash landed in a rice paddy and was killed."[29]

This air attack left about forty enemy vehicles wrecked and burning. Another flight of Marine Corsairs and U.S. Air Force (USAF) F-51s arrived and continued the work of destruction. "Our air [VMF323 'Death Rattlers' and USAF F-51 aircraft] hit this column east of Kosong," Craig declared. "Between the ground elements and our air, we annihilated practically this entire column."[30]

When the ground troops reached the scene later in the afternoon, they found 31 trucks, 24 jeeps, 45 motorcycles, and much ammunition and equipment destroyed or abandoned. Craig, long a devoted fan of motorcycles, tried to figure out how he could "rescue" one of the undamaged vehicles.[31]

At the height of the action, Master Sergeant Herbert Valentine, flying an OY observation plane, spotted a speeding NKPA jeep with what appeared to be a high-ranking officer in the rear seat. Valentine and his observer decided to "strafe" the jeep with their .38-caliber pistols. After making several passes without hitting anything—and being shot at by the occupants—they made one last run. The driver took one look too many, missed a turn, and drove off a cliff with the officer still sitting rigidly in the seat. There was a hot debate within the aircrews on whether to paint this "airborne victory" on the nose of the aircraft.[32]

The marine advance stopped that night four miles west of Kosong. The Special Action Report noted for August 12, 1950, that:

> At 0630 the 1st Battalion passed through the 3rd Battalion and continued the advance ... fifty enemy-abandoned motorcycles with sidecars, twenty Russian-built jeeps, and numerous quantities of small arms were passed, burned or camouflaged beside the road, all having been abandoned by the enemy as a result of the rapid movement of the brigade and air strikes.[33]

On the morning of the 12th, the brigade got off to an early start. Enemy resistance was light and the 1st Battalion quickly gained 11 miles, passing through evidence of considerable enemy disorganization. Andrew Geer wrote that a captured enemy officer admitted: "Panic sweeps my men when they see the Marines with the yellow leggings coming at them." The Marines' canvas leggings appeared to be yellow in color.[34]

Bloody Gulch

The brigade CP opened at Kosong, and its leading elements were just 4,000 yards short of its objective when Craig received an urgent order to send one battalion back toward Chindong-ni to assist Army units that had been overrun (two Army artillery battalions, the 555th Field Artillery Battalion and the 90th Field Artillery Battalion). "You're to go back at once," Craig told Taplett, "and contact General Kean of the 25th Division. I'll arrange to have your battalion trucked back. You're to find out what the hell the situation is." By late afternoon the 3rd Battalion, via truck convoy, had completed the move, and Lieutenant Colonel Taplett was attempting to make sense of the chaotic situation. Taplett recalled that several Army units in the area showed little concern for what happened to their comrades and were doing nothing to help out. "I flew over the abandoned artillery positions," Craig said. "Abandoned 155mm howitzers and trucks were clearly visible. I could see the Marines quickly overrun the enemy and recapture the guns."[35]

The 555th Field Artillery lost all eight of its 105-mm howitzers in the two firing batteries located there. The 90th Field Artillery Battalion lost all six 155-mm howitzers of its A Battery. The loss of "Triple Nickel" artillerymen has never been accurately computed. The day after the enemy attack, only 20 percent of the battalion troops were present for duty. The battalion estimated at the time that from 75 to 100 artillerymen were killed at the gun positions and 80 wounded, with many of the latter unable to get away. Five weeks later, when the 25th Division regained Taejong-ni, it found in a house the bodies of 55 men of the 555th Field Artillery.[36]

The First Battle of the Naktong Bulge

Craig was deeply concerned because the brigade was deep in enemy territory and there were no friendly troops on his right flank, and "with the 5th RCT (Army) heavily engaged and unable to advance, the area to our north was exposed. There were many North Korean troops in the area and we were out on a limb." Nevertheless, Craig planned on resuming the advance at daylight and securing Sachon. It was not to be. Lieutenant General Walker directed that the drive on Sachon be terminated and that the brigade urgently return to Chindong-ni. The situation was critical. Craig received the orders late that afternoon to make a tactical withdrawal the next morning and return to Chindong-ni.[37]

The suddenness of the order caught the brigade strung out on the road between Kosong and Sachon and his leading battalion engaged. Lieutenant Colonel Stewart had to resort to penciling a note to Roise of the 2nd Battalion: "I wrote on a little piece of brown paper, 'These are your trucks; move to Naktong at once.'"[38]

On the 13th, the brigade commenced its withdrawal from Sachon as ordered, blowing all bridges, laying anti-tank mines, and destroying all facilities that could be used by the North Koreans. Craig recounted that, as the last man of the rear guard passed his deserted CP "I stood there for a few moments looking around at the town and area which we had come so far to capture and were now giving up. It seemed so unnecessary that we had to pull out and give it up. It was a lonesome sight ... I turned and got in my helicopter and flew out wondering why such things had to be. The brigade had paid a price, a total of 315 casualties, 66 killed or died of wounds and 240 wounded, and 9 missing."[39]

The official Marine Corps history noted:

> The communist drive to this sensitive area [Kosong/Sachon] came closest of all [to] the NKPA thrusts to the vital UN supply port of Pusan. Up to that time the NKPA units spearheading the advance—the 6th Infantry Division and the 83rd Motorcycle Regiment—had never suffered a reverse worth mentioning since the outset of the invasion. Then the counterattack by the 1st Provisional Marine Brigade hurled the enemy back 26 miles in 4 days from the Chindong-ni area to Sachon.[40]

Craig had no sooner settled down at his new Chingdong-ni CP when at 1:30am on the 14th: "I received orders from the Eighth Army to detach the brigade from the 25th Division and to report to the commanding general of the 24th Division, General Church. The brigade commenced moving our heaviest equipment that night, and in the morning sent the troops by truck and rail to our rendezvous area, a place called Miryang, 75 miles away." The 7,000-man North Korean 4th "Seoul" Division, the title given for its vital role in capturing the capitol, had forded the Naktong River during the night of August 6. It broke through the battered 24th

Infantry Division lines and threatened Taegu, the temporary seat of the South Korean government and the headquarters of Lieutenant General Walker's Eighth Army.[41]

The Naktong River, the second largest in Korea, formed a moat one-quarter to one-half-mile wide and six feet deep, almost the entire length of the American perimeter. At the confluence of the Naktong and the Nam there is a bulge, four miles east–west and five miles north–south. The 24th Division, which occupied a series of strongpoints on the high ground east of the river, called the "Naktong Bulge."[42]

The brigade went into bivouac at Miryang on the 15th. "We camped in a grove of trees and were able to set up our field kitchen," Craig reported. "This was the first time that the brigade had had hot rations since they landed and the first time they were able to bathe."[43]

Craig got to the CP early in the morning and lay down under a tree. When he woke up at daylight and looked around, lo and behold, he spotted the famed war correspondent for the *New York Herald Tribune*, Maggie Higgins, sleeping under a nearby tree in the midst of hundreds of Marines. "I always had much respect for her," Craig said. "I went by helicopter to confer with Brigadier General Church regarding an attack to drive the enemy from the pocket [Bulge]. I received an overlay of the proposed attack plan and then returned to brigade CP." Lieutenant General Walker told Church: "I am going to give you the Marine brigade. I want this situation cleaned up—and quick."[44]

On August 16, "The 3rd Battalion relieved elements of the Army's 34th Regiment prior to daylight on August 17."[45] The brigade then jumped off on the 17th. In a series of attacks over the next three days, the brigade hit the North Koreans head on and succeeded in stopping them and forcing them back across the Naktong River. Their withdrawal became a rout. Joe Stewart observed the action: "As they retreated back across the river, I actually observed for the first time in my life the panic retreat of an enemy force, with our tanks lined up taking pot shots into scores of fleeing enemy troops. Then the air caught the remnants going back across the river."[46]

> The first flight from the USS *Sicily* [VMF-212] attacked the ridge ahead of the advancing Marines near a bend in the Naktong River. Two tanks and a fieldpiece

were attacked; one tank was dismantled by a 500-pound bomb, another destroyed with rockets. At this time, Marine ground forces, aided by our close air support, drove the retreating enemy into the Naktong river. While several thousands of them were attempting to swim across this, this flight commenced to attack, strafing with 20mm explosives and incendiaries. The enemy was killed in such numbers that the river was definitely discolored by blood.[47]

Craig said, "That division was never heard from again."[48] Special Action Report for 1st Provisional Marine Brigade (1st Tank Battalion), noted that:

> The tank platoon was still in the process of replenishing ammunition at 2000 when three enemy tanks were reported approaching the lines. In a matter of seconds, the platoon was on the road moving forward. About 300 yards from the enemy, our advance was held up by trucks parked in the middle of the road and abandoned by their drivers. Tank crewmen drove these trucks from the road enabling the tanks to continue the advance. Upon order from the platoon leader, the first section loaded a 90mm/APC cartridge. Immediately upon rounding the bend in the road at a range of 100 yards, the lead tank came face to face with an enemy tank.[49]

"The 1,359 air strikes by Marine air resulted in great damage to enemy personnel and equipment at and near the front lines, and in decelerating the North Korean advance toward Pusan. The North Koreans were forced almost totally to abandon daylight attacks and daylight work of all kinds."[50]

Extracts from Craig's field notebook August 19, 1950:

> To the front by jeep all day. During the three-day operation some 1,200 enemy were killed. We captured many small arms and 122mm Russian artillery pieces, including antitank guns and mortars. Knocked out four Russian made tanks ... our casualties amounted to over 600. Our total casualties to date are 785 killed and wounded. Brigade faced elements of four regiments of enemy [4th North Korean Division].

On August 20, Craig drove to the cemetery established by the U.S. Army near Miryang with the idea of checking on the burial of Marine dead and arranging for a memorial service there on the following morning. "I was most surprised to find its condition." The dead from the Naktong battle had been gathered up and deposited in the cemetery. They were in a bad state of decomposition and were lying in rows without cover. The Marine dead were mostly buried. The stench was terrific and the whole scene was macabre. "I thought what a depressing effect this would have on my men ... certainly would not help morale ... and decided to call off the memorial service. I talked to my graves registration officer, who assured me that all Marines would be suitably interred before dark. It was soon after this that I was notified that the cemetery was in good shape and I held memorial services at which representatives of all Marine units that had lost men attended."[51]

After the heavy fighting in the Naktong bridgehead, the brigade was pulled out of the line for a much needed rest and refit. They looked like a bunch of rag pickers—rotting uniforms, worn-out field shoes, missing equipment—when they arrived at "The Bean Patch," an open field large enough to accommodate the brigade. The men camped out in the open, under the stars, having ditched their shelter halves during the fighting. Eight hundred replacements arrived to fill the badly depleted ranks and the third infantry company—Lem Shepherd had lived up to his word. President Syngman Rhee presented Purple Heart medals, but the most important event occurred with the arrival of a beer ration and letters from home. A rumor floated among the men: "We're goin' to join the division and make a landing in th' rear of these bastards." For once, the scuttlebutt was true. The brigade staff was alerted to start planning for the withdrawal from the perimeter. Joe Stewart caught a plane to Japan, but no sooner had he reached the terminal than he received a message: "Return to Korea at once; all hell has broken loose!"[52]

The Second Battle of the Naktong Bulge

On September 1, the NKPA launched a massive assault—13 infantry regiments, 3 security regiments and the remnants of three armored regiments—against Walker's thinly deployed forces. They struck five separate points, but their heaviest attack was against the U.S. 2nd Division in the Naktong Bulge. Troops from four North Korean divisions, supported by armor and artillery, slammed into the American front lines, penetrating almost three miles and slicing the division in two. Hundreds of U.S. soldiers were killed, wounded, or missing, and the victorious NKPA were close to a breakthrough. All the ground that the 1st Provisional Marine Brigade had seized was lost at such a heavy cost. Walker's forces needed help, so the call went out to the "Fire Brigade."[53]

Craig noted: "Heavy attack by enemy along 2nd Infantry Division–25th Infantry Division front commencing at 0330. My brigade put on alert. At 1100 received orders to be prepared to move...."[54]

Craig rushed by helicopter to the 2nd Division CP for a meeting with its commander, Major General Lawrence B. Keiser, and the Eighth Army's chief of staff. "Situation is critical with several companies cut off by enemy. Much infiltration by enemy to rear of units." Pressure was brought on him to attack at once. Craig refused, saying "I explained that it was more or less impossible unless I committed my units piecemeal and without air support." The conversation boiled over. "I insisted that the attack be delayed until all my troops arrived and I had my air support properly coordinated."[55]

Extract from Craig's field notebook September 2, 1950:

> The Army wanted me to attack on a very broad front. I also objected to this. I knew that if we were committed to combat piecemeal that we would be defeated in detail and the Marine Corps would be finished in Korea, and in the public eye. General Kaiser and 8th Army finally agreed and we firmed up plans for the attack on a narrow front. H-hour was set for 0800 September 3rd.

Craig stood his ground—the brigade would fight as a united air-ground team. Finally, the Army backed down. "This was the only heated discussion I had in Korea with the Army," Craig related. During the meeting Keiser apologized to Craig for losing the ground the brigade had won at such a high cost. "General Craig, I'm horribly embarrassed that you have to do this. My men lost the ground that you took in a severe fight." General Shepherd, who was at the meeting, related: "Eddie, in his very gallant manner, said: 'General, it might have happened to me.'" Shepherd was upset with the Army's defeat. "We turned them [the Naktong objectives] over to the Army. The next day they lost the ground and Eddie had to go back and recapture the positions. He lost a lot of boys retaking the same damn ground that he'd taken two or three days before. If that had happened to me, I might have been tempted to say to the Army commander 'Well, you damn fool, why couldn't you hold it?'"[56]

Special Action Report, 5th Marines, for September 1, 1950 noted:

> Fifth Marines received a warning order to stand by for immediate movement, on order ... to reinforce U.S. Army forces. At 1100 orders were received directing 1st Battalion to prepare for movement to Miryang to be used as Eighth Army reserve for the Naktong River area. At 1630 all units of this command boarded a train in the vicinity of the bivouac area for transportation and proceeded to Miryang.[57]

All during September 2, a heavy haze covered the area, which would have hindered air support, so the attack was postponed until the morning of September 3. The 2nd Battalion, 5th Marines jumped off in the attack against Objective No. 1, Obong-ni Ridge, a dominant terrain feature. The communists had pushed the Army lines back, the line of departure had been lost, and the Marines had to fight to regain it. A platoon of tanks moved forward to give support and, as was his leadership style, Craig moved closer to the action. "I brought up a company of tanks, who fired point-blank into antitank guns manned by the North Koreans. These were knocked out pretty promptly, and our troops made a very good advance through a difficult area." Automatic weapons fire forced Craig and his aide to take cover behind one of the tanks. Buck recalled: "The tank platoon commander, Second Lieutenant Bob Winters, was halfway out of the hatch firing .50-caliber tracers to point out targets for his 90mm cannon." Winters suddenly slumped over the turret, bleeding profusely from a neck wound.[58]

Disregarding the enemy fire, Craig and Buck climbed up, pulled the wounded officer off the tank, and dragged him to cover. Craig leaned over the groggy but still conscious officer, giving him words of encouragement. "It was a shock to discover the officer was the son of an old friend of mine. He looked at me as he lay there and smiled, pointing to the tank and said 'General, I've got a bottle of whiskey in the hull; you can have it.'" It was a magnanimous gesture, worth its weight in gold—but it remained in the tank. "I never took the whiskey," Craig declared. He never ate or drank anything his troops did not have.[59]

Artillery and air strikes supported the attack, pounding the enemy positions. Gull-wing Vought F4U-4B Corsairs doused the NKPA with napalm in an almost seamless demonstration of air–ground coordination. Response time averaged seven minutes from the air request to the run on the target. One Army commander reported: "The Marines on our left were a sight to behold. Not only was their equipment superior to ours, but they had squadrons in direct support. They used it like artillery. It was 'Hey, Joe, this is Smitty, knock off the left of that ridge in front of Item Company.' They had it day and night."[60]

The fight continued for three more days before the brigade seized its last objective. One of the highlights of the action occurred when the 1st Battalion overran an enemy division command post. Marines found fully erect tents, a treasure trove of documents, piles of abandoned or destroyed equipment, and two T-34 tanks in perfect operating condition. The area had been saturated with artillery and air strikes. Hundreds of North Korean bodies bore mute testimony to the accuracy of the American firepower.[61]

On September 5, Craig received the message: "directing the withdrawal of the brigade to the port of Pusan for embarkation on ships which would join up at sea with the 1st Marine Division for the Inchon and advance on Seoul."[62]

CHAPTER 18

The Great Gamble—Inchon

The brigade received orders on September 5 to proceed to Pusan to prepare to embark for an amphibious operation. Walker was not happy and said he wouldn't release the regiment—"If I lose the 5th Marines I will not be responsible for the safety of the front." His intransigence caused a great deal of consternation among the Navy and Marines operational planners. Major General O. P. Smith talked to Major General Edward M. "Ned" Almond, MacArthur's chief of staff, about the release; "he passed it off." O. P. Smith said "Gen Walker will let them go at the proper time ... and stalled, so finally I sat down and wrote a dispatch and [formally] requested that the 1st Brigade be released to the 1st Marine Division on September 1st in order to prepare and mount out for the Inchon operation. It was not fair to General Craig to put him in the position of requesting release from combat commitments. I decided to put myself on record regarding the brigade and sent a dispatch to X Corps requesting that the brigade be released from combat commitments on September 1 in order to plan for the forthcoming operation and mount out."[1]

The stalemate was kicked upstairs to MacArthur. "Tell Walker, he will have to give up the 5th Marines." Smith said: "I finally got them detached on the September 5, and we had to land on the 15th."[2]

The remarkable performance by "Warrior Six" (Brigadier General Craig) and the "Fire Brigade" stabilized the defense of the Pusan Perimeter, gave the defenders a much-needed morale boost, and gained time for MacArthur to plan and execute a "master stroke," the Inchon Landing.

Craig's brigade movement order:

> This my opn order 22-50 x commencing at 2400 5 Sept Brig moves by rail and motor to staging area Pusan for further operation against the enemy x prior to commencement of movement 5th Mars will stand relieved by elms of 2nd Inf Div commencing at darkness ... conceal from the enemy activities connected with your withdrawal ...
> Brig. Gen. Edward Craig

The brigade proceeded to Pusan. "As the men arrived, weapons were cleaned, necessary extra equipment was issued, and the men were provided beer to quench their thirst. I managed to get a number of truck-loads of beer from the Army ... and soon my men had their first cold drink in over a month." Many of the parched Marines slaked their thirst with copious amounts of brew. A medical officer wrote in his diary: "Entries this date terminated early because, in addition to foul weather, it got considerably drunk out." The issuance of alcohol was the source of controversy. "Some of those boys are underage" was the complaint, which could not stand up to the argument: "If they're old enough to fight, they're old enough to drink!"[3]

MacArthur's genius was never more on display than in his insistence on an amphibious operation even as the North Korean Army was on the verge of crushing U.S. and South Korean resistance and seizing all of Korea. The great Marine Corps historian Colonel Joe Alexander commented to General Shepherd during an interview: "I think Inchon was MacArthur's greatest hour." Shepherd responded: "No question about it," and went on to say: "He [MacArthur] was, in my opinion, the greatest military leader of our century."[4]

The Worst Possible Place

An amphibious assault is perhaps the most complicated of all operations in war. Of all the Korean west coast seaports, Inchon was probably the least desirable when considered strictly from the viewpoint of hydrographic considerations. In fact, there was great opposition to MacArthur's plan from all quarters. Rear Admiral James H. Doyle, perhaps the Navy's finest amphibious practitioner, warned him: "General, I have not been asked, however, the best I can say is that Inchon is not impossible." Doyle's comment was made at the end of a very detailed brief for MacArthur, who responded: "If we find that we can't make it, we will withdraw." Doyle, a veteran of all the major World War II amphibious landings in the Pacific, replied: "No, General, we don't know how to do that. Once we start ashore, we'll keep going."[5]

Shepherd, no slouch when it came to landing on a hostile shore, was unhappy and had reservations. "From the various reports that we had, it appeared that Inchon was a pretty damn tough spot to take. Initially, I was lukewarm about making an amphibious landing on the center of a well defended city. I was thinking about World War II, and the Japanese, and how they fought from house to house, and it was tough going. I was afraid we would run into similar difficulties at Inchon and that it would cost the lives of many Marines to take the city." Despite their misgivings, planning continued at a feverish pace; time was running out. MacArthur set D-day for September 15, when there was sufficient water to float the landing craft.[6]

MacArthur viewed the Inchon-Seoul operation as the opening move in a strategic bid to crush the North Korean Army. The seizure of the seaport city, only 25 miles from Seoul, would enable him to move rapidly against the capital and cut the NKPA lines of communication and supply. Seoul was also the hub of an excellent railroad system and a road network that fanned north and south. Kimpo, the nation's best airport, lies between the two cities. Inchon was the key to the kingdom. No other port was satisfactory. MacArthur wanted the place—and being who he was, nothing was going to keep it from him—not hydrographic conditions, not opposition, and certainly not the North Korean Army. "We shall land at Inchon and I shall crush them!" After attending MacArthur's brief on Inchon, the Chief of Naval Operations, Admiral Forest P. Sherman, is quoted as saying: "I wish I had that man's optimism."[7]

Commander in Chief of the Far East (CINCFE) General Douglas MacArthur, sent a message to the JCS, September 8, 1950:

> There is no question in my mind as to the feasibility of the operation and I regard its chance of success as excellent. I go further and believe that it represents the only hope of wresting the initiative from the enemy and thereby presenting

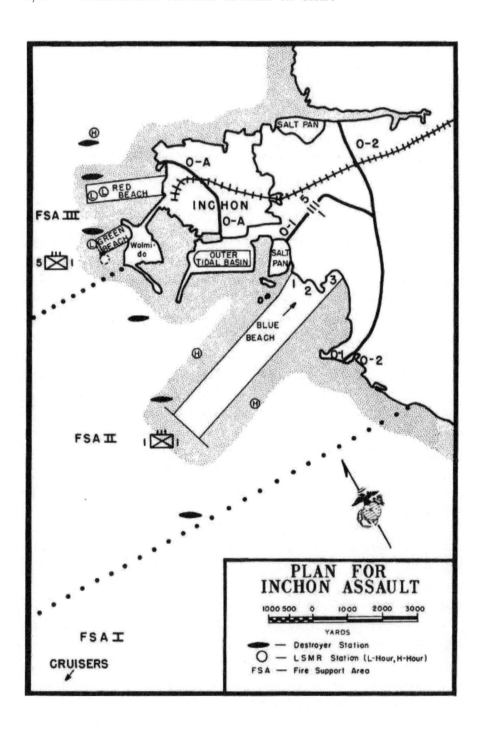

PLAN FOR
INCHON ASSAULT

an opportunity for a decisive blow. To do otherwise is to commit us to a war of indefinite duration, of gradual attrition, and of doubtful results ... There is no slightest possibility ... of our forces being ejected from the Pusan beachhead. The envelopment from the north will instantly relieve the pressure on the south perimeter and, indeed, is the only way that this can be accomplished ... This, indeed, is the primary purpose of the movement. Caught between our northern and southern forces, both of which are completely self-sustaining because of our absolute air and naval supremacy, the enemy cannot fail to be ultimately shattered.[8]

The JCS response to MacArthur on the same day:

We approve your plan and President has been so informed.[9]

Command of the operation, code-named Chromite, fell to Major General Almond, an officer with no experience in amphibious operations. The Navy wanted Shepherd to command the operation because of his background in landing on hostile beaches—and Shepherd wanted the job—but it was not to be. "MacArthur told me himself," Shepherd said, "Lem, I would like you to command this landing at Inchon. It's a Marine show, and you should be in command. But unfortunately, I have promised it to my chief of staff, Ned Almond. Since you can't command this corps landing, I want you to accompany me on my staff as my amphibious advisor." Shepherd was greatly disappointed but agreed to the temporary assignment, which gave him the opportunity to provide input on the landing plan.[10]

MacArthur's dictate to seize Inchon on September 15 created almost impossible parameters for the planning staffs of Amphibious Group One (PhibGru-1) and the 1st Marine Division. They had only about 20 days to prepare, probably the shortest period ever allotted for a major amphibious assault. Inchon's natural conditions—a extreme tidal range with an average range of 29 feet and a maximum observed range of 36 feet, combined with torturous shipping channels, fast currents, mud flats, and high seawalls—gave them fits.[11]

Major General Almond and Major General Smith (Commanding General 1st Marine Division) did not get along, which added to the difficulties. They were two different personalities. Smith was a cautious individual, a fine staff officer who carefully considered every contingency before taking action. Almond, on the other hand, was aggressive and anxious for his X Corps to push ahead faster than Smith wanted. "I'll admit that I shortly lost confidence in the higher command out there," Smith admitted.[12]

It seemed obvious to Smith that neither Almond nor his staff appreciated the difficulties inherent in the Inchon operation. In a letter to the commandant, Smith wrote: "It was only after a week of close study of all the factors involved that I was able to convince myself that the operation was feasible from the standpoint of the landing force." Colonel Alpha L. Bowser, Smith's operations officer, found "They [X Corps staff] had no capability of understanding what we were doing or how we were doing it. They were standing around wringing their hands. I took a piece of paper that was brought to me by a corps staffer, folded it up very neatly and stuck it through the front of his shirt and told him to blow...." Shepherd tried to mediate between the two. "I talked to O. P. and told him to play the game. 'Don't get so mad with Almond, he's trying to do the right thing.'" Almond didn't help matters. The first time he met Smith, Almond addressed him as "son." There was only a year age difference separating the two.[13]

Despite the friction, a landing plan quickly took shape. Inchon was divided into three color-coded landing beaches, Red, Green, and Blue. Two battalions of the 5th Marines would land over Red; one battalion at Green (Wolmi-Do); and the 1st Marines—two battalions abreast—over Blue Beach. The extreme tidal range—enough water to float landing—dictated two landings a day: one at first light and the other at twilight. It was a bold plan that depended on split second timing and a hell of a lot of luck![14]

Extracts from Craig's field notebook:

10 September 1950
Position (moored)
35-06.2N 129-02.6E

At 1820 commenced loading cargo and equipment of the 1st Marine Division. USS *Henrico* (APA 45), Capt. John E. Frado

11 September 1950
On the night of 10 September 1950, all companies were alerted to make preparations to board ship on order because of an approaching typhoon. Actual embarkation of the battalion commenced at 1400, 11 September 1950.

BLT [Battalion Landing Team] 1/5 and H & S Company, 5th Marines were the major units embarked. Special Action Report, 1/5

Uniform and Equipment for Embarkation

> (1) Individual arms and equipment (2) Utility with steel helmet camouflage cover, green side out, and leggings (3) Field Transport Pack with the following minimum content: 1 belt, with trouser, w/o buckle; 1 Buckle, metal, trouser, belt; 1 Cap, utility; 1 Coat, utility; 2 Drawers, cotton, pr.; 1 Jacket, field; 2 Shirts, flannel; 1 Shoes, field, pr.; 3 Socks, woolen, pr.; 1 Trouser, winter service; 2 Trousers, utility; 2 Undershirts, cotton; 1 Razor, w/blades; 1 Soap Box, w/soap; 1 Toothbrush, w/case; 1 Comb; 1 Soap, shaving; 1 Toothpaste; 1 Mirror; 1 Handkerchief; 1 Legging Laces; 1 Towel; 1 Sewing Kit; 1 Sleeping Bag, w/2 blankets.
> Administrative Plan Number 3-50, 1st Marine Division

12 September 1950
At 1300 completed embarkation of troops having embarked 1649 military personnel and 7 civilian war correspondents (Marguerite Higgins, John O. Davies, Richard Ferguson, Lionel Crane, Frede Vidar, Larry Keighly; John Shaw). USS *Henrico* (APA 45) Capt. John E. Fradd

12 September 1950
USS *Henrico* sailed from Pusan, at 1450 and was underway for a period of three days.
Special Action Report. 1/5

September 13 was a blustery, overcast afternoon when MacArthur's black 1941 Cadillac pulled up to the entrance of the Dai Ichi Building, MacArthur's headquarters in Tokyo. Three officers climbed in, MacArthur and Shepherd in the back—protocol required the most senior to sit on the right—and Almond in front. At a signal, the MP escort wheeled out of the driveway, sandwiching MacArthur's beflagged sedan between their two vehicles. Shepherd made small talk with the "great man" during the drive to Haneda Airport. As they approached the gate, the clouds lifted briefly, revealing a rainbow. "Lem," said MacArthur, "there is my lucky rainbow. This operation is going to be a success. You know I commanded the Rainbow Division in France during World War I and I have always believed that a rainbow is my lucky omen."[15]

Shepherd thought divine intervention might have played a hand. "It was an unusual coincidence that a rainbow should appear in the sky just prior to the general's embarkation on what was considered to be a hazardous amphibious operation with a typhoon threatening to disperse the convoy of ships enroute to Inchon. Although MacArthur placed a great confidence in his own decisions, I will always believe the rainbow that appeared in the sky at that psychological moment must have reassured him that the Inchon landing would be a successful operation."[16]

On September 12, Craig's ship, USS *Henrico* (APA-45), left Pusan. The brigade was dissolved and it became part of the 1st Marine Division, with Craig as the assistant division commander and second in command of the landing for the attack on Inchon. While at sea, Craig was handed a frantic NKPA message: "Enemy radio intercepts states our convoy sighted and our intentions deduced; calls on all troops to repel our landing at Wolmi-Do and Inchon." Just hours remained before naval gunfire began blasting the North Korean beach defenses.[17]

Extracts from the log of USS *Collett*:

13 September 1950
0916 Formed column led by USS *Mansfield* (DD 728) and proceeded up Flying Fish Channel toward Inch'on, Korea. Anchored in harbor. Adjusted heading at anchor to bring guns to bear.
1302 Commenced prearranged firing on targets, primarily gun emplacements.
USS *Mansfield* (DD 728) Cmdr. E.H. Headland

1302 Fire shifted to target area no. 2 but not before enemy commenced fire from that area. Within minutes there were at least 50 short and 50 over, plus continuous small arms fire.
USS *Collett* (DD 730) Cmdr. R.H. Close

1303 Commenced counter battery fire on target no. 2.
1308 Gurke (DD 783) asked where counter battery was coming from and Collett informed that it was in target area indicated on chart as "D."
1310 Received hit no. 1 (forward head).
1312 Received hit no. 2 (Steward's living space).
1326 Received hit no. 3 (Wardroom).
1335 Received hit no. 4 (Fireroom and Plot).
1336 Received hit no. 5 (Steward's living space)
1337 Requested permission from CTG 90.6 to get underway and shift our position. Our rate of fire was considerably diminished in local control as the smoke obscured the targets and necessitated frequent check of fire until targets again became visible. We did not seem to be giving as good as we were taking since

some of the enemy guns had found the range and I hoped that the damage to the computer might be such that the guns could be put back in director control ... My request did not indicate a lack of initiative, but simply a consideration that part of our mission was to locate enemy batteries which we were doing very effectively. I felt that a sound decision could be better made by someone with a broad view, mine having become somewhat limited by numerous splashes close aboard.
1338 Permission granted by CTG 90.6 to withdraw.[18]

The log of USS *Rochester* recorded:

1350 Commenced firing main battery to starboard in accordance with D minus 2 day schedule at enemy positions on Wolmi-Do.[19]

While the log of USS *Mansfield* noted:

1400 Underway. Proceeding out of harbor at flank speed.
1415 Received counter battery fire from Wolmi-Do. A total of 25 splashes were observed in the immediate vicinity of which five were close aboard.[20]

Land the Landing Force: Wolmi-Do Island

The key to the port of Inchon was the island of Wolmi-Do. It had to be taken prior to the main landing at Inchon. Craig was to land on Wolmi-Do on the afternoon of D-day and set up an advance CP for the division, and to take such immediate action as the tactical situation required. As the afternoon high tide surged up Flying Fish Channel, LCVPs and amphibian tractors carrying the assault elements of the 1st and 5th Marines gunned across the line of departure toward their landing beaches:

"A" Company, with the mission of taking battalion objective No. 1 (Cemetery Hill on Wolmi-Do) ... landed amid heavy small arms fire and intermittent mortar fire coming from trenches and bunkers on the beach, from the exposed left flank, and from Cemetery Hill.[21]

The log of USS *Dehaven* noted:

1708 Shifted main battery ... and fired on large grey building after observing machine gun fire from Wolmi-do Marines. Area quickly became dark at H-hour due to heavy overcast and smoke. Commenced firing 40-mm and 20-mm along

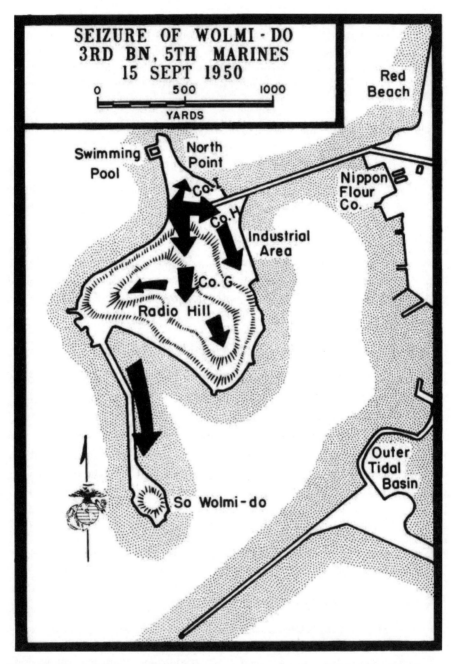

Brigadier General Craig established his first command post on Wolmi–Do Island to, as ordered by O. P. Smith, "function at discretion"

entire seawall on RED Beach and Cemetery Hill. First landing wave heading in to beach.[22]

Two free boats carrying Craig, his personal staff, and a jeep and trailer landed on Wolmi-Do's Green Beach. As his LCVP bottomed out, the ramp dropped and Craig stepped out on the sand. "I went ashore on the morning of D-day ... established my CP near the shoreline and went to the top of [Cemetery] hill ... where I established an observation post (OP)." From the OP, he could clearly see Red Beach where Lieutenant Colonel Ray Murray's 5th Marines had stormed ashore. Craig inspected the North Korean positions, finding them heavily dug in. "Apparently this was done at the last minute ... and it was a very thorough job. I believe if our naval gunfire had not done such a fine job of shore bombardment, our casualties might have been very heavy. As it was, it was such an effective bombardment ... that the island was practically denuded of cover and vegetation. There was very little that could live there when the Marines landed."[23]

In accordance with O. P. Smith's orders that outlined Craig's duties ashore on D-day—"If everything goes all right on Wolmi-Do during D-day, I would like you to go ashore on the [afternoon] tide and set up an advance CP. We will give you a dispatch to that effect sometime during the day of D-day. I would expect you to function at discretion. There may be decisions to be made which you can best make on the spot. If there is time and you feel the matter should be referred to division, do so."[24]

In a personal interview with the author, General Craig related that he was very proud of the fact that Smith gave him such latitude to "act as he saw fit," particularly since he did not get to talk with the division commander before the landing. Craig took it that Smith had high regard for his professional competence. Smith's hand-written letter reads:

Office of the Commanding General
First Marine Division
(Secret) 8 September 1950

Dear Eddie:

I am sending over this note by Lt.Col. Moore. I had already talked to [Col. Edward W.] Snedecker [brigade chief of staff] and Col. [Joseph L.] Stewart [brigade G-3] about the operation, but I believe it would be well to repeat my ideas about your participation.

If everything goes all right on Wolmi-Do during D-Day, I would like for you to go ashore on the evening tide and set up an advance CP. We will give you a dispatch to that effect some time during the day of D-ay. I would expect you to function at discretion. There may be decisions to be made which you can best make on the spot. If there is time and you feel that the matter should be referred to Division, do so. In any event, keep us advised. In this connection I am thinking primarily of Red Beach. I believe we will be better able to handle the situation at Blue Beach from the Mt McKinley [command ship].

Depending on the situation, it is my intention to land on Wolmi-Do on the evening tide of D+1. We do not want to clutter up the island with a lot of CP vans, etc. What we hope to do is soup up your communications and bring in a minimum of personnel. At the first opportunity, we will displace the CP beyond the city. At this time, we will move forward the rest of the personnel from the Mt. McKinley and personnel and equipment from the other ships. I appreciate the beating you are taking in coming out of action and mounting out. Only Marines could do what you are doing. We had a narrow squeak in getting you at all. We had 100% backing of the Navy in finally putting it across. Within a week after we land, the 7th Marines will be with us.

The Brigade has done a splendid job in South Korea and we are all proud of you. You have put the rest of us on the spot. I am confident we can all give a good accounting of ourselves, when the chips are down.

I regret that I could not get down to see you, but I could not work it in. I am looking forward to seeing you on Wolmi-Do.
Sincerely,
(Signed) Oliver P. Smith

Smoke hid Blue Beach. All that Craig could see was a line of amphibian tractors floundering through the mud flats. Several tractors were stuck belly deep in the muck. However, just in front, movement caught his attention. Five North Koreans leaped out of hiding, fled across the causeway linking Wolmi-Do with the city, and escaped despite a flurry of rifle-fire, much to the chagrin of several sharpshooters. Late in the afternoon, Craig's five-man command group set up his CP tent on a flat area close to the beach. They erected the tent over the hole that they had laboriously dug for his protection. Craig turned in—but almost immediately exited, exclaiming: "The damn thing stinks like shit!" Upon closer inspection, it turned out the diggers had excavated a North Korean crapper! Craig slept in the trailer that night, while the others chose a less odiferous location.[25]

The assault waves barely cleared Red Beach when the first of eight LSTs literally plowed into the seawall. The landing ships lived up to their nickname—"large slow targets"—when the North Koreans started shooting them up. Craig was incensed to see "sailors manning the bow gun—a 40mm automatic cannon—fire directly onto the beach and hit some of our Marines. They then traversed the gun around and fired directly across our front. It was one of the instances of wild firing that I saw during their landing—and it was promptly stopped by the Navy—but it did result in some of our men being injured." During the night, the landing force consolidated their lines and waited for the expected North Korean counterattack, which fortunately did not occur.[26]

Army–Marine Friction

By 7:30am on D+1, the 1st Marine Division was clear of Inchon and advancing toward Seoul, 20 miles away. Almond was already pressuring Smith to move quickly and seize the capital. "What Gen[eral] Almond tried to get me to agree to was that we capture Seoul by September 25. And, he explained frankly, that was exactly three months after the date that the North Koreans had invaded South Korea. They [MacArthur and Almond] wanted to be able to get out a communiqué saying that on September 15, three months later, they [North Koreans] had been thrown out." Smith was not happy with Almond's abbreviated time schedule and told him so. "I couldn't guarantee anything; that was up to the enemy. We'd do the best we could and go as fast as we could." Nevertheless, both Almond and MacArthur pushed for a quick resolution to the campaign. MacArthur believed the easy Inchon victory meant that Seoul would fall quickly. The Marines believed MacArthur's headquarters just wanted a public relations communiqué bolstering his reputation.[27]

Craig was well forward watching the Marine's progress, as was his style. "I had my driver, Corporal Adams, take me to a small knoll overlooking the road. Sniping was heavy and the Marines were having a stiff fight at a small pass. One of our tanks was knocked out, when suddenly the enemy gave up the fight and retreated." As he watched the action, a mud-wattle hut beside him caught fire and erupted in flames. The fire set off a large quantity of ammunition that the North Koreans had stored there. Craig jumped into a ditch. "Metal and debris were flying all around. Adams, however, was not going to lose his jeep, which he took great pride in. He dashed over to the vehicle as I yelled for him to take cover, he jumped in, started the motor, and drove it to safety."[28]

That afternoon, after returning from the front, Craig passed through a small village. The road narrowed, and Adams slowed the jeep to pass a group of Korean peasants. An old man reached out to give something to Craig. "Without thinking, I reached out to take it. It was an American hand grenade. I quickly squeezed it to make sure the handle was not up or the pin pulled. The pin was still in, and I heaved a sigh of relief. We stopped and the old man made gestures indicating he had found it by the road and was simply returning it. He was showing his goodwill and friendship for us."[29]

Crossing the Han River

Extracts from Craig's field notebook, September 19, 1950:

> 1st Marines and 5th Marines jumped off at 0700. Moderate resistance in 1st Marines zone of action. Five enemy tanks knocked out by our tanks and bazookas of the 5th Marines. Many enemy dead testify as to opposition. 5th Marines advanced to within two and a half miles of Kimpo Airfield. General MacArthur visited division CP … he spoke highly of the work of the 1st Marine Provisional Brigade. Conferred with Colonel Murray regarding plans to cross Han River.

Craig was concerned about crossing the Han River because, in essence, the crossing was a small amphibious operation. "I knew we were going faster than we had planned, and we were making every effort to get to the river as quick as we could. The eyes of the world were upon us. It would have looked bad for the Marines, of all people, to reach a river and not be able to cross." It was the responsibility of X Corps to supply the pontoon bridging, and Craig was assured by the corps engineer officer that everything was ready—pontoons, powerboats, and so forth. Unfortunately, the equipment was not ready, adding to the Marines' disillusionment with Almond's command. One of the reasons the Army was given the top job, rather than the Marines, was because they were supposed to be better at running a land campaign.[30]

Extracts from Craig's field notebook, September 19, 1950:

> The [X] Corps has made no definite long range plans for crossing—appears to be a planning breakdown. Some material available for bridging, but insufficient for complete bridge. Made a low level reconnaissance by helicopter of the Han River banks and proposed landing area. Crossing will take place commencing at 0400 tomorrow by 5th Marines, with 3rd Battalion in assault, followed by 2nd Battalion.

Craig had the division's engineer battalion break out their own equipment, which included pneumatic pontoon rafts and some bridging material. They constructed big rafts to ferry tanks and other critical material across, while the infantry crossed in amtracs and six-wheel-drive amphibious vehicles [DUKWs]. In the meantime, the Army sweated getting enough material to construct a bridge—flying it in from all over the far east—in time for MacArthur to enter the city.

Shortly after nightfall on September 20, Captain Kenneth J. Houghton led a team of 13 swimmers across the Han River. If they "found the other bank clear of the enemy they were to signal the rest of his reconnaissance company to follow in LVTs." Craig reported: "Attempt by Capt[ain] Houghton and his reconnaissance company during the night met with heavy resistance on far side of the Han River ... three LVTs abandoned."[31] Hours later, 3rd Battalion, 5th Marines crossed the river on LVTs against moderate resistance. Lieutenant Colonel Taplett recounted: "The 3/5's success opened the floodgates as the remainder of the Fifth Marines and supporting division troops poured across the river and the advance on Seoul continued."[32]

Craig had been checking the disposition of the 5th Marines and was on his way back to the division CP in his jeep when he came across four Marines "with some naked prisoners standing in the road. As we [driver and aide] drove up, small arms and machine gun fire started to fall around us from a house about fifty yards off the road to our left. We abandoned the jeep and dove for the cover afforded by a high bank and culvert under the road."[33]

"We were joined by the four Marines and prisoners. The enemy fire continued, and it was then that a Marine by the name of Gus Scafidi took three other Marines and attacked the house from the flank. It was a brave thing to do and I felt great pride in our men as I watched them from the cover of the road. Using grenades and rifles they finally charged the house and threw a grenade into the door ... wiping out the machine gun crew. Gus returned with his men and, with obvious pride, reported the gun knocked out."[34]

"In talking with him I learned that his detail had been in a truck going to the front with communication equipment when fired on originally by the three prisoners. Instead of stepping on the gas they had stopped, attacked, and captured the three snipers and then attacked the house."[35]

"I arrived back at the division CP late that evening with the three shivering naked prisoners on the hood of my jeep. [The prisoners were stripped to make sure they weren't carrying concealed weapons.] It had been a full day starting with the crossing of the Han River early that morning and ending with Gus and his attack on the house."[36]

Liberation of Seoul

After the division crossed the Han River, there was increasing pressure to capture Seoul. MacArthur asked Shepherd every morning: "Lem, when are your Marines going to capture Seoul?" O. P. Smith received the same pressure from Almond. "What General Almond tried to get me to do was to agree to capture Seoul by the September 25. And he explained frankly—that was exactly three months after the date that the North Koreans had invaded South Korea ... and I told him i couldn't guarantee anything, that was up to the enemy."[37]

The liberation of Seoul was, by far, larger than any previous single Marine combat objective. The city was a sprawling metropolitan area with a population of more than 2 million people, including thousands of terrified refugees. The city proper consisted of solidly constructed multifloored office buildings that often fronted wide boulevards. The broad avenues offered excellent fields of fire for the defenders, who threw up barricades every four hundred to six hundred yards. They piled dirt and rubble-filled rice bags eight feet high and six feet deep, reinforced with trolley cars, automobiles, and streetcar rails; anything to act as a barrier. They sowed mines around each barricade and supported them with machine guns and anti-tank weapons. The improvised strongpoints, stretching across the entire street, were centered on intersections for maximum effectiveness.

The makeshift barricades were almost impervious to machine gun and small arms fire. Their destruction took a coordinated effort by infantry, tanks, engineers, and supporting arms to destroy them. However, even successful attacks often left a trail of killed and wounded Marines. Rifle companies in both regiments melted away. In the close-quarter door-to-door fighting, it was shoot first, ask questions later. Private First Class Morgan Brainard described the stress: "The tension from these little forays whittled us pretty keen. I think if one's own mother had suddenly leapt out in front of us she would have been cut down immediately." Captain Robert H. Barrow's company quickly found another use for their new rocket launchers: "We employed it in a very effective manner in Seoul. In many instances [our] 3.5 [gunners] simply shot at some of those fragile houses, killing all the occupants." The civilian population was caught in the crossfire; Seoul became a killing ground. It would not "be captured without great difficulty" as MacArthur told Shepherd.[38]

"General Smith was responsible for making the plan for the capture of Seoul insofar as the 1st Marine Division was concerned" Craig pointed out. The 1st Marines were to cross the Han in the Yongdungp'o area and join the 5th Marines north of the river, forming the division right, while the 7th Marines were to move up from Inchon and go into the line north of the 5th Marines, which then would form the center of a three-regiment line. The plan contemplated that the 1st Marine Division, without the help of other ground units, would capture the city. But that same day, General Almond introduced one change in the plan—he indicated that the ROK Marines and the ROK 17th Regiment were also to be committed to securing the city.[39]

MacArthur wanted the city wrapped up by September 25, three months to the day that North Korea had launched its assault. "It was a meaningless goal. It's easy to pass along pointless orders, except if you're the one who has to carry them out," Captain Barrow (later Commandant of the Marine Corps) angrily declared.[40]

"At about 2000 on the [night of the] 25th, we received a dispatch from X Corps, saying that air reconnaissance had reported large groups of enemies moving out of the city and that enemy resistance in Seoul had ceased," Craig related. "We were ordered to attack immediately, 'NOW.'" Smith was incredulous, as all his front-line units had been engaged all day and were expecting a counterattack. Craig was skeptical. "There was no doubt in our minds but that there was a strong enemy force still in front of us." Murray asserted that Taplett's battalion was engaged in a hard fight for a portion of Seoul, and nobody was withdrawing or retreating or doing anything else."[41]

Smith said: "ordering us to counterattack at night on two- or three-hour notice shook my confidence, which left us no time to make a reconnaissance." He called the X Corps chief of staff and complained. All he got for his trouble was "After all, General Almond dictated that order, and he wants it carried out." Craig, a superb tactician, felt the order violated every tenant in the book. "A night attack requires at least a day's notice, careful observations of the terrain ... and a thorough briefing of all small-unit commanders."[42]

Nevertheless, an order was an order, and the two regiments were ordered into the attack. The indomitable Private First Class Brainard groused: "We were all rousted out and mustered down on the darkened street by platoons. Scuttlebutt said we were going into the heart of Seoul in a surprise attack." Just as the order was relayed to Murray's 5th Marines, they were hit with a counterattack. Puller's 1st Marines delayed for a 15-minute artillery barrage and then requested a second—just in time to catch the North Koreans in a counterattack. Craig was elated. "This barrage caught them squarely. I believe the enemy had thought that after our first preparation, there would be no more ... and started his attack."[43]

All hell broke loose, when a reinforced battalion of the North Korean 25th Brigade hit 3/1's roadblock on Ma po Boulevard. First Lieutenant Ed Simmons, weapons company commander, heard the unmistakable sounds of tanks. Their first shot missed him by inches, but killed his radio operator, who had been standing at his side. The Marines opened up with everything they had: rifles, rocket launchers, mortars, machine guns, and artillery, including three battalions of 105mm howitzers. The area quickly turned into a nightmarish scene of exploding shells and glowing tracers set against a backdrop of burning buildings. The attack went on all night, ending shortly before dawn. However, one North Korean self-propelled gun remained in the fight and continued to fire at Simmons' command post. He grew tired of the threat, brought up a 75mm recoilless rifle, and "gave the gunner a project." In the grey half-light of dawn, the crew spotted the vehicle and scored a direct hit.[44]

In an interview with a correspondent from the *New York Times*, Almond allowed as how "Nothing could have been more fortunate than the tank-led enemy counterattacks. It gave us a greater opportunity to kill more enemy soldiers and destroy his tanks more easily than if we had had to take the city house by house." While the Marines of the 1st Marine Division were slugging it out in the nighttime battle, Almond sent a message to MacArthur, timing it to arrive just before midnight on the 25th. "Three months to the day after the North Koreans launched their surprise attack south of the 38th Parallel, the combat troops of X Corps recaptured the capital city of Seoul." Unfortunately, his message had little effect on the North Koreans. It took four more days of heavy combat—and 500 Marine casualties—before Seoul was finally liberated. Smith recalled that Almond's headquarters "never admitted that the fighting went on after that."[45]

Taplett's 3/5 won bragging rights by being the first unit to raise a flag over Government House. One of his companies spotted a large North Korean flag waving from a pole in front of the building. Several men ducked through a hole in the wall surrounding the burned-out building. The flag's halyards were snarled and wouldn't shake free, so three Marines stood on each other's shoulders, a la gymnastic act, and cut it down. They attached Old Glory to the shortened lines and with a shout, "Run her up," claimed victory over the 1st Marines.[46]

Liberation Ceremony

After three days of savage street by street, building by building, fighting, the Marines drove the North Koreans out of Seoul at a cost of more than 700 casualties.

> Three months to the day after [the] North Koreans launched their surprise attack south of the 38th Parallel, the combat troops of X Corps recaptured the capital city of Seoul ... The liberation of Seoul was accomplished by a coordinated attack of X Corps troops ... By 1400 hours [on] 25 September, the military defenses of Seoul were broken ... The enemy is fleeing the city in the northeast.[47]

At 10:00am on September 29, MacArthur's plane named SCAP (acronym for Supreme Commander, Allied Powers) landed at Kimpo Airfield. An impeccably dressed MacArthur and his wife stepped onto the runway and climbed into the lead sedan. Other lesser dignitaries found room in one of the other four sedans or scrambled for space in one of the four jeeps that comprised the convoy. Elaborate preparations had been made to ensure not only the safety of the celebrants, but also the proper decorum of the proceedings. The latter rationale may have been the reason why the Marines were not invited to the party.[48]

"The Marines were not represented in the ceremonies at the palace except General Smith, myself, Colonel Puller, my aide, and one or two other officers. You'd think that they'd have the decency to give some of the honor to the men who captured the place." The five Marines wore combat gear and one, Puller, had a hard time even getting in. An Army MP, complete with white gloves and white bootlaces, barred his battered jeep from entering a "sedan only" entrance. Puller solved the dilemma in short order by ordering his driver to "run him over."[49]

Extracts from Craig's field notebook, September 27, 1950:

> I observed attack on Seoul from the edge of the city. Many places burning ... heavy artillery fires and bombing ... much of the city ruined. Report from a POW indicates some American POWs shot and burned with gasoline ... these were Army prisoners captured by enemy in South Korea. Counterintelligence Corps ascertained that there are a number of POWs buried in grounds of Seoul's Muhok Girls High School.

The National Palace still smelled of smoke and charred wood. The observers could clearly hear the sounds of distant small arms fire and artillery explosions. Craig noted that "The fighting was still going on in some parts of the city, but publicity gave the idea that the city had been captured completely when, as a matter of fact, it had not ... we were still taking casualties."[50]

The interior of the Palace was ringed with "a detachment of Army military police wearing knife-pressed, tailor-made OD [olive drabs] with gleaming black airborne boots laced with white nylon parachute cords." Their snazzy appearance was in sharp contrast to the "out of sight" grungy Marines who were really providing security. Craig said, rather tongue in cheek, that "The MPs looked more or less out of place at that time." Smith commented dryly: "The Marines were a little caustic about it."[51]

Craig's aide, Jack Buch, recalled that the palace had glass ceiling panels that were weakened after all the shelling. Shards of glass were constantly fluttering down onto the concrete floor, making a tinkling noise as they hit. Buck kept his helmet on, just to be on the safe side. He watched as MacArthur escorted Syngman Rhee to a small podium in front of the 100 or so senior officer guests. MacArthur recited the Lord's Prayer and, after a short speech, turned to Rhee, saying: "Mr. President, I return your country to you."[52]

After the ceremony, Craig and Buck stopped at what had been one of Seoul's better hotels. "It was a classic nice place," Buck recalled, "except for the dead North Koreans littering the winding staircase." Ever the explorer, Buck cautiously made his way to the basement. In the dim light, he saw a sight that would have made even the hardest gunnery sergeant smile with joy—stack after stack of the finest booze money could buy, or in Buck's case, what he could "appropriate." As the duly appointed representative of the assistant division commander, he loaded several cases of the hoard into his jeep and rode off into the sunset. Later, after a dinner of barely edible C-rations, Smith, Craig, and several of the division staff sipped an excellent cabernet, out of canteen cups.[53]

CHAPTER 19

North to the Yalu

With the liberation of Seoul and the restoration of the South Korean government, the only mission that remained was the destruction of the North Korean Army. Battered remnants of that Army were desperately attempting to escape north across the 38th Parallel. MacArthur, basking in the glow of one of the most decisive operations in military history, was intent on crushing them. All he needed was approval to cross the boundary. On September 27 the JCS, in the name of the president, gave its consent, with the proviso that "At the time of such operations there has been no entry into North Korea by major Soviet or Chinese communist forces, no announcement of intended entry, nor a threat to counter our operations in North Korea." There was great concern at the highest levels of the U.S. Government that either of the two countries might enter the war. MacArthur shared no concerns.[1]

On October 1, MacArthur authorized the release of a broadcast calling for the surrender of the North Korean Army, who did not dignify it with a reply. However, two days later, the Chinese forwarded their intentions through a third-party intermediary. The Indian ambassador was told "If the Americans crossed the 38th Parallel, China would intervene." This message was immediately relayed to the State Department, but the secretary pooh-poohed it, because the Indian diplomat "was not a good reporter." Retired Admiral Kichisaburo Nomura, Japan's ambassador to the United States in 1941, said: "If you go north of the 38th Parallel, they'll come in. They'll have to do that now to save face, [to] live up to their own words." The 1st Cavalry Division crossed the 38th Parallel on October 9.[2]

MacArthur's complicated strategy was "OpnPlan 9–50," in which he assured the JCS that there was "no indication of Soviet or Chinese intervention," that assigned Walker's Eighth Army the task of seizing the North Korean capital, Pyongyang. Almond's X Corps was directed to make an amphibious landing at Wonsan on the east coast and drive due west, linking up with Walker, thereby trapping the North Koreans between them. The plan further stipulated that at some future date, both commands would attack north to a line approximately fifty to one hundred miles south of the Manchurian border. Smith thought the plan was "really unrealistic because the central mountain chain was swarming with these North Koreans who were making their way north to reorganize, and they had [all] their weapons with them."[3]

The senior leadership of the division not only lacked confidence in the plan, but also with the corps commander. Almond was seen as a vain, overly aggressive officer, who let his ambitions overrule his judgement. Smith saw him as "egotistical. He was a MacArthur man, and nothing could change it. MacArthur was God." Almond's aggressiveness would have serious consequences for X Corps in the drive north during the dead of a Korean winter. Smith was also very concerned "over the lack of realism in the plans for the corps and the tendency of the corps to ignore the enemy capabilities when a rapid advance was desired. I found in my dealings with the Army, particularly with X Corps, that the mood was either one of extreme optimism or of extreme pessimism. There did not seem to be any middle ground."[4]

Wonsan and the Drive North

Extracts from Craig's field notebook, September 30, 1950:

> Received a new plan for embarking the 1st Marine Division as part of X Corps for an amphibious landing on East coast of Korea [at Wonsan]. Time and space factors given appear short for proper preparation, and the question of getting our tanks and heavy equipment back across the Han River is critical. Also, execution of the plan will depend on whether the United Nations and our State Department will give the go signal on crossing the 38th Parallel.

Authorization: 30 September 1950
Personal From: Joint Chiefs of Staff
Personal For: General of the Army Douglas MacArthur

Secretary of Defense Sends
Reference present report of supposed announcement by Eighth Army that ROK Divisions would halt on 38th Parallel for regrouping: We want you to feel unhampered tactically and strategically to proceed north of 38th Parallel. Announcement above referred to may precipitate embarrassment in UN where evident desire is not to be confronted with necessity of a vote on passage of 38th Parallel, rather to find you have found it militarily necessary to do so.
Signed G.C. Marshall

On October 7, 1950, patrols from the 1st Cavalry Division crossed the 38th Parallel, followed two days later by the rest of the division, which started fighting its way north. The 1st Marine Division was ordered to make an amphibious landing at Wonsan on the east coast. "It was my opinion at the time that the reason we were doing this [landing] was because Almond wanted to make another amphibious landing come hell or high water."[5]

"We moved rapidly back to Inchon, holding ceremonies at the cemetery on the way back for those who had been killed in action," Craig recounted. "One of the incidents at this cemetery was the fact that the UN flag was raised, and that was all, until we complained. We demanded that an American flag be raised, which was done."[6]

"Received information that D-day will be postponed due to a large number of mines off Wonsan," Craig noted. And again, the next day, "landing postponed another 24 hours due to possibility of mines broken loose from moorings by rough seas and floating in swept channels...."[7]

Extracts from Craig's field notebook, October 19–21, 1950:

D-day postponed due to large number of mines off Wonsan. Two minesweepers lost so far trying to clear lane for transports. Word received that an administrative landing would be made due to Wonsan being in hands of ROK Army. Received word over Voice of America Radio that I had been selected for promotion to major general. Landing postponed 24 hours ... and another 24 hours ... and another 24 hours ... landing now scheduled for 25 September.

The amphibious assault was quickly termed Operation *Yo-Yo*, as the invasion fleet steamed back and forth for five days while the Navy cleared the estimated 2,000 mines in the harbor and sea approaches. As already mentioned, in the process of clearing the mines, the Navy lost two minesweepers, USS *Pledge* (AM-277) and USS *Pirate* (AM-275).

While the sweeping was going on, South Korean troops captured the city after a hard-fought battle. In addition, MAG-33 flew in and occupied the airfield. To add insult to injury, Bob Hope waited for the Marines on the beach, much to their chagrin. Finally, on October 25, the division began an administrative landing. "It was quite a letdown," Craig recalled.[8]

"The Allied drive north was going so well; there was almost an end to the war atmosphere," Craig said. The *Stars and Stripes*, an Army-air force newspaper, quoted MacArthur as saying: "This war is definitely coming to an end shortly." Signs appeared throughout the area, saying "Drive carefully—the Marine you hit might be your relief." In fact, the division received a directive stating that when the war was over, the entire outfit, minus one regiment, would immediately return to the States. However, in the meantime, there were still armed North Korean troops in the area. "Shortly after our arrival," Craig related, "there were guerrilla activities to the south and west of us and it was necessary to send a battalion of the 1st Marines to Kojo and Majon-ni."[9]

Extracts from Craig's field notebook, October 27–31, 1950:

> 1st Battalion, 1st Marines at Kojo under attack by estimated 1,500 North Koreans resulting in 67 casualties and one platoon cut off ... investigated 1st Marines situation. It appeared to me that the 1st Battalion took up poor tactical positions—too spread out without depth. General Almond at CP for conference [said] there is some evidence that Chinese Army units have crossed the Yalu River into Korea. Sixteen Chinese communist troops from 124th Division have been captured.

The entire division bivouacked among the low-lying hills and rice paddies west of Wonsan. There were a few buildings for the command posts, but most of the men lived in tents scattered over a distance of ten to 12 miles. On November 1, the division received orders to send a regiment "to relieve a South Korean unit in contact with enemy troops on the road leading to the Chosin Reservoir." The South Koreans were fighting hard but were forced to give up ground. There were rumors their attackers were Chinese "volunteers." The 7th Marines were given the mission of relieving the South Koreans and immediately proceeded by truck and train to Hamhung. Before leaving, however, the regimental commander, Colonel Homer L. Litzenberg, talked to his officers and NCOs. "We can expect to meet Chinese communist troops, and it is important that we win this first battle."[10]

Lieutenant Colonel Raymond G. Davis' 1st Battalion, 7th Marines was in the regiment's vanguard and caught up with the South Korean soldiers just south of Sudong. His mission was to secure the Changjin Power Plant above Chinhung-ni. During his jeep reconnaissance, Davis' Korean Army interpreter talked with several villagers, who reported that Chinese soldiers were in the area. Davis returned to his battalion perimeter. Sometime after midnight, he was awoken by "God-awful sounds of bugles and shepherd's horns and whistles." An illumination round outlined enemy soldiers heading toward his position. Several were killed and one taken prisoner, who was interrogated and confirmed the attackers were members of the 124th Division of the Chinese Communist Forces (CCF).[11]

The Chinese continued to attack. At dawn an enemy force approached along the railroad track toward a tunnel. Davis described the resultant action as a "real turkey shoot." "They were near where we had set up our six heavy water-cooled machine guns. Not one of the Chinese made it. The final count was 600 dead!"[12]

Another group slipped past Davis' right flank and hit Major Webb Sawyer's 2nd Battalion, setting in motion an ugly brawl for possession of the high ground, which lasted all the next day. By the afternoon of November 3, the only Chinese in the regimental area were dead—but at a high cost. More than 200 Marine battle casualties were evacuated. Smith remarked: "Litzenberg went on up the road and had quite a fight. He had 43 killed and a couple of hundred wounded, but they absolutely decimated the 124th CCF Division." The 7th Marines had won their first battle with the Chinese.[13]

"The first prisoners—Chinese prisoners—captured by the 7th Marines were within 18 miles of Hungnam, and it was a definite Chinese division, the 124th," Craig declared. "There was no doubt in the minds of the Marines that there was an organized group of Chinese troops to our front. If higher headquarters did not realize there was a Chinese buildup in this area, I do not know why."[14] "We kept sending back reports to X Corps that they [7th Marines] were running into Chinese. Willoughby [MacArthur's intelligence chief, G-2] just insisted that there were no Chinese and MacArthur agreed with him, I suppose, because they didn't seem to be concerned."[15]

Martin Ross, in his book *Breakout: The Chosin Reservoir Campaign*, wrote that Almond did not even mention Sudong in his command diary. Willoughby announced on November 3 that there were only 16,500 to 34,000 Chinese "volunteers" in the country. Captain Donald France, the 7th Marines intelligence officer, told Almond: "General, there's a shitload of Chinamen in those mountains."[16]

Extracts from Craig's field notebook, November 3–10, 1950:

> 7th Marines unable to advance toward reservoir due to Chinese communist troops roadblocks ... a little over 100 casualties in 48 hours. Near Hungnam I saw some 250 dead civilians lying in rows. They had been shot by the communists prior to retreating. All [the dead] were political prisoners. The regiment [now] making good progress against a regiment of CCF troops. We have had 45 killed and 200 wounded in past 48 hours. Very cold! The line of communications for this regiment is fast becoming critical due to distance and enemy situation. Due to [X] Corps orders requiring a large dispersion of the three infantry regiments, the division is not at present in a favorable position for combat as a unit. The road to the Chosin Reservoir very steep and narrow, over 4,000-foot mountains with sheer cliffs ... only a few places where vehicles can pass.

Extracts from Craig's field notebook, November 15–19, 1950:

> It is exceedingly cold and men are having a tough time ... mountains and roads [are icy] in the area, covered with snow and it was 11 degrees below zero.

Out on a Limb

On November 15, Almond ordered the 1st Marine Division to attack north to Yudam-ni then west to assist the Eighth Army in its drive to the Yalu. He envisioned that the Army's 7th Infantry Division would cover the division's right flank. On that day, the 1st Marine Division was spread out from "hell to breakfast." Litzenberg's 7th Marines had just reached the medium-sized town of Hagaru-ri at the base of the Chosin Reservoir; Murray's 5th Marines were spread along the coast from Koto-ri to Majon-dong, a distance of 20 miles as the crow flies; and Puller's 1st Marines were still 50 miles to the rear.

As Craig recalled, "Before he left our command post, General Almond stressed the need for speed. We had reached Hagaru at the south end of the reservoir, and now he wanted Litzenberg to head northwest to Yudam-ni, 14 miles away, while Murray was to take the 5th Marines up the east shore. 'We've got to go barreling up that road.' General Smith's involuntary response was 'NO!' However, Almond pretended not to hear it. After he departed, General Smith said 'We're not going anywhere until I get this division together and the airfield built.'" Smith admitted that "What I was trying to do was slow down the advance and stall until I could pull ... our outfit together." He was so alarmed that he wrote a letter, out of channels, to the commandant, stating: "I believe a winter campaign in the mountains of North Korea is too much to ask of the American soldier or Marine, and I doubt the feasibility of supplying troops in this area during winter ..." General Matthew B. Ridgway, who took over the Eighth Army, had high praise for Smith's protective tactics: "As it turned out, these textbook precautions were all that enabled this magnificent fighting force to battle its way out of the entrapment in one of the most successful retrograde movements in American military history."[17]

Craig was not happy about Almond's orders to move north. "I was very jittery about the situation up there. There was a great concern in the mind of General Smith and myself and various other officers concerning the dispersal of the division, one regiment in the Wonsan area, one on the road to the reservoir, and the 5th Marines being split at one time into three parts in various sectors around Hamhung. General Smith was much concerned what might happen if we did run into heavy organized resistance. It was for this reason that he exerted every means at his disposal to concentrate the regiments and bring them together on the march to the reservoir."[18]

The 5th Marine Regiment's Historical Diary notes for November 23, 1950:

> Thanksgiving services were held at H & S Company, 1st and 2nd Battalion areas. The Thanksgiving dinner of turkey, cranberry sauce, shrimp cocktail, vegetables, dressing, fresh potatoes, pumpkin and mince pies, coffee, fruitcake, candies, nuts, oranges, apples, and other items were served to the 1st and 2nd Battalions and H & S Company and attached units.[19]

On November 26, Craig received an upsetting Red Cross message: "Father not expected to live ..." General Smith sent a "dispatch to General Shepherd at Pearl Harbor and said unless I [Smith] receive an answer within 12 hours I am going to grant Craig leave to go home." Both officers were acutely aware that Craig was very close to his father, a well-known retired Army doctor. They were also aware that in World War II, Craig's corps commander had refused him leave to attend his dying wife. Smith, hearing nothing, granted his assistant 10 days' emergency leave, starting on the 27th. "Eddie Craig was a very fine person," Smith declared, "I was very fond of him."[20]

The flight to San Antonio took five days, and during that time, Craig was out of touch and did not learn about the Chinese intervention. "It was a great shock to me when I did see them [newspaper headlines], 'Eighth Army in Retreat; Marine[s] Still Trapped' ... The newspapers unanimously predicted the destruction of the 1st Marine Division." The commandant called Craig and ordered him back to Korea immediately. Smith thought that "Almond or somebody else in the Army chain of command wired the commandant to complain about only one general officer in the division." Craig left the States on December 7—his father passed away two days later—and reported back to the division on December 11, too late to participate in the withdrawal. To his dying day, Craig deeply regretted being absent during the division's fight from the Chosin Reservoir.[21]

The 5th Marine Regiment's diary for November 27 noted:

> The MSR [Main Supply Route] from Hagaru-re to Yudam-ni was frozen but passable. The grade and sharp curves made it very dangerous. Control points were required because it was usable only to one-way traffic in many places. Because of the extreme cold and bad road conditions ten trucks were rendered temporarily unserviceable. The weather was bitter cold.[22]

Attack of General Winter

"Before we went up the mountain on our Marine Corps birthday, November 10, it was quiet enough for me to go swimming in the nearby stream—even though the water was a trifle cold for a guy from Atlanta." Ten days later the temperatures dropped below zero. "On our second or third day up on the plateau, the Siberian winds attack, lowering the temperatures suddenly to 16 degrees below zero. Vehicles died, everything froze, troops were frostbitten."[23]

The diary for the 5th Marine Regiment noted:

> 28 November 1950
> The MSR from Hagaru-ri to Yudam-ni was severed by enemy action during the night.
>
> The regimental aid station moved to join the 7th Marines aid station in a relatively less exposed position. Evacuation of patients was impossible except that a few of the most seriously wounded were taken out by helicopter. Shortly after noon, patients began to come in by the truckload and the medical sections were rapidly swamped. The tents and courtyard of the aid station area were filled. Patients eventually filled the twenty-two tents, four civilian houses and the remainder were put in straw and covered with a large tarpaulin. It was estimated that nearly 500 were being held by midnight. About dark, battalion aid stations began holding patients instead of evacuating them to the regimental aid stations ... 74 bullet holes were counted in the 5th Marines aid station tent after the previous night's action. Personnel report for the period 6pm 28 November: 16 killed in action, 136 wounded in action, two missing in action, 91 non-battle casualties, eight returned to duty, four prisoners taken.[24]
>
> CO 5th Marines Date/Time/Group
> To: 1/5; 2/5; 3/5; 1/11; H&S Co.; 4.2 Motor Co.
> All hands make sure that every shot counts.
>
> By 28 November it was known that the enemy had cut the MSR between Hagaru-ri and Yudam-ni. The commanding officers of the 5th and 7th Marines in joint operations consolidated positions at Yudan-ni. The 2nd Battalion, 5th Marines was withdrawn from its advance position and other subordinate unit positions adjusted to form a perimeter around Yudam-ni.
>
> The night of 28–29 November was free of any strong enemy attacks. However, on the 29th, the 3rd Battalion and 1st Battalion were pressed continuously

throughout the day. "I" Company repulsed three strong enemy attacks. Air strikes by Marine aircraft aided materially in breaking up these attacks.[25]

VMF-212 diary notes:

29 November 1950
Approximately six inches of snow fell during the night which delayed operations until 0850. Thirty-four Close Air Support and two reconnaissance sorties were flown in support of X Corps.[26]

On that day, VMF-312 flew "A total of 31 sorties and 75.7 hours [...] All 31 flights were sent to the Hagaru-ri area. On the first flight in the morning ... ridges containing a heavy concentration of communist troops were hit and all armament expended. Very little reconnaissance work was done as all of the planes were needed to fend off the communist attack with close air support."[27] The next day:

30 November 1950
Snow still covered the runway [at Yonpo] except a narrow strip down the center which had been blown clean by the previous day's operations. Forty-six close air support sorties represented the day's efforts in support of the X Corps element in contact around the Chosin Reservoir. A total of 31 sorties and 824 hours were flown.[28]

The 5th Marine Regiment's historical diary records:

30 November 1950
During the night 29/30 November minor enemy action was encountered in vicinity of Yudam-ni. On 30 November, 5th Marines subordinate units moved to new positions replacing elements of the 7th Marines. The two regiments received orders from division to expedite return by way of the MSR to Hagaru-ri. Enemy occupies positions to NW, NE, and SW of present 6th and 7th Marines. Capable of cutting MSR and from any direction. 5th and 7th on 30 Nov[ember] and 1 Dec[ember] adjust positions to protect Yudam-ni and conduct operation to clear MSR to Hagaru-ri.[29]

December 1, 1950
Orders issued to segregate litter patients from those able to walk in preparation for the trip to Hagaru-ri.[30]

The division brought out all the dead, according to General Smith. "We flew out 130 bodies from Hagaru-ri. We didn't want to bury them in that God-forsaken place ... the Corps [X Corps] wanted us to quit [but] we just stalled them. We sent them [the dead] all out. Then when we got to Koto-ri we had a very limited [air] strip; we couldn't fly out the dead, so we buried 113 there." The North Koreans recovered these remains and turned them over at Panmunjom.[31]

2 December 1950
A company-sized task force of Army troops from Hagaru-ri, supported by tanks, moved out [on the 2nd] to bring in any organized units of three shattered battalions which might have been left behind. Known as Task Force Anderson after Lieutenant Colonel Berry K. Anderson, senior Army officer at Hagaru-ri, the column met heavy CCF opposition and was recalled when it became evident that only stragglers remained. [Lieutenant Colonel] Beall and his men kept up their rescue work until the last of an estimated 1,050 survivors of the original 2,500 troops had been saved. A Marine reconnaissance patrol counted more than 300 dead in the abandoned trucks of the Task Force Faith convoy, and there were apparently hundreds of MIA. The 385 able-bodied soldiers who reached Hagaru-ri were organized into a provisional battalion and provided with Marine equipment.[32]

3 December 1950
Approximately 100 additional casualties were loaded on passing vehicles near the top of the pass between Yudam-ni and Hagaru-ri while many walking wounded accompanied the column. Most of these casualties came from F/7 which had been isolated ... for several days. Others had become casualties during the attack to capture Toktong Pass and from snipers along the way. Approximately 900 casualties were brought out in the convoy. Subsequently, about 80 percent of all casualties were found to have frostbite.[33]

4 December 1950
The column was halted several times by defended roadblocks that were cleared. The battalion continued to move until 1530 at which time B and C Companies were set in position to cover the withdrawal of division elements. H&S Company, supply train and Weapons Company proceeded on to Hagaru-ri, arriving there at 2100.

At 2pm on December 4 the last elements of the rear guard, 3/7, entered the perimeter and the four-day operation passed into history. Some 1,500 casualties were brought to Hagaru-ri, a third of them being non-battle category, chiefly frostbite cases. It had taken the head of the column about 59 hours to cover the 14 miles, and the rear units 79 hours.[34]

5 December 1950

Litter patients continued to be evacuated by air during the day. A "screening" line was set up for walking patients to determine the seriousness of their wounds or illnesses and only those considered not able to make the remainder of the move were given air evacuation. Total evacuation for the day by all units was 1,300.[35]

6 December 1950

1st Battalion [7th Marine Regiment]—to move out at 0430 to clear the ground to the right of the river;

2nd Battalion [7th Marine Regiment]—supported by tanks, to attack as advance guard along the MSR;

Provisional Battalion (31/7)—to clear the ground to the left of the MSR.

3rd Battalion [7th Marine Regiment]—to bring up the rear of the regimental train, with George Company disposed along both flanks as security for the vehicles.[36]

The weather was bitterly cold as the convoy moved out and the 5th Marines fought a heavily contested rear-guard action all night to protect the rear of the division train.[37]

The Marines fought their way through several roadblocks until the column reached the Funchilin Pass where the Chinese had blown a critical bridge that left a 24-foot gap in the road. "At this point water from the Chosin Reservoir was discharged from a tunnel into large steel pipes, which descended sharply down the mountainside to the turbines of the power plant in the valley below. The bridge covered the pipes, creating a roadway. There was no possibility of a bypass because of the cliff on one side and a sheer drop on the other. If the gap was not covered, the division would have [had] to abandon all its rolling stock, including tanks and artillery."[38]

General Smith had foreseen the destruction of the bridge and talked with Craig about it. "Smith was sure that they [the Chinese] wanted us to come across, and that they were going to blow the bridge after we crossed, thus completely isolating us. It was shrewd of Smith to understand that." During a visit by Almond, Smith mentioned his concern about the bridge. Craig said that Almond "seemed to have little respect for the Chinese as fighting men, it was as if he didn't care."[39]

The division engineer, Lieutenant Colonel John H. Partridge, proposed a solution to Smith. "He was kind of a grouchy guy," Smith said after questioning the solution. "I could see that he was mad at the time by my questioning. He told me: 'I got you across the Han River, I got you the airfield [Hagaru], and I'll get you a bridge!'" Smith responded with "Okay, we'll take that."

Partridge had the USAF air drop eight sections (2,500 pounds each) of a Treadway bridge and winched four of them across the gap with specialized trucks. The bridge was completed in three-and-a-half hours, just as the head of the convoy reached it.[40]

> December 9, 1950
> On this date the 1st Marine Division was poised on the top of the plateau in preparation for the hazardous trek down through the Sudong Gorge. As the first echelon of Marines started down the hill, flights of four planes hit communist troops on either side of the canyon.[41]

Evacuation

The 1st Marine Division received word that they would be evacuated, rather than defend Hungnam. The Marines were not happy. They were prepared to defend the port city. Shepherd, on orders from the Chief of Naval Operations, "on the recommendation of Admiral Joy, I was charged specifically to supervise the evacuation of naval forces (Marines) from Hungnam. With the situation as it was, Admiral Joy did not want another Dunkirk." In Shepherd's opinion, "The 1st Marine Division and the rest of X Corps could hold on to the port and airfield indefinitely." Puller was more pithy: "Why the hell they withdrew, I'll never know ... Not all the Chinese in hell could have run over us."[42]

> December 11, 1950
> When the train arrived at Hamhung, troops were disembarked, placed aboard Army trucks for movement to the regimental bivouac area. Yonpo Airfield. All personnel were billeted in the bivouac area ... with tents, stoves, galleys with hot food, water, and a security guard. The remainder of the day and the morning of the following day [the] personnel spent the time resting, reading mail, and making preparations for going aboard ship.[43]

> The Hungnam evacuation plan, as outlined in X Corps OpnO 10-50, issued on December 11, provided for the immediate embarkation of the 1st Marine Division and the 3rd ROK Division. A smaller perimeter than the original concept

was to be defended meanwhile by the 7th and 3rd Infantry Divisions, with the latter having the final responsibility. Major units were to withdraw gradually by side-slipping until only reinforced platoons remained as covering forces holding strong points. Plans called for naval gunfire and air support to be stepped up as the perimeter contracted.[44]

"Thousands and thousands of Koreans were endeavoring to board the ships at Hungnam and be evacuated before the arrival of the communists," Craig related. "It is difficult for me to look these poor refugees in the eye. I was ashamed that we were leaving them behind." In a massive effort, the Navy evacuated more than 91,000 refugees, 105,000 military, 17,500 vehicles, and thousands of tons of cargo.[45]

MacArthur made periodic reports to the United Nations. In report number 11, he gave an account of the Chosin Reservoir operation: "In this epic action the Marine Division and attached elements of the 7th Infantry Division marched and fought over 60 miles in bitter cold along a narrow, tortuous, ice-covered road, against opposition from six to eight Chinese Communist Force Divisions, which suffered staggering losses." Smith was complimentary to MacArthur but could not say the same for Almond's leadership of X Corps. He was too much of a gentleman to publicly disparage his boss, but that did not hold true of Puller. A *Time* magazine reporter asked Puller, "What is the most important lesson that the Marines have learned in Korea so far?" Puller did not blink an eye: "Never serve under X Corps!"[46]

Epilogue

"The period after the pull-out from the Chosin Reservoir was one of let down for most of us," Craig explained.

"Not that we were idle, we were very busy in fact. I had the feeling that we had been let down by those in Washington, and in turn that we had let down the Koreans. Thousands and thousands of Koreans were endeavoring to board the ships at Hungnam and be evacuated before the arrival of the communists. Thousands were eventually evacuated but many were also left. It became difficult for me to look these poor refugees in the eye. I had seen the hope and happiness in these same people when the United Nations forces liberated them in South Korea and in Seoul. Now they looked at me with wonder in their eyes that so powerful a force as we had landed was pulling out and leaving them. Many of them looked at us with contempt for not continuing the fight."

"I was ashamed in my own mind too. I felt that if those in Washington wanted to win the Korean War that sufficient troops could have been sent out to win. Our Marines and soldiers thought they were fighting in Korea to win a war, suffering untold hardships because they were fighting for what they thought was a principle—our way of life against communism. I felt that my men had been led down. I was even more certain of that when I later arrived in Washington, D.C. for duty."

"From Hungnam I flew to Pusan, and then by jeep to Masan, where I made arrangements for the arrival and re-equipping of the division. In the Pusan-Masan area I had again to face the uncomprehending stares of the Koreans. They could not believe that the Marines had pulled out from the north. I was ashamed to look them in the eye. It had been just a few months previously that my 1st Provisional Marine Brigade had fought so gallantly in this same area and driven the communists north. Now we were back in the same campsite from which we started, only this time it was a reinforced Marine division."

"My first night at Masan was spent in an old Japanese officers' quarters; there were no windows, no furniture and no heat. It was in the middle of a cold winter and as we sat around a candle which furnished the only light, my aide, Captain John Buck, suggested that he go down to the town and see if he could find a hibachi to warm the place a little. When he returned, we spent two hours trying to get it started and warmed up. Finally, we gave up. The air was too cold. We ate our cold 'C' rations, spread our sleeping bags, and shivered through the night."

"We did not have much time to get reorganized and re-equipped before we received orders to proceed north to Pohang to operate against a communist division that had infiltrated into several towns."

"It was during this time [January 24, 1951] that I was promoted to major general and ordered back to the United States. After a short leave, I reported to Headquarters Marine Corps for duty as the Director,

Marine Corps Reserve. Little did I realize that this would be my last duty station."

"I was given three days to work into the job before I was ordered to be on a selection board for reserve colonels for over a month, which gave me little time for my primary duty. On top of that, I was ordered to the Manpower Board at the Pentagon. A woman from the Defense Department headed the board. I was surprised and angered when I saw her deliberately stop a Navy captain, who was delivering a briefing on personnel, and tell him to go back and redo the brief, [that] it was not satisfactory." "It was soon apparent to me that the Korean War was not an important subject in Washington, and from talking to some who I knew, I found that it was intended to end the war in a stalemate."

"President Truman summarily relieved General MacArthur. This act embittered me toward the administration. I could see there was no chance of uniting Korea under the policies then in effect. I also felt that my experience in Korea should be used to better advantage than as Director of the Reserve. I had whole notebooks filled with recommendations on various vital matters affecting equipment and tactics, etc. No one at headquarters seemed to be interested in these, and my only outlet was a few minutes of recorded questions from a public information officer, which was written up and filed away."

"A general's conference was held at headquarters each Friday morning. At the first one I attended, I had expected that some time would be devoted to the Korean War, and what the 1st Marine Division was doing. Instead, it was a shock to see eight young women Marines in new style uniforms march into the conference room. At great length a discussion was then held as to what changes should be made."

"After this important matter was attended to, a discussion was held as to whether Marines from Quantico should be required to wear the old style battle jackets on liberty ... It was then that the G-2 and G-3 Sections brought in a big map of the Korean area and announced they were ready to give a briefing on the situation in Korea. I was delighted to think that I would get the latest dope from Korea. Instead, the senior general announced, after looking at his watch, that it was time for lunch and that the briefing on Korea would be delayed until the following Friday."

"This really shook me. I got to my feet and walked out of the room in disgust. I could not believe that such indifference could be real. I felt that justice was not being done to the men in Korea, and that I did not want to be part of the Washington scene. I was probably a little quick on the trigger after what I had gone through in Korea, but when I arrived home that night I told my wife that I was going to turn my suit in. The next day I sent in my written request for retirement to take effect on June 1, 1951."

"The Commandant had been absent from Washington on leave and when he arrived back he called me into his office and advised me against retirement. Later the Secretary of the Navy had me in on the day I was to retire and told me that if I would withdraw my request that he would personally see that the whole matter was stopped. However, I was determined to go through with it and told him that my mind was made up. Accordingly, I was retired as requested ... I had no one to blame but myself."

"My wife and I went to Mexico and it was a couple of weeks later while there that I started to regret my hasty action, and I have regretted it to this day. I had no gripes against the Marine Corps itself. I will always love the corps. It was just the Washington set-up at the time, and I felt that I did not want to be a part of it, too many men were dying and being wounded trying to win a war they couldn't possibly win under the administration. It was not the Marine Corps' fault; it was the fault of those in power in our government at the time. The generals' conference I alluded to was just a circumstance in the big picture which triggered my request after 34 years of service."[47]

Eddie Craig lived a full, active life, maintaining a vigorous correspondence with old friends and comrades. He was often cited as reference for official Marine Corps publications about World War II and Korea. He passed away on December 11, 1994—at the age of 98. Jack Buck, his former aide, took him to lunch on the last day of his life. Upon returning to his home in El Cajon, California, Craig went to his room and sat on the bed. Buck followed. Craig turned to him and said, "I think the end is near. I'm just waiting for the bugler to sound Taps."

His wife, Marion Mackle Craig. passed away two years later. They are buried at Fort Rosecrans National Cemetery.[48]

Awards and Decorations

Lieutenant General Craig's personal decorations include:
  Navy Cross
  Navy Distinguished Service Medal
  Silver Sat Medal
  Legion of Merit with Gold Star
  Bronze Star with "V" Device
  Air Medal with Service Star
  U.S. Navy Presidential Unit Citation with three stars
  Navy Unit Commendation
In addition, his decorations and medals also include the Presidential Unit Citation; Navy Unit Citation; two Korean Presidential Unit Citations; Victory Medal; Haitian Campaign Medal, 1919; Marine Corps Expeditionary Medal with one Bronze Star, Dominican Republic 1919–21; China 1924; Second Nicaraguan Campaign Medal, 1929–30; American Defense Service Medal with Fleet Clasp; American Campaign Medal; Asiatic-Campaign Medal; Asiatic-Pacific Campaign Medal with four Bronze Stars; World War II Victory Medal; China Service Medal, 1947; Navy Occupation Medal, Japan 1946; and the Korean Campaign Medal.

Navy Cross Citation

The President of the United States of America takes pleasure in presenting the Navy Cross to Colonel Edward A. Craig (MCSN: 0-196),

United States Marine Corps, for extraordinary heroism as Commanding Officer of the Ninth Marines, THIRD Marine Division, during action against enemy Japanese forces on Guam, Marianas Islands, from 21 July to 10 August 1944. An aggressive and inspiring leader, Colonel Craig constantly directed his men in combat in the face of intense enemy fire from the time of landing with the assault elements of his regiment until organized resistance ceased. On 30 July, charged with capturing a portion of high ground on the force beachhead line and making contact with the Army on Mount Tenjo, Colonel Craig remained with his leading assault elements during the entire advance and, by his coolness under fire, provided inspiration for his officers and men. Personally directing the final assault on Mount Chachao, he kept casualties at a minimum by his expert judgment. When one of his battalions encountered heavy enemy resistance near an important road junction during the advance to the northern end of Guam on 3 August, he took a position beside a tank advancing with the assault troops and, despite a constant stream of rifle and machine-gun fire, fearlessly remained there throughout the entire action of several hours to direct the attack which annihilated several hundred of the enemy. His outstanding ability, courageous leadership and devotion to duty were important factors in the success of the campaign and reflect the highest credit upon Colonel Craig and the United States Naval Service.

Legion of Merit Citation

The President of the United States of America takes pleasure in presenting the Legion of Merit with Combat "V" to Colonel Edward A. Craig (MCSN: 0-196), United States Marine Corps, for exceptionally meritorious conduct in the performance of outstanding services to the Government of the United States while serving as Assistant Chief of Staff, G-3 with a landing force during the operations against the enemy on Iwo Jima, Volcano Islands, from 19 February to 20 March 1945. During the planning phase, beginning on 13 October 1944, Colonel Craig was charged with the responsibility of formulating and preparing the detailed plans for the operation, and exhibited great professional skill in the performance of that difficult task. From D-Day until the island was secured he had charge of operation orders for the entire landing force, and displayed technical ability and resourcefulness of a very high degree. He frequently visited units in contact with the enemy in order to determine by personal observation the progress of the battle, and by his exemplary conduct contributed immeasurably to the success of the operation. His outstanding enterprise, initiative, sound judgment and inspiring devotion to duty at all times were in keeping with the highest traditions of the United States Naval Service.

Navy Distinguished Service Medal Citation

The President of the United States of America takes pleasure in presenting the Navy Distinguished Service Medal to Brigadier General Edward A. Craig (MCSN: 0-196), United States Marine Corps, for exceptionally meritorious service to the Government of the United States in a duty of great responsibility as Commanding General of the First Provisional Marine Brigade (Reinforced) during action against enemy aggressor forces in the Korean Area, from 7 July 1950 to 13 September 1950; and as Assistant Division Commander of the FIRST Marine Division (Reinforced) from 14 September to 31 December 1950. As Brigade Commander, Brigadier General Craig displayed outstanding ability in preparing the Brigade for combat and in supervising its rapid embarkation and movement overseas and assembly in the combat area. He led the Brigade in a series of effective actions within the Pusan bridgehead in South Korea, including two decisive attacks wherein his forces routed the enemy in the Chinju Area and the heroic action in which his forces attacked and destroyed numerically superior enemy forces holding a bridgehead east of the Naktong River, driving the remnants of the enemy force from key positions within our perimeter. As Assistant Division Commander, he rendered invaluable assistance to the Division Commander during the planning and execution of an amphibious landing by the Division against strongly defended Inchon and during the inland advance and seizure of Kimpo Airfield and Yongdungp'o. Brigadier General Craig further assisted in supervising and coordinating the crossing of the Han River against stubborn enemy opposition, and the subsequent defeat of hostile forces in Seoul, Korea. He continued to render invaluable assistance during operations of widely separated Division Units, directing the administrative support of forward elements of the Division that were isolated from their source of supplies. Upon retirement of the Division from the Chosin Reservoir Area, he coordinated the movement of various Division elements, supervising not only the preparation of bivouac areas to receive the returning troops but also the arrangements for embarkation of Division Units. His personal courage, professional skill and inspiring leadership throughout these operations reflect the highest credit upon Brigadier General Craig and the United States Naval Service.

Silver Star Citation

The President of the United States of America, authorized by Act of Congress July 9, 1918, takes pleasure in presenting the Silver Star (Army Award) to Brigadier General Edward A. Craig (MCSN: 0-196), United States Marine Corps, for conspicuous gallantry and intrepidity in action as Assistant Division Commander, FIRST Marine Division (Reinforced), in the amphibious landing resulting in the capture of Inchon, Korea, on 15 September 1950 in the Inchon-Seoul operation. His actions contributed materially to the success of this operation and were in keeping with the highest traditions of the military service.

Legion of Merit Citation (2nd Award)

The President of the United States of America takes pleasure in presenting a Gold Star in lieu of a Second Award of the Legion of Merit with Combat "V" to Brigadier General Edward A. Craig (MCSN: 0-196), United States Marine Corps, for exceptionally meritorious conduct in the performance of outstanding services to the Government of the United States as Assistant Division Commander of the FIRST Marine Division, Reinforced, Fleet Marine Force, prior to and during the amphibious assault on Inchon, Korea, the subsequent attack and liberation of Seoul, Korea, and the continuation of the advance to Wonsan, Korea, from 13 September to 2 November 1950. General Craig discharged his responsibilities wisely and with meticulous attention to detail, effectively supervising the preparatory stages of the Division participation in the operations and by his actions contributed materially to the success of the operation. On numerous occasions he fearlessly exposed himself to enemy fire when visiting the assault units to gain first-hand knowledge of the progress of the attack and was of outstanding assistance in solving the many complex and difficult problems of tactics and joint action with other United Nations units. General Craig's skilled service and exemplary conduct throughout this period were in keeping with the highest traditions of the United States Naval Service. (Brigadier General Craig is authorized to wear the Combat "V.")

Duty Stations

Edward A. Craig was born on November 22, 1896, in Danbury, Connecticut. He attended St. John's Military Academy, Delafield, Wisconsin, and upon graduation in 1917, reported for active duty as a second lieutenant in the Marine Corps on August 23, 1917.

In November 1917, he was assigned to duty with the Eighth Marine Regiment, and in April 1919 was ordered to foreign shore duty in Haiti, and later with the 2nd Provisional Brigade of Marines in the Dominican Republic.

He returned to the United States in December 1921, where he served as Commanding Officer, Marine Detachment, Naval Ammunition Depot, Puget Sound, Washington, until again ordered to foreign shore duty, on this occasion to the Marine Barracks, Olongapol, Philippine Islands.

He was ordered to sea duty in February 1924, as Commanding Officer of the Marine Detachment aboard the USS *Huron*, and during part of this period was on temporary detached duty ashore in China, where he took part in guarding the International Settlement at Shanghai and the American Legation at Peking.

He returned to the United States in March 1926, and after serving with the 4th Marine Regiment at San Diego, California, was assigned in June of that year as aide-de-camp to the Major General Commandant at Headquarters Marine Corps, Washington, D.C. He remained there until May 1929, when he was ordered to Nicaragua for duty with the Nicaraguan National Guard.

Two and a half years later he joined the Marine Corps Base at San Diego, California, where he remained until June 1933. During this period he was on temporary duty in Nicaragua under the State Department from June to November 1932.

Following a short interval of three months during which Craig was Commanding Officer, Marine Detachment, Receiving Ship, Disciplinary Barracks, San Diego, he returned to the Marine Corps Base where he performed duties as a Company Commander in the 6th Marines, Fleet Marine Force. In July 1936, he was detailed as G-1 (Personnel Officer) 2nd Marine Brigade.

Craig joined the Marine Corps Schools at the Marine Barracks, Quantico, Virginia, in July 1937, as a student in the Senior Course. Upon graduation in May the following year, he again returned to the Marine Corps Base at San Diego where he served as instructor in the Platoon Leaders' Course, Inspector-Instructor of Reserve Battalion Field Training, and Base Adjutant.

From June 1939 to June 1941, he was Marine Officer and Intelligence Officer on the Staff of the Commander, Aircraft Battle Force aboard the USS *Yorktown* and USS *Enterprise*, and for an interval of four months was stationed at the Naval Air Station at Pearl Harbor.

In July 1941, he again joined the Marine Base at San Diego and in October the same year was appointed Provost Marshall and Commanding Officer of the Guard Battalion where he performed duties until March 1942, when he joined the 2nd Marine Division as Commanding Officer, 2nd Pioneer Battalion.

In June 1942, he was detailed as Executive Officer of the 9th Marines, in which position he remained until October when he became Commanding Officer, Service Troops, 3rd Marine Division, and sailed with the division for the South Pacific in February 1943.

General Craig assumed command of the 9th Marines at Guadalcanal in July 1943, and as part of the 3rd Marine Division, led the regiment in the landing at Empress Augusta Bay on Bougainville in November 1943.

Remaining as Commanding Officer of the regiment, he took part in the invasion and subsequent recapture of Guam, Marianas Islands, in July and August 1944, where he was awarded the Navy Cross.

He was ordered to the V Amphibious Corps in September 1944, where he became Corps Operations Officer, in which capacity he planned and participated in the landing and assault on Iwo Jima in February 1945. He returned to the United States in July 1945 and assumed duties as Chief of Staff of the Marine Training Command, San Diego Area. From October 1945 to July 1946 he served as Commanding Officer of the Redistribution Regiment of the Marine Training and Replacement Command, San Diego Area.

After six months as Chief Instructor of the Troop Training Unit, Amphibious Forces, Pacific Fleet, during which time he was in charge of the Specialized Amphibious Training of Eighth Army Troops in Japan, he was promoted to brigadier general and again ordered overseas as Assistant Division Commander, 1st Marine Division (Reinforced), Tientsin, China. On June 1, 1947, he was assigned as Commanding General, 1st Provisional Marine Brigade, Fleet Marine Force, on Guam, where he remained for two years.

Upon his return, General Craig assumed duties as Assistant Division Commander, 1st Marine Division, at Camp Pendleton, Oceanside, California. With the reactivation of the 1st Provisional Marine Brigade, General Craig was named Commanding General in July 1950. The brigade sailed for duty in Korea a few days later and participated in the fighting around the Pusan perimeter. When the 1st Marine Division subsequently arrived in Korea, he once again became Assistant Division Commander and took part in the landing at Inchon and operations in northeast Korea. He was appointed to the rank of Lieutenant General in January 1951. In March 1951, he returned to the United States, and assumed duties at Marine Corps Headquarters as Director of the Marine Corps Reserve until his retirement on June 1, 1951, after serving for 33 years. He died on December 11, 1994 at his home in El Cajon, California, at the age of 98.

Endnotes

Chapter 1

1   Richard D. Camp, *Leatherneck Legends: Conversations with the Marine Corps' Old Breed* (Minneapolis, MN: Zenith Press, 2006), 58. Hereafter: *Leatherneck Legends*.

2   Ibid.

3   Lieutenant General Edward A. Craig. Oral History transcript (Quantico, VA: Oral History Collections, Marine Corps University Archives), 5. Hereafter: Craig interview.

4   Edward A. Craig, *Incidents of Service. 1917–1951* (Unpublished manuscript). Hereafter: *Incidents*.

5   Camp, *Leatherneck Legends*, 59.

6   Craig interview, 4.

7   Scott Vasquez and Michael B. Williams, Naval Postgraduate School Master's Thesis, "Reengineering the Marine Corps Officer Promotion Process for Unrestricted Officers."

Chapter 2

1   Annette Amerman, *United States Marines in the First World War I Anthology, Selected Bibliography, and Annotated Order of Battle* (Quantico, VA: Marine Corps History Division, 2016), 33. Hereafter: USMC in the 1st World War.

2   Charles A. Fleming, et al., *Quantico, Crossroads of the Marine Corps* (Washington, D.C.: History and Museums Division, Headquarters USMC, 1978), 30.

3   Camp, *Leatherneck Legends*, 61.

4   Craig interview, 4.

5   Bradley E. Gernand and Michelle A. Krowl, *Quantico: Semper Progredi, Always Forward* (Virginia Beach, VA: The Donning Company Publishers, 2004), 70.

6   Ibid. 72.

7   Craig, *Incidents*.

8   Camp, *Leatherneck Legends*, 60; Gernand and Krowl, *Quantico: Semper Progredi, Always Forward*, 66.

9   Camp, *Leatherneck Legends*, 60.
10 Craig, *Incidents*.
11 Camp, *Leatherneck Legends*, 60.
12 Craig interview, 10.

Chapter 3

1   Craig interview, 11.
2   Ibid, 5.
3   Ibid.
4   Ibid, 6.
5   Ibid.
6   Ibid.
7   Craig, *Incidents*.

Chapter 4

1   Camp, *Leatherneck Legends*, 61.
2   Ibid.
3   Ibid.
4   Amerman, *USMC in the 1st World War*, 141.
5   Clyde H. Metcalf, *A History of the United States Marine Corps* (New York: G.P. Putnam's Sons, 1939), 457.
6   Camp, *Leatherneck Legends*, 62.
7   Amerman, *USMC in the 1st World War*, 141.
8   Craig interview, 13.
9   Ibid.
10 Ibid, 15.
11 Craig, *Incidents*.
12 Craig interview, 16.
13 Ibid.
14 Ibid, 17.

Chapter 5

1   Camp, *Leatherneck Legends*, 63.
2   Captain Stephan M. Fuller and Graham A. Cosmas, *Marines in the Dominican Republic 1916–1924* (Washington, D.C.: History and Museums Division, Headquarters, U.S. Marine Corps, 1974), 28.

3   Craig interview, 20.
4   Craig interview, 19.
5   Craig interview.
6   "War in Asia," *Time* (August 14, 1950).
7   Craig interview, 19.
8   Camp, *Leatherneck Legends*, 64.
9   Fuller, *Marines in the Dominican Republic 1916–1924*, 28.
10 Craig interview, 21.
11 Camp, *Leatherneck Legends*, p. 67.
12 Ibid.
13 Ibid. 68.

Chapter 6

1   Leo J. Daugherty III, *Counterinsurgency and the United States Marine Corps, Vol. 1, The First Counterinsurgency Era, 1899–1945* (Jefferson, NC: McFarland & Co., 2015) 131. Hereafter: *Counterinsurgency*.
2   Craig interview, 21.
3   Benjamin R. Beede (ed.), *The War of 1898 and U.S. Interventions 1898–1934, An Encyclopedia* (New York and London: Routledge, 1994), 23.
4   Camp, *Leatherneck Legends*, 68.
5   Craig interview, 37.
6   Ibid.
7   Ibid, 38.
8   Craig, *Incidents*.
9   Camp, *Leatherneck Legends*, 68.
10 Ibid.
11 Ibid.
12 Ibid.

Chapter 7

1   Camp. *Leatherneck Legends*, 64.
2   Ibid, 65.
3   Ibid, 70.
4   Craig, *Incidents*.
5   Camp, *Leatherneck Legends*, 68.
6   Ibid.
7   Craig, *Incidents*, 41.

Chapter 8

1   Camp, *Leatherneck Legends*, 69.
2   Ibid.
3   Ibid.
4   Ibid.
5   Ibid.
6   Ibid. 70.
7   Ibid, 69.
8   Ibid, 70.
9   Ibid.
10 Ibid. 71.
11 Ibid.
12 Ibid.
13 Craig, *Incidents*.
14 Ibid.
15 Ibid.
16 Ibid.
17 Ibid.
18 Ibid.
19 Ibid.
20 Ibid.
21 Ibid.
22 Ibid.
23 Ibid.
24 Ibid.

Chapter 9

1   Craig, *Incidents.*
2   Ibid.
3   Craig, *Incidents*.
4   Ibid.
5   Ibid.
6   Ibid.
7   Ibid.
8   Ibid.
9   Ibid.
10 Camp, *Leatherneck Legends*, 73.
11 Ibid.
12 Craig, *Incidents*.
13 Ibid.

14 Ibid.
15 Ibid.
16 Ibid.
17 Ibid.
18 Ibid.
19 Ibid.
20 Ibid.
21 Camp, *Leatherneck Legends*, 74.
22 Ibid.
23 Ibid.
24 Ibid, 75.
25 Craig, *Incidents.*
26 Ibid.
27 Ibid.
28 Ibid.
29 Ibid.
30 Ibid.
31 Ibid.
32 Ibid.
33 Camp, *Leatherneck Legends*, 74.
34 Craig, *Incidents.*
35 Ibid.
36 Ibid.
37 Camp, *Leatherneck Legends*, 76.
38 Ibid, 77.
39 Ibid, 77–78.
40 Ibid.
41 Craig, *Incidents.*
42 Craig interview, 97.
43 Ibid.

Chapter 10

1 Craig, *Incidents.*
2 Ibid.
3 Ibid.
4 Ibid.
5 Ibid.
6 Ibid.
7 Ibid.
8 Ibid.
9 Ibid.

10 Ibid.
11 Ibid.
12 Ibid.
13 Ibid.
14 Ibid.
15 Leo J. Daugherty III, *The Marine Corps and the State Department: Enduring Partners in United States Foreign Policy 1798–2007* (Jefferson, NC: McFarland & Co., 2009), 49.
16 Craig, *Incidents.*
17 Ibid.
18 Ibid.
19 Ibid.
20 *Foreign Relations of the United States Diplomatic Papers, Vol. 1* (Washington, D.C.: U.S. Government Printing Office, 1954), 647.
21 Craig, *Incidents.*
22 Ibid.
23 Ibid.
24 Ibid.
25 Ibid.
26 Ibid.
27 Ibid.
28 Ibid.
29 Ibid.
30 Ibid.
31 Ibid
32 Ibid.
33 Ibid.
34 Ibid.
35 Ibid.
36 Ibid.
37 Ibid.
38 Ibid.
39 Ibid.
40 Ibid.
41 Ibid.

Chapter 11

1 Craig, *Incidents.*
2 Ibid.
3 Camp, *Leatherneck Legends*, 107.
4 Craig, *Incidents.*

5   Camp, *Leatherneck Legends*, 108.

6   Craig, *Incidents*.

7   Ibid.

8   Ibid.

9   Ibid. General Craig related the story of his wife to me. He called Vogel a "son of a bitch," which totally surprised me, as I never heard him swear in the many years I knew him—it was totally out of character.

10 Ibid.

11 Camp, *Leatherneck Legends*, 109.

12 Craig, *Incidents*.

13 L. D. Burrus, *The Ninth Marines: A Brief History of the Ninth Marine Regiment* (Washington, D.C.: Infantry Journal Press, 1946), 38; Craig interview, 121.

14 Craig, *Incidents*.

15 Ibid.

16 Craig interview, 121.

17 Ibid, 125.

18 Craig, *Incidents*.

19 Ibid.

20 Ibid.

Chapter 12

1   Saburo Hayashi and Alvin D. Coox, *Kogun: The Japanese Army in the Pacific War* (Quantico, VA: The Marine Corps Association, reprint, 1959), 73.

2   Major John N. Renz, USMC., *Bougainville and the Northern Solomons* (Washington, D.C.: Headquarters USMC: Historical Section, USMC, 1948) 25.

3   Craig, *Incidents*.

4   Craig, *Incidents*.

5   Craig interview, 125.

6   Burrus, *The Ninth Marines, 1942–1945*, 40.

7   Craig interview, 126.

8   Renz, *Bougainville and the Northern Solomons*, 34. Major General Oscar F Peatross, USMC, *Bless 'em All: The Raider Marines of World War II* (Irvine, CA: Review Publications, 1995) 251.

9   Camp, *Leatherneck Legends*, 113.

10 Renz, *Bougainville and the Northern Solomons*, 34.

11 Ibid, 33

12 Peatross, *Bless 'em All*, 248.

13 Camp, *Leatherneck Legends*, 114.

14 Craig interview, 125.

15 Shaw, *Isolation of Rabaul*, 220. Combat Report of the Third Marine Division in the Bougainville Operations, November 1–December 28, 1943.

16 Camp, *Leatherneck Legends*, 114. Renz, *Bougainville and the Northern Solomons*, 32–33.
17 Report of Operations of Second Raider Regiment (Provisional), Enclosure A, January 3, 1944, 1530. Peatross, *Bless 'em All*, 250.
18 Renz, *Bougainville and the Northern Solomons*, 42.
19 Craig interview.
20 Arthur, *The Third Marine Division*, 66.
21 Ibid.
22 Renz, *Bougainville and the Northern Solomons*, 42–46.
23 Craig, Incidents.
24 Renz, *Bougainville and the Northern Solomons*, 49, 50.
25 Ibid, 51.
26 Craig interview, 128.
27 Craig, *Incidents*.
28 Camp. *Leatherneck Legends*, 115.
29 Craig interview.
30 Camp, *Leatherneck Legends*, 114.
31 Ibid.
32 Craig, *Incidents.*
33 Ibid.
34 Camp, *Leatherneck Legends*, 115.
35 Craig, *Incidents.*
36 Ibid.
37 Ibid.
38 Ibid.
39 Ibid.
40 Craig interview, 129.
41 Camp, *Leatherneck Legends*, 116.
42 Craig interview, 130.

Chapter 13

1 Martin Boyle, *Yanks Don't Cry: A Marine's Eye-view of Four Heroic Years in a Japanese Prisoner of War Camp* (New York: Bernhard Geis Associates, Random House, 1963), 21.
2 Craig, *Incidents.*
3 Ibid.
4 Camp, *Leatherneck Legends*, 120.
5 Ibid, 126.
6 Ibid, 127.
7 Camp, *Leatherneck Legends,* 126.
8 Ibid, 119.
9 Ibid, 127.

10 Ibid.
11 Craig, personal correspondence with author.
12 Ibid.
13 "War in Asia," *Time* (August 14, 1950).
14 Camp, *Leatherneck Legends*, 127–128.
15 Ibid.
16 Craig, *Incidents*.
17 Ibid.
18 Ibid.
19 Ibid.
20 Camp, *Leatherneck Legends*, 133; Craig, personal correspondence with author.
21 Camp, *Leatherneck Legends,* 133.
22 Ibid.
23 Ibid, 134.
24 Ibid.
25 Ibid.
26 Ibid, 135.
27 Ibid.
28 Craig, *Incidents.*
29 Ibid.
30 Ibid.
31 Military Awards Branch (MMMA), Headquarters, U.S. Marine Corps, Quantico, VA 22134.

Chapter 14

1 Craig, *Incidents.*
2 Craig, *Incidents.*
3 Camp, *Leatherneck Legends*, 158.
4 Ibid, 159.
5 Ibid, 160.
6 Ibid. 160
7 Ibid, 160–161.
8 Ibid, 161.
9 Howard M. Conner, *The Spearhead: The World War II History of the 5th Marine Division* (Washington, D.C.: Infantry Journal Press, 1950), 25.
10 Camp, *Leatherneck Legends*, 161.
11 Ibid, 161
12 Ibid, 163.
13 Ibid, 163.
14 Ibid, 163.
15 Ibid, 164.

16 Ibid, 164.
17 Ibid, 164.
18 Ibid, 164–165.
19 Ibid, 165.
20 Ibid, 165.
21 Ibid, 166.
22 Ibid, 166.
23 Ibid, 166.
24 Ibid, 167.
25 Ibid, 167.
26 Craig, *Incidents*.
27 Jeter A. Isley and Philip A. Crowl, *The U.S. Marines and Amphibious War: Its Theory and Its Practice in the Pacific* (Princeton, NJ: Princeton University), 490.Camp, *Leatherneck Legends*, 167.
28 Camp, *Leatherneck Legends*, 168.
29 Craig interview, 143.

Chapter 15

1   Craig, *Incidents*.
2   Ibid.
3   Ibid.
4   Ibid.
5   Ibid.
6   Ibid.
7   Ibid.
8   Ibid.
9   Raymond G. Davis, *Oral History interview* (Quantico, VA: Oral History Collection, Marine Corps Archives, 1979). Hereafter: Davis Oral History interview.
10 Ibid.
11 Craig, *Incidents*.
12 Ibid.
13 Davis Oral History interview.
14 Camp, *Leatherneck Legends*, 192.

Chapter 16

1   General Paik Sun Yup, *From Pusan to Panmunjom* (McLean, VA: Brassey's, Maxwell Macmillan, 1992), 1.
2   Ibid, 1.
3   Camp, *Leatherneck Legends*, 195.

4 Ibid, 195.
5 Ibid, 195.
6 Ibid, 196.
7 Ibid.
8 Ibid
9 Ibid, 197.
10 Ibid, 197.
11 Ibid.
12 Ibid, 203–204.
13 Ibid, 204.
14 Ibid.
15 Ibid, 205.
16 Ibid.
17 Ibid.
18 Ibid, 199–200.
19 Ibid, 200; *First Provisional Marine Brigade Special Action Report*, August 2–September 6, 1950.
20 Craig, *Incidents.*
21 Ibid.
22 Camp, *Leatherneck Legends*, 204.
23 Oliver P. Smith, Oral History interview (Quantico, VA: Oral History Collection, Marine Corps Archives, 1973), 185. Hereafter: Smith interview.
24 Clifton La Bree, *The Gentle Warrior: General Oliver Prince Smith, USMC* (Kent, OH & London: Kent State University Press, 2001), 103.
25 Craig interview, 4.
26 Craig, *Incidents.*
27 Craig interview, 4.
28 Raymond Murray, *Oral History Transcript* (Washington, D.C.: History and Museums Division, Headquarters, USMC, Marine Corps University Special Collections, 1988), 183.
29 Craig, *Incidents.*
30 Andrew Greer, *The New Breed: The Story of the U.S. Marines in Korea* (New York, NY: Harper & Brothers, 1952), 5.
31 Ibid, 4.
32 John C. Chapin, *Fire Brigade: U.S. Marines in the Pusan Perimeter* (Washington, D.C.: Marine Corps History and Museums Division, 2000), 7.
33 Camp, *Leatherneck Legends*, 202.
34 Ibid; *First Provisional Marine Brigade, Special Action Report*, August 2, 1950–September 6, 1950.
35 Craig, *Incidents.*
36 Smith interview, 196.
37 Craig, *Incidents.*

38 Ibid.
39 Ibid. In an interview with General Shepherd, the author was told by him "that when he passed away, he told his wife to marry Eddy Craig because he was such a good man."
40 Ibid.
41 Jack Buck interview with author.
42 Camp, *Leatherneck Legends*, 207.
43 Greer, *The New Breed*, 6.
44 Craig interview.
45 Craig, *Incidents*.
46 Craig interview with author. Robert D. Heinl, Jr., *Victory at High Tide: The Inchon-Seoul Campaign* (New York, NY: J.B. Lippincott Company, 1966), 21.
47 Craig, *Incidents*.
48 Ibid.
49 Ibid.
50 Ibid.
51 Ibid.
52 Camp, *Leatherneck Legends*, 211.
53 Ibid.
54 Robert D. Taplett, *Dark Horse Six: A Memoir of the Korean War, 1950–1951* (Williamstown, NJ: Phillips Publications, 2002), 13.
55 Camp, *Leatherneck Legends*, 211.
56 Ibid, 212.

Chapter 17

1 Roy E. Appleman, *South to the Naktong, North to the Yalu: June–November 1950* (Washington, D.C.: Office of the Chief of Military History, Department of the Army, 1961), 252. Hereafter: *South to the Naktong*.
2 Craig interview.
3 Camp, *Leatherneck Legends*, 213.
4 Craig, *Incidents*.
5 Ibid.
6 Ibid.
7 Ibid.
8 Craig interview.
9 Ibid.
10 Craig, *Incidents*.
11 Ibid.
12 Ibid.
13 Special Action Report, 5th Marines. August 7, 1950.
14 Craig, *Incidents*.

15 Ibid.

16 Ibid.

17 Malcolm W. Cagle and Frank A. Manson, *The Sea War in Korea* (Annapolis, MD: Zenith Press, 2006), 63.

18 Craig, *Incidents.*

19 Ibid.

20 Camp, *Leatherneck Legends*, 214.

21 Ibid.

22 Ibid.

23 Craig interview.

24 Craig, *Incidents.*

25 Lynn Montross and Nicholas A. Canzona, *U.S. Marine Operations in Korea 1950–1953: Volume III: The Chosin Reservoir Campaign* (Washington, D.C.: Historical Branch, G-3, Headquarters U.S. Marine Corps, 1957), 171.

26 Craig, *Incidents.*

27 Special Action Report, 3rd Battalion, 5th Marines, October 7, 1959.

28 Craig interview.

29 Greer, *The New Breed: The Story of the U.S. Marines in Korea*, 39.

30 Craig interview.

31 Appleman, *South to the Naktong*, 255.

32 Camp, *Leatherneck Legends*, 215.

33 Special Action Report, 5th Marines, August 12, 1950.

34 Greer, *The New Breed*, 40.

35 Craig, *Incidents.*

36 Appleman, *South to the Naktong*, 256.

37 Craig, *Incidents.*

38 Camp, *Leatherneck Legends*, 219.

39 Craig, *Incidents.*

40 *U.S. Marine Operations in Korea, Vol. 1*, 68.

41 Ibid, 70.

42 Camp, *Leatherneck Legends*, 217.

43 Craig, *Incidents.*

44 Ibid.

45 *Special Action Report, 3rd Battalion, 5th Marines*, August 16, 1950.

46 Camp, *Leatherneck Legends*, 217.

47 Cagle, *The Sea War in Korea*, 65.

48 Craig, *Incidents.*

49 *Special Action Report. 1st Provisional Marine Brigade (1st Tank Battalion)*, August 17, 1950.

50 Cagle, *The Sea War in Korea*, 67.

51 Craig, *Incidents.*

52 Ibid.

53 Camp, *Leatherneck Legends*, 218.
54 Craig interview.
55 Camp, *Leatherneck Legends*, 218.
56 Ibid, 219.
57 *Special Action Report, 5th Marines*, September 1, 1950.
58 Camp, *Leatherneck Legends*, 218.
59 Ibid.
60 John P. Condon and Peter B. Mersky, *Corsairs to Panthers: U.S. Marine Aviation in Korea* (Washington, D.C.: U.S. Marine Corps Historical Center, 2002), 8.
61 Camp, *Leatherneck Legends*, 220.
62 Craig, *Incidents*.

Chapter 18

1 La Bree, *The Gentle Warrior*, 109–110.
2 Smith interview, 202.
3 Craig, *Incidents*.
4 Camp, *Leatherneck Legends*, 211.
5 Ibid, 228–229.
6 Ibid, 229.
7 Ibid.
8 *History of the Joint Chiefs of Staff: The Joint Chiefs of Staff and National Policy 1950–1951: The Korean War*, 88.
9 Ibid, 89.
10 Camp, *Leatherneck Legends*, 229–230.
11 Ibid, 230.
12 Smith interview, 199.
13 Camp, *Leatherneck Legends*, 230.
14 Ibid.
15 Ibid, 231.
16 Ibid.
17 Ibid, 234.
18 Log of USS *Collett* (DD730) Cmdr. R. H. Close, September 13, 1950.
19 Log of USS *Rochester* (CA-124) Capt. Edward Woodyard, September 13, 1950.
20 Log of USS *Mansfield* (DD-728), Cmdr. E. H. Headland, September 13, 1950.
21 Special Action Report, 1/5, October 7, 1950.
22 Log of USS *Dehaven* (DD-727) Cmdr. O.D. Lundgren, September 13, 1950.
23 Craig, *Incidents*.
24 Ibid.
25 Ibid.
26 Ibid.
27 Smith interview.

28 Craig, *Incidents*.
29 Ibid.
30 Ibid.
31 Montross, *U.S. Marine Operations in Korea 1950–1953, Vol.2* (Washington, D.C.: Historical Branch, Headquarters Marine Corps, 1955), 192.
32 Taplett, *Dark Horse Six*, 140.
33 Craig, *Incidents*.
34 Ibid.
35 Ibid.
36 Ibid.
37 Camp, *Leatherneck Legends*, 249.
38 Ibid, 247–248.
39 Craig, *Incidents*.
40 Camp, *Leatherneck Legends*, 248.
41 Craig, *Incidents*; Murray interview, 223.
42 Smith interview.
43 Camp, *Leatherneck Legends*, 249.
44 Ibid, 249–250.
45 Ibid, 250.
46 Ibid.
47 X Corps communiqué, September 26, 1950.
48 Camp, *Leatherneck Legends*, 251.
49 Craig, *Incidents*.
50 Ibid.
51 Craig interview; Smith interview.
52 Buck interview with author.
53 Ibid.

Chapter 19

1   Camp, *Leatherneck Legends*, 253.
2   Ibid.
3   Ibid, 254.
4   Ibid.
5   Murray interview, 224.
6   Craig, *Incidents*.
7   Ibid.
8   Ibid.
9   Ibid.
10 Montross, *History of U.S. Marine Corps Operations in Korea 1950–1953, Vol. III*, 98.
11 Camp, *Leatherneck Legends*, 258.

12 Ibid, 259.

13 Smith interview.

14 Craig, *Incidents.*

15 Murray interview, 226.

16 Martin Russ, *Breakout: The Chosin Reservoir Campaign* (New York, NY: Penguin Books, 2000), 300.

17 Craig, *Incidents.*

18 Craig interview, 59.

19 Historical Diary, 5th Marine Regiment, November 23, 1950.

20 Smith interview, 237.

21 Craig, *Incidents.*

22 Historical Diary, 5th Marine Regiment, November 27, 1950.

23 Camp, *Leatherneck Legends,* 262.

24 Historical Diary, 5th Marine Regiment, November 28, 1950.

25 Historical Diary, 5th Marine Regiment, December 1950.

26 Historical Diary, VMF-212, November 29, 1950.

27 Historical Diary, VMF-312 December 1950.

28 Historical Diary, VMF-212, November 30, 1950.

29 Historical Diary, 5th Marine Regiment, November 30, 1950.

30 Historical Diary, 5th Marine Regiment, December 1, 1950.

31 Smith interview, 239.

32 Montross, *U.S. Marine Operations in Korea 1950–1953,* Vol. III, 245.

33 Narrative History, 5th Marine Regiment, December 3, 1950

34 Special Action Report, 1/5, December 4, 1950. Montross, *U.S. Marine Operations in Korea 1950–1953*, Vol. III, 275

35 Historical Diary, 5th Marine Regiment, December 5, 1950.

36 7th Marine Regiment, OPNO 14-50, December 6, 1950.

37 Historical Diary, 5th Marine Regiment, December 6, 1950.

38 Montross, U.S. Marine Operations in Korea 1950–1953, Vol. III, 309.

39 Hampton Sides, *On Desperate Ground: The Marines at the Reservoir, The Korean War's Greatest Battle* (New York, NY: Doubleday, 2018), 124.

40 Smith interview, 251.

41 Historical Diary, VMF-312, December 9, 1950.

42 Shepherd interview.

43 Special Action Report, 1/5, December 11, 1950.

44 Montross, *U.S. Marine Operations in Korea, Vol. III.,* 339.

45 Ibid.

46 Camp, *Leatherneck Legends,* 280.

47 Craig, *Incidents.*

48 Ibid.

Bibliography

Personal Papers

Craig, Lieutenant General Edward A. *Incidents of Service: 1917–1951*, unpublished manuscript given to author, 1980.

Craig, Lieutenant General Edward A. Field Notebook.

Craig, Lieutenant General Edward A. Personal Letters, Private collection of Author.

Oral Histories and Presentations

Craig, Lieutenant General Edward A., USMC. Oral History Transcription of Lieutenant General Edward A. Craig, USMC (1968). Marine Corps Archives, Marine Corps University Special Collections, Quantico, VA, 1967.

Davis, General Raymond G., USMC (Retired). Interview by Benis M. Frank. Oral history transcription. Marine Corps Archives, Marine Corps University Special Collections. Quantico, VA, 1978.

Lejeune Leadership Institute, Marine Corps University. *A Case Study Brigadier General Edward A. Craig, USMC and the Fire Brigade at the Pusan Perimeter*, August 1950. Marine Corps University, 2019.

Litzenberg, Colonel Homer L., USMC (Retired). Inchon Landing to CCF Counteroffensive. Oral History interview. Marine Corps Archives, Marine Corps University Special Collections. Quantico, VA, 1951.

Murray, Major General Raymond, USMC. Oral History Transcription. Marine Corps Archives, Marine Corps University Special Collections. Quantico, VA, circa 1968.

Smith, General Oliver P., USMC (Retired). Interview by Benis M. Frank. Oral History transcription. Marine Corps University Special Collections. Quantico, VA, 1973.

Published Sources

Books

Alexander, Colonel Joseph H. USMC (Retired). *Battle of the Barricades: U.S. Marines in the Recapture of Seoul.* Marines in the Korean War Commemorative Series. Washington, D.C.: Marine Corps Historical Center, 2000.

Amerman, Annette D. "Over Here! Marines in Texas During World War I," *United States Marine Corps in the First World War,* Anthology, Selected Bibliography, and Annotated Order of Battle. Quantico, VA: History Division, USMC, 2016.

Appleman, Roy E. *South to the Naktong, North to the Yalu: June–November 1950.* Washington, D.C.: Office of the Chief of Military History, Department of the Army, 1961.

Arthur, First Lieutenant Robert A., USMCR and First Lieutenant Kenneth Cohlmia, USMCR. *The Third Marine Division.* Washington, D.C.: Infantry Journal Press, 1948.

Beede, Benjamin R., editor. *The War of 1898 and U.S. Interventions, 1898–1934: An Encyclopedia.* New York and London: Routledge, 1994.

Boyle, Martin. *Yanks Don't Cry: A Marine's Eye-view of Four Heroic Years in a Japanese Prisoner of War Camp.* New York: Bernhard Geis Associates, Random House, 1963.

Burrus, First Lieutenant L. D., USMCR, editor. *The Ninth Marines: A Brief History of the Ninth Marine Regiment.* Washington, D.C.: Infantry Journal Press, 1946.

Camp, Richard D. *Leatherneck Legends: Conversations with the Marine Corps' Old Breed.* Minneapolis, MN: Zenith Press, 2006.

Cagle, Commander Malcolm W., USN. and Commander Frank A. Manson, USN. The Sea War in Korea. Annapolis, Md.: U.S. Naval Institute, 1957.

Chapin, Captain John C., USMCR (Retired). *Fire Brigade: U.S. Marines in the Pusan Perimeter.* Marines in the Korean War Commemorative Series. Washington, D.C.: Marine Corps History and Museums Division, 2000.

Condon, Major General John P., USMC (Retired) and Commander Peter B. Mersky, USNR (Retired). *Corsairs to Panthers: U.S. Marine Aviation in Korea.* Marines in the Korean War Commemorative Series. Washington, D.C.: Marine Corps Historical Center, 2002.

Conner, Howard M. *The Spearhead: The World War II History of the 5th Marine Division.* Washington, D.C.: Infantry Journal Press, 1950.

Daugherty, Leo J., III. "Counterinsurgency and the United States Marine Corps," Vol. 1, *The First Counterinsurgency Era, 1899–1945.* Jefferson, N.C.: McFarland & Co.,2015.

_____. The Marine Corps and the State Department: Enduring Partners in United States Foreign Policy 1798–2007. Jefferson, NC: McFarland & Co., 2009.

Estes, Kenneth W. *Into the Breach at Pusan: The 1st Provisional Marine Brigade in the Korean War.* Norman, OK: University of Oklahoma Press, 2012.

Fleming, Lieutenant Colonel Charles A., USMC, Captain Robin L. Austin, USMC, and Captain Charles A. Braley III, USMC. *Quantico: Crossroads of the Marine Corps.* Washington, D.C.: History and Museum Division, Headquarters U.S. Marine Corps, 2016.

"Foreign Relations of the United States Diplomatic Papers," Vol.1. Washington, D.C.: U.S. Government Printing Office, 1954.

Fuller, Captain Stephan M., USMC and Graham A. Cosmas. *Marines in the Dominican Republic 1916–1924.* Washington, D.C.: History and Museums Division, Headquarters, U.S. Marine Corps, 1974.

Garand, Georg W. and Truman R. Strobridge. *History of U.S. Marine Corps Operations in World War II: Western Pacific Operations*, Volume IV. Washington, D.C.: Historical Branch, Headquarters, U.S. Marine Corps, 1971.

Gernand, Bradley E. and Michelle A. Krowl. *Quantico: Semper Progredi, Always Forward.* Virginia Beach, VA: The Donning Company Publishers, 2004.

Greer, Andrew. *The New Breed: The Story of the U.S. Marines in Korea.* New York, NY: Harper & Brothers, 1952.

Hammel, Eric M. *Chosin: Heroic Ordeal of the Korean War.* New York, NY: The Vanguard Press, 1981.

Hayashi, Saburo and Alvin D. Coox. *Kogun: The Japanese Army in the Pacific War.* Quantico, VA: The Marine Corps Association, reprint, 1959.

Heinl, Colonel Robert Debs, Jr., USMC. *Victory at High Tide: The Inchon-Seoul Campaign.* J.B. Lippincott Company, New York, 1966.

_____. *Soldiers of the Sea: The United States Marine Corps, 1775–1962.* Annapolis, MD: United States Naval Institute, 1962.

Hough, Lieutenant Colonel Frank O., USMCR, Major Verle E. Ludwig, USMC., and Henry I. Shaw, Jr. *Pearl Harbor to Guadalcanal: History of United States Marine Corps in World War II, Vol. 1.* Washington, D.C.: Historical Branch, G-3, Headquarters, U.S. Marine Corps, 1958.

Isley, Jeter A. and Philip A. Crowl. *The U.S. Marines and Amphibious War: Its Theory and Its Practice in the Pacific.* Princeton, NJ: Princeton University Press, 1951.

Johnson, Wray R. *Biplanes at War: U.S. Marine Corps Aviation in the Small Wars Era, 1915–1934.* Lexington, KY: University Press of Kentucky, 2019.

Knox, Donald. *The Korean War: Pusan to Chosin.* San Diego: Harcourt Brace Jovanovich Publishers, 1985.

La Bree, Clifton. *The Gentle Warrior: General Oliver Prince Smith, USMC.* Kent, Ohio & London: Kent State University Press, 2001.

Lodge, Major O.R., USMC. *The Recapture of Guam.* Washington, D.C.: Historical Branch, G-3, Headquarters U.S. Marine Corps, 1954.

Metcalf, Lt. Col. Clyde H. *A History of the United States Marine Corps.* New York, NY: G.P. Putnam's Sons, 1939.

Montross, Lynn and Captain Nicholas A. Canzona, USMC. *U.S. Marine Corps Operations in Korea 1950–1953: Volume III, The Chosin Reservoir Campaign.* Washington, D.C.: Historical Branch, G-3, Headquarters U.S. Marine Corps, 1957.

Montross, Lynn, Major Hubard D. Kuokka, USMC and Major Norman W. Hicks, USMC. *U.S. Marine Corps Operations in Korea 1950–1953: Volume IV: The East-Central Front*. Washington, D.C.: Historical Branch, G-3, U.S. Marine Corps, 1962.

O'Brien, Cyril J. *Liberation: Marines in the Recapture of Guam*. Marines in World War II Commemorative Series. Washington, D.C.: Marine Corps Historical Center, 1994.

Peatross, Major General Oscar F., USMC (Retired). *Bless 'em All: The Raider Marines of World War II*. Irvine, CA: Review Publications, 1995.

Renz, Major John N., USMC. *Bougainville and the Northern Solomons*. Washington, D.C.: Headquarters USMC: Historical Section, USMC, 1948.

Russ, Martin. *Breakout: The Chosin Reservoir Campaign*. New York, NY: Penguin Books, 2000.

Shaw, Henry I., Jr. and Major Douglas T. Kane, USMC. *Isolation of Rabaul: History of U.S. Marine Corps Operations in World War II, Vol.2*. Washington, D.C.: Historical Branch, G-3, Headquarters U. S. Marine Corps, 1963.

Shaw, Henry I., Jr. et al. *Central Pacific Drive: History of U. S. Marine Corps Operations in World War II. Vol.3*. Washington, D.C.: Historical Branch, G-3, Headquarters U. S. Marine Corps, 1966.

Sides, Hampton. *On Desperate Ground: The Marines at the Reservoir, The Korean War's Greatest Battle*. New York: Doubleday, 2018.

Simmons, Brigadier General Edwin H., USMC (Retired). *Frozen Chosin: U.S. Marines at the Changjin Reservoir*. Marines in the Korean War Commemorative Series. Washington. D.C.: Marine Corps Historical Center, 2002.

———. *Over the Seawall: U.S. Marines at Inchon*. Marines in the Korean War Commemorative Series. Washington, D.C.: Marine Corps Historical Center, 2000.

Sloan, Bill. *The Darkest Summer: Pusan and Inchon 1950: The Battles that Saved South Korea—and the Marines—from Extinction*. New York, NY: Simon & Schuster, 2009.

Smith, Charles R., editor. *U.S. Marines in the Korean War*. Washington, D.C.: History Division, USMC, 2007.

Smith, Major Julian C., USMC, et al. *A Review of the Organization and Operations of the Guardia Nacional de Nicaragua*. Quantico, VA: Marine Corps Schools, 1937.

Smith, S. E. editor. *The United States Marine Corps in World War II*. New York: Random House, 1969.

Schnabel, James F. and Robert J. Watson. *History of the Joint Chiefs of Staff: The Joint Chiefs of Staff and National Policy, Vol. III, 1950–1951, The Korean War Part I*. Washington, D.C.: Office of Joint History, 1998.

Taplett, Robert D. *Dark Horse Six: A Memoir of the Korean War, 1950–1951*. Williamstown, NJ.: Phillips Publications, 2002.

Toland, John. *In Mortal Combat: Korea, 1950–1953*. New York, NY: William Morrow and Company, 1991.

Utz, Curtis A. *Assault from the Sea: The Amphibious Landing at Inchon*. Fiftieth Anniversary of the Korean War Commemorative Edition. Washington, D.C.: Naval Historical Center, 2000.

Weintraub, Stanley. *MacArthur's War: Korea and the Undoing of an American Hero.* New York, NY: The Free Press, 2000.

Yup, General Paik Sun. *From Pusan to Panmunjom.* McLean, VA: Brassey's, Maxwell Macmillan, 1992.

Articles

Camp, Richard D. "Recollections of General Edward A. Craig and the Recapture of Guam." *Leatherneck*, Magazine of the Marines, July 2019, 30–35.

Camp, Colonel Richard D. "A U.S. Marine in the Guardia Nacional." *Naval History*, August 2021, 20–25.

"War in Asia." *Time*, The Weekly Newsmagazine, August 14, 1950, 14–26.

Unpublished Documents

Combat Report, Third Marine Division, Bougainville Operation, November 1–December 28, 1943.

Special Action Report, First Tank Battalion, First Provisional Marine Brigade, August 2–September 6, 1950.

Vasquez, Scott and Michael B. Williams. "Reengineering the Marine Corps Officer Promotion Process for Unrestricted Officers." Master's Thesis, Naval Postgraduate School, 2002–2003.

Interviews by Author

Buck, Lieutenant John A.

Craig, Lieutenant General Edward A.

Davis, General Raymond G.

Shepherd, General Raymond G.

Index

References to maps are in *italics*.

LEADERSHIP IN ACTION

CASEMATE

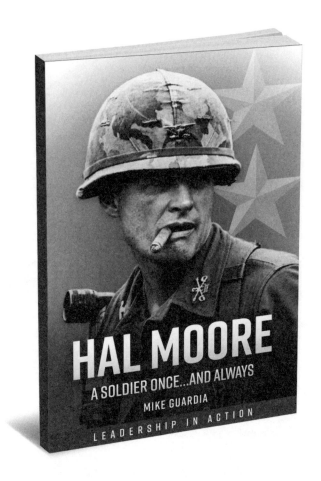

Finalist 2013 Army Historical Society Distinguished Writing Award.

Hal Moore, one of the most admired American combat leaders of the last 50 years, is best known for his book *We Were Soldiers Once … and Young* and the subsequent movie *We Were Soldiers*. At the beginning of the Vietnam War, Moore commanded the 1st Battalion of the 7th Cavalry at Ia Drang in the first full-fledged battle between U.S. and North Vietnamese regulars. Drastically outnumbered and nearly overrun, Moore led from the front, and though losing 79 soldiers, accounted for 1,200 of the enemy before the Communists withdrew. Moore graciously allowed the author Mike Guardia interviews and granted full access to his files and collection of letters, documents, and never-before-published photographs, to write this fully illustrated biography.

9781636240527

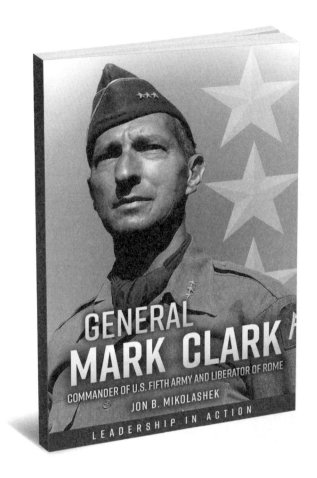

GENERAL MARK CLARK

COMMANDER OF U.S. FIFTH ARMY AND LIBERATOR OF ROME

JON B. MIKOLASHEK

LEADERSHIP IN ACTION

A skilled staff officer, Mark Clark rose quickly through the ranks, and by the time America entered World War II he was deputy commander of Allied Forces in North Africa. Several weeks before Operation *Torch*, Clark landed by submarine in a daring mission to negotiate the cooperation of the Vichy French. He was subsequently named commander of U.S. Fifth Army and tasked with the invasion of Italy. The brutal Italian campaign has been long overshadowed by events in northern Europe, and likewise, the senior U.S. commander in Italy has been largely overlooked. Jon Mikolashek remedies this situation, shedding much-needed historical light on one of America's most important fighting generals in this "warts and all" biography.

9781636240510

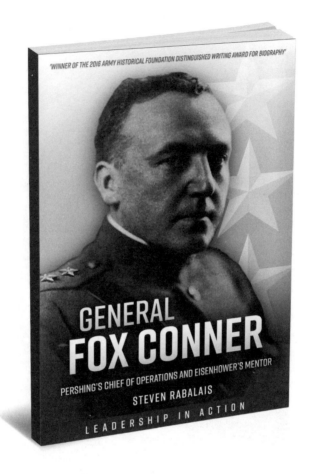

Winner of the 2016 Army Historical Foundation Distinguished Writing Award.

John J. Pershing considered Fox Conner to have been "a brilliant soldier" and "one of the finest characters our Army has ever produced." During World War I, General Conner served as chief of operations for the American Expeditionary Force in Europe. In the early 1920s, Conner transformed his protégé Eisenhower from a struggling young officer on the verge of a court martial into one of the American army's rising stars. Steven Rabalais presents the first complete biography of this significant, but now forgotten, figure in American military history.

9781636240503

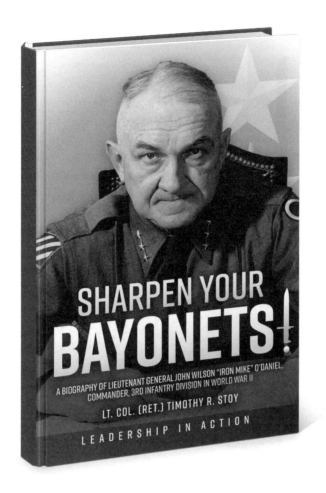

LTC Timothy Stoy paints a vivid picture of warrior John Wilson "Iron Mike" O'Daniel, one of the U.S. Army's great fighting generals of the 20th century. He began his military career with the Delaware Militia in 1914, served on the Mexican border in 1916, received a Distinguished Service Cross in World War I, was Mark Clark's man for hard jobs in the early days of World War II, and commanded the storied 3rd Infantry Division from Anzio to the end of the war in Europe. "Iron Mike "commanded I Corps in Korea 1951–1952 and ended his career as the Chief of the Military Assistance Advisory Group in Vietnam in the early days of American involvement there.

9781636242408

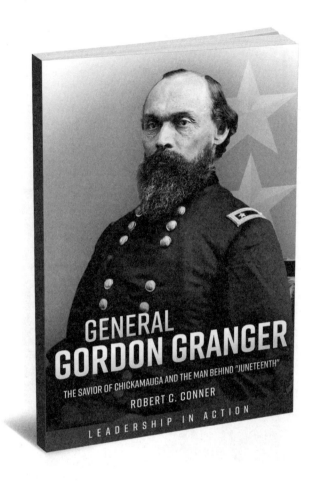

Civil War General Gordon Granger saved the Union army from catastrophic defeat at the Battle of Chickamauga, and went on to play major roles in the Chattanooga and Mobile campaigns. Immediately after the war, as commander of U.S. troops in Texas, his actions sparked the "Juneteenth" celebrations of slavery's end, which continue to this day. In this long-overdue biography, Robert C. Conner presents the life of a colorful commander who fought through the war in the West from its first major battles to its last, and even left his impact on the Reconstruction beyond.

9781636241302